Creating a Website with WordPress

Studio Visual Steps

Creating a Website with WordPress

For anyone who wants to create their own professional website

www.visualsteps.com

This book has been written using the Visual Steps™ method.
Cover design by Studio Willemien Haagsma bNO

© 2015 Visual Steps
Author: Studio Visual Steps

First printing: July 2015
ISBN 978 90 5905 422 6

Resources used: Some of the computer terms and definitions seen here in this book have been taken from descriptions found online at the WordPress help section.

Do you have questions or suggestions?
E-mail: info@visualsteps.com

Would you like more information?
www.visualsteps.com

Website for this book:
www.visualsteps.com/wordpress

Subscribe to the free Visual Steps Newsletter:
www.visualsteps.com/newsletter

Table of Contents

Foreword

For many people today, creating and updating a personal website has become a fun and enjoyable hobby. A website can be used to share information about your family history, favorite genre of music, business or even to post the latest news and event information for a local club or organization. Thanks to a variety of software and online services, creating a website has never been easier. With the free, user-friendly *WordPress* software, you can make your own personal and professional website in no time at all.

This book, shows you step by step exactly what to do. You start off by choosing an attractive theme (template) with which to build your website. Then you fill the website with your own text, pictures, videos and hyperlinks. You can even include a photo gallery, a pull-down menu with links to other pages, or an online form enabling people to contact you. These are just a few of the things that can be added to your website. *WordPress* offers a wide variety of plugins and widgets that can easily add extra functionality to your website.

By using this book and the software from *WordPress*, you will have everything you need to create your own website!

 Alex Wit

P.S.
Your comments and suggestions are most welcome. Our email address is:
mail@visualsteps.com

Visual Steps Newsletter

All Visual Steps books follow the same methodology: clear and concise step-by-step instructions with screenshots to demonstrate each task.
A complete list of all our books can be found on our website **www.visualsteps.com**
You can also sign up to receive our **free Visual Steps Newsletter**.
In this Newsletter you will receive periodic information by email regarding:
- the latest titles and previously released books;
- special offers, supplemental chapters, tips and free informative booklets.
Also, our Newsletter subscribers may download any of the documents listed on the web page **www.visualsteps.com/info_downloads**

When you subscribe to our Newsletter you can be assured that we will never use your email address for any purpose other than sending you the information as previously described. We will not share this address with any third-party. Each Newsletter also contains a one-click link to unsubscribe.

Introduction to Visual Steps™

The Visual Steps handbooks and manuals are the best instructional materials available for learning how to work with the computer. Nowhere else can you find better support for getting to know your PC or *Mac*, your iPad or iPhone, Samsung Galaxy Tab, the Internet and a variety of computer applications.

Properties of the Visual Steps books:
- **Comprehensible contents**
  Addresses the needs of the beginner or intermediate user for a manual written in simple, straight-forward English.
- **Clear structure**
  Precise, easy to follow instructions. The material is broken down into small enough segments to allow for easy absorption.
- **Screenshots of every step**
  Quickly compare what you see on your screen with the screenshots in the book. Pointers and tips guide you when new windows or alert boxes are opened so you always know what to do next.
- **Get started right away**
  All you have to do is turn on your computer or laptop and have your book at hand. Perform each operation as indicated on your own device.
- **Layout**
  The text is printed in a large size font and is clearly legible.

In short, I believe these manuals will be excellent guides for you.

dr. H. van der Meij
Faculty of Applied Education, Department of Instructional Technology, University of Twente, the Netherlands

What You Will Need

To be able to work through this book, you will need a number of things:

Windows

The primary requirement for working with this book is that you have a computer or laptop running the US or English version of *Windows 10, 8.1, 7* or *Vista*.

This book can also be used on a Mac computer. You will see slightly different windows than the ones shown in this book. Always look for a comparable button, option or function that is being discussed or explained in the text. When using *WordPress* on a Mac it is recommended that your website is hosted by a hosting provider that supports *WordPress*.
Configuring a WordPress website on a Mac that is hosted by a provider that does not support WordPress as a standard (see *section 1.5 Setting Up Your Web Space with a Regular Provider* up to and including *section 1.11 Installing WordPress*) is very different from the examples shown in this book. The hosting provider may offer additional information regarding *WordPress* support. You can also find more information on the *WordPress* website.

In order to work with this book and *WordPress* you will need an active Internet connection.

The FTP program *FileZilla*. In *Chapter 1 Starting with WordPress* you can read how to install this program.

Web space by a hosting provider. You can read more about this topic in *Chapter 1 Starting with WordPress*.

Prior Computer Experience

If you want to use this book, you will need some basic computer skills. If you do not have these skills, it is a good idea to read one of the following books first:

Windows 10 for the Beginning Computer User - ISBN 978 90 5905 461 5
Windows 8.1 for SENIORS - ISBN 978 90 5905 118 8
Windows 7 for SENIORS - ISBN 978 90 5905 126 3
Mac OS X Yosemite for SENIORS - ISBN 978 90 5905 360 1

A complete catalog of all of our books can be found at our website:
www.visualsteps.com

How To Use This Book

This book has been written using the Visual Steps™ method. The method is simple: place the book next to your desktop computer or laptop and execute all the tasks step by step, directly on your own device. With the clear instructions and the multitude of screenshots, you will always know exactly what to do. This is the quickest way to become familiar with *WordPress*.

In this Visual Steps™ book, you will see various icons. This is what they mean:

Techniques
These icons indicate an action to be carried out:

 The mouse icon means you need to do something with the mouse.

 The keyboard icon means you should type something on your keyboard.

 The hand icon means you should do something else, for example, turn on the computer or carry out a task previously learned.

In addition to these icons, in some areas of this book extra assistance is provided to help you successfully work through each chapter.

Help
These icons indicate that extra help is available:

The arrow icon warns you about something.

The bandage icon will help you if something has gone wrong.

$\mathscr{G}_1$ Have you forgotten how to do something? The number next to the footsteps tells you where to look it up at the end of the book in the appendix *How Do I Do That Again?*

In this book you will also find a lot of general information and tips. This information is displayed in separate boxes.

Extra information
Information boxes are denoted by these icons:

 The book icon gives you extra background information that you can read at your convenience. This extra information is not necessary for working through the book.

 The light bulb icon indicates an extra tip for using a program or service.

The Website Accompanying This Book

On the website that accompanies this book, **www.visualsteps.com/wordpress**, you will find additional information about this book.
Please, take a look at our website **www.visualsteps.com** from time to time to read about new books and gather other useful information.

Test Your Knowledge

Accompanied with some Visual Steps books, you can test your knowledge online on the **www.ccforseniors.com** website. By answering a number of multiple choice questions you will be able to test your knowledge of the Mac. If you pass the test, you can also receive a free *Computer Certificate* by email, if you wish.
Participating in the test is **free of charge**. The computer certificate website is a free service from Visual Steps.

For Teachers

This book is designed as a self-study guide. It is also well suited for use in a group or a classroom setting. For this purpose, we offer a free teacher's manual containing information about how to prepare for the course (including didactic teaching methods) and testing materials. You can download the teacher's manual (PDF file) from the website which accompanies this book: **www.visualsteps.com/wordpress**

The Screenshots

The screenshots used in this book indicate which button, folder, file or hyperlink you need to click on your computer screen. In the instruction text (in **bold** letters) you will see a small image of the item you need to click. The line will point you to the right place on your screen.
The small screenshots that are printed in this book are not meant to be completely legible all the time. This is not necessary, as you will see these images on your own computer screen in real size and fully legible.

On the next page you will see an example of an instruction text and a screenshot. The line indicates where to find this item on your own computer screen.

Click Documents

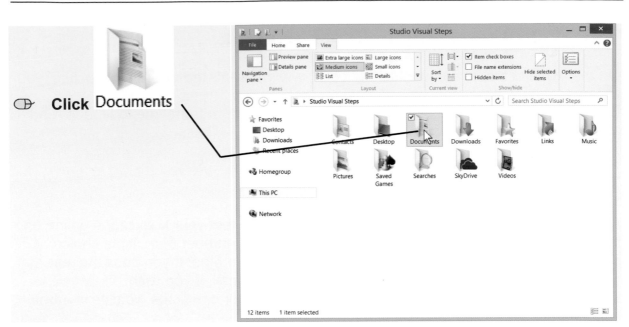

Sometimes the screenshot shows only a portion of a window. Here is an example:

Click Medium icons

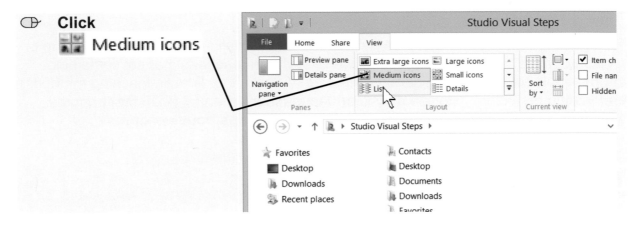

It really will **not be necessary** for you to read all the information in the screenshots in this book. Always use the screenshots in combination with the image you see on your own computer screen.

1. Starting with WordPress

The *WordPress* program was originally intended for creating and maintaining *blogs*. A blog is a kind of diary, where users can share their experiences, thoughts, and feelings with others.
In the meantime, the need to create a website has become increasingly urgent. *WordPress* has been adapted over the years, in order to turn it into a program with which you can easily build and maintain a website with little technical knowhow.

WordPress is actually a *Content Management System (CMS)*. A Content Management System is a system that lets you manage the content of a website. If you wanted to create or maintain a website starting from scratch, you would need to be adept at several programming languages such as *HTML, JavaScript* or *PHP.* You would enter the program code one line at a time by hand. This code tells your Internet browser, for example, *Internet Explorer*, just how the website needs to look. With *WordPress* you build and edit the website by using links and editing boxes, without having to change anything in the code. It is a lot like filling in a form. This way, it is easier for you to focus on the appearance and content of the website, without needing to worry about the code.

Before you can start working with *WordPress*, you will need to set up the program. You will need to acquire some *web space* from a *hosting provider*, for example. A hosting provider rents web space. You can upload your website to this space. Other people will then be able to visit your website on the Internet.
The web space is also used for working with the *WordPress* program itself. Contrary to most other programs, you do not work with *WordPress* on your computer, but directly online. This means that *WordPress* must be installed on the web space provided by your hosting provider, instead of on your computer.

In this chapter you will learn:

- how *WordPress* works;
- what you need to use for *WordPress* and your website;
- how to set up your web space;
- how to download and unzip *WordPress*;
- how to adjust the configuration file for *WordPress*;
- how to set up *FileZilla*;
- how to upload *WordPress* to your web space;
- how to install *WordPress*;
- how to view the *WordPress* home website.

✎ Please note:

In this book we use the domain name and database name of the sample website www.visualstepswordpr.com. You will need to replace these names with your own domain name and database name.

1.1 Working with WordPress

There are various ways of building a website. One of the methods is building the website with programming code that describes how the website should look. There are many different programming languages used to create websites, of which HTML, JavaScript and PHP are the best known. By using the correct code with their accompanying settings, you can display the colors on a web page and decide how the text will be positioned, for example. The advantage of this method is that you can determine exactly how the website will appear. The downside is that it takes time and requires a lot of work. Plus you need to know various programming languages before you can build and maintain your website.

An example of the HTML code underlying the Visual Steps website:

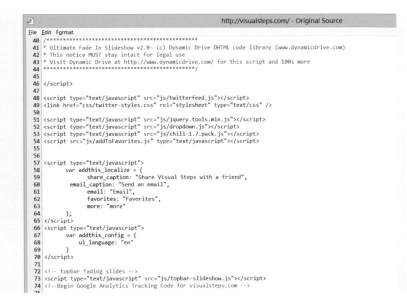

In order to simplify building and maintaining a website, you can use a so-called *WYSIWYG* editor. WYSIWYG stands for: What You See Is What You Get. This type of program helps you build a website without entering any code. You place text and photos directly in the editor, and then the program generates the necessary code to display them on the website. In this way you can totally focus on the layout and content of your website. It makes building a website a lot easier. The only disadvantage is that you cannot adjust *every* detail of the website according to your own preferences.

An example of the WYSIWYG editor *Website X5*:

WordPress also contains a WYSIWYG editor. In the editor you can place text and photos that will be rendered on your web page. With the aid of sample pages or templates, you can build your own website by adjusting text, photos, and other components. This functionality gives *WordPress* its status as a Content Management System (CMS).

An example of the *WordPress* CMS:

CMS programs such as *WordPress* also deviate in other aspects from the regular programs you use on your computer. For instance, the program does not run on your computer but is web based. This means you need to be online in order to use the program. The program is actually running on the space provided to you through a hosting provider. A hosting provider is a company that offers web space on the Internet for a fee. In order to create a *WordPress* website and make it accessible to others, *WordPress* must be installed to the web space provided to you by a hosting provider. In the next couple of sections you will read how to do this. Programs that work in this way are called *server-sided* programs. A server is another name for a computer owned by a hosting provider. Server-sided means that the program runs on the provider's computer and not on your own computer.

So, you will be working on the Internet while building or maintaining your website. You can view any changes you have made immediately in your Internet browser. This method is a bit like maintaining a *Facebook* page.

CMS programs such as *WordPress* work with a *database*. A database is sort of like a big file cabinet where all your data is kept. *WordPress* stores the data needed for your website, in other words your text, images, settings and more in a database. You can add, edit and delete this data. When somebody visits your website, the data is retrieved from the database and displayed on the visitor's screen. He or she will see a web page with text and images.

One of the big advantages of this method is that the content of the website is separated from the layout features of the website, while in the program code, these two elements work together. You can adjust the layout of your website just as quickly and easily as it is to add a new photo or text to your website. For example, you can simply select another *theme* from the multitude of available *WordPress* themes to give your website a whole new look.
A theme is a template for a website. It determines the overall look and feel of your website; the layout, style, and arrangement. If you install a different theme, your entire website will look different right away, usually without affecting the text and photos. You can read more about themes in *Chapter 3 Working with Themes*.

Another great thing about *WordPress* is that it is an *open source* program. Not only can you use the program for free, but anyone can create an addition to the program in order to improve it. The administrators of the *WordPress* main program keep a close watch on these additions, and will check whether they really improve it. As a result of the *open source* nature of *WordPress*, you can make use of many extra features that have been built by other users. In *Chapter 5 Adding Extra Components* and *Chapter 6 Useful plug-ins* you can read more about these additions.

1.2 Necessary for WordPress

Since *WordPress* is a special kind of program, you will need to use a slightly different method to set up the program, other than the one you are used to with regular computer programs.

You will need these items in order to work with *WordPress*:

- **Web space for your website and a domain name.**
  A domain name is the web address for your website, such as www.mysite.com. A new domain name will only cost you a small monthly fee and you can choose from a multitude of webhosting companies. It is good to check whether the hosting provider supports working with *WordPress*. If that is

the case, the provider will already have taken measures to enable an easy installation of *WordPress*, and may already have set up a database. Then you will be on your way with just a few mouse-clicks, and you just need to fill in a *WordPress* form to get started. In the *Background Information* at the end of this chapter you can read more on the topic of hosting providers.

- **A MySQL database in which the content of the website is stored.**
  MySQL is a type of standard database. It is put at your disposal by the hosting provider, and is usually set up right away by the hosting providers that support *WordPress*.
  You can also create a MySQL database yourself. Many hosting packages include at least one MySQL database. You can read more about databases in *section 1.4 Setting Up Your Web Space with a Provider that Supports WordPress* and *section 1.5 Setting Up Your Web Space with a Regular Provider*.
- **An FTP program to upload files to your web space.**
  An FTP program is used to copy files to a computer on the Internet, such as a hosting provider's computer, or to download files from the Internet to your own computer. The free *FileZilla* program is an example of an FTP program. You will only need to use an FTP program if you need to manually install *WordPress* yourself, and if the hosting provider does not support *WordPress*. In *section 1.9 Installing and Setting Up FileZilla* you can read more about this.

In order to properly use the most recent version of *WordPress*, your hosting provider needs to have the correct version of a number of components already installed. At the time of writing this book, these were the version numbers:

- MySQL version 5.0 or higher. This is the software for managing the database.
- PHP version 5.2.4 or higher. This is the language used by *WordPress*.
- Mod_rewrite Apache module. This is the software that is used by the server (the hosting provider's computer).

You can find this relevant information on the hosting provider's website, for example, in the FAQ (Frequently Asked Questions) section, or by viewing the various hosting packages on offer. You can also use the search box on the website to search for the keyword 'WordPress'. If you cannot find any information, you might be able to fill in a contact form, or send an email to your provider. On the following page is an example of the text you can use if you want to contact your hosting provider.

Dear Sir/Madam,

I would like to use WordPress in my web space and therefore would like to know if you support the following requirements for the use of WordPress:

- MySQL version 5.0 or higher.
- PHP version 5.2.4 or higher.
- Mod rewrite Apache module.

I would also like to know whether there are any restrictions for using plugins and widgets with WordPress.

Many thanks for considering my request.

Kind regards,

[Your name and, if you wish, your address]

If you choose a hosting provider with specific *WordPress* support, this information is usually provided right on their home page, or on the pages with specific information about the various hosting packages. In such a case, the hosting provider will already have ensured that all requirements for adequately using *WordPress* are met.

➥Please note:

Hosting providers that do not offer specific support for *WordPress*, sometimes require you to enable or disable a specific setting, in order to work with the program. These are often so-called safe mode settings. If *WordPress* does not work properly after it has been installed, you can check with your provider to see if a safe mode setting is causing the problem.

➥Please note:

Your Internet provider that supports your access to the Internet may also offer free web space. This space is usually not suited for working with *WordPress*, because there are often restrictions for using PHP and there is usually no database available.

1.3 Necessary for Your Website

For this book the subject of our website will be 'Gardening as a hobby'. You can learn how to work with *WordPress* by following the instructions and building the website as seen in our examples. You can also use the instructions in this book to build a website about another topic of your own choice. Then you will not need to delete the sample website from your web space after working through this book.

An example of a website created with *WordPress*:

Although you can edit your website with *WordPress* even after you have built it, it is much wiser to think about a good basic design beforehand, and to consider what type of information you want to place on your website.

These are important topics when considering a basic design:

- **Which colors do you want to use?**
  It is important to choose colors that match, and that do not make it difficult to read the content of the website. Do not choose too many different colors, because this can make the website appear chaotic.
- **What text do you want to place on your website?**
  The text should contain information about the website's subject, contact data, and news. Keep the amount of text in balance. Too much text on a website can be unpleasant, difficult to read and may even lead the visitor to look somewhere else. The text needs to be concise but still clear enough. Visitors will just as quickly abandon a website if it contains too little information.
- **Which photos and images do you want to place on your website?**
  In the early days of the Internet you would come across websites with only text and nothing else. Nowadays, it has become important to make the website livelier by including photos and images. For example, you can place photos of your hobby, or of yourself, and you can use other images to embellish your website. Just like we have used photos of flowers for our sample website about gardening as a hobby. In this way you can lend a certain atmosphere to your website. Make sure that all the photos and images on your website are of a high quality. Blurry images or those with red eyes are never a pretty sight on a website.
- **Which pages do you want your website to contain?**
  A good arrangement of your website pages is also important. This makes the website clear and easy-to-follow for visitors. There are often some standard pages that appear in almost every website: home, news, contact, or about me.

If you wish you can add more pages, depending on the subject of the site. And you can also distribute the information over multiple pages. This is a good way of making sure there is not too much information on a single page. Keep in mind that you can always add pages in *WordPress* later on, if you wish.

- **Which additional components do you want to include on your website?** You can add all sorts of extra features in *WordPress*. Such as a calendar or a photo gallery.

If you want to build your own website right away, with this book as a guideline, it is useful to have a number of good images available, right from the start. You can make up the texts as you go, and change or expand them later on, if you wish.

1.4 Setting Up Your Web Space with a Provider that Supports WordPress

The first step to take if you want to use *WordPress*, is to set up your web space. One of the operations is setting up your database, among other things. Here there are two options: either your provider offers special support for *WordPress*, or not.

Does your provider offer no special support for *WordPress*?

☞ **Continue with *section 1.5 Setting Up Your Web Space with a Regular Provider***

If you have a subscription with a hosting provider that supports the use of *WordPress*, you will often be able to use a wizard on the provider's website to initiate the set up. You will not need to change a lot of settings before you start building your website. The hosting provider's website will offer additional information about this topic. Usually, you can find this information on the *WordPress* pages of the website, or you may also have been given information in the email your provider has sent to you after you have subscribed.

For this book we have used the hosting services provided by SiteGround. This hosting provider offers specific support for working with *WordPress*. It is quite easy to set up your web space for using *WordPress* with this provider.
Among other things, this means that a database for *WordPress* will automatically be created. Also, the most recent version of *WordPress* will be installed, and in future you will automatically be notified when newer versions (*updates*) of the program become available.

Please note:

Even if your hosting provider supports *WordPress*, setting up the program may be a bit different from the way it is described in this section. Please read the information on your hosting provider's website regarding the setting up of *WordPress*, or read the email sent to you by your hosting provider.

This is how *WordPress* is installed when SiteGround is the hosting provider:

☞ **Open your web hosting service's website, for example, www.siteground.com** 🐾1

Please note:

Sometimes, the login information for your hosting manager or control panel is different from the login information (user name and password) for your hosting account. The same login information may be needed for using an FTP program (see *section 1.8 Adjusting the WordPress Configuration File*). Read the information sent to you by your hosting provider, the information on the FAQ pages (Frequently Asked Questions), or the Help information on the provider's website.

Please note:

Take into account that the system distinguishes between lower and upper case letters when entering user names and passwords.

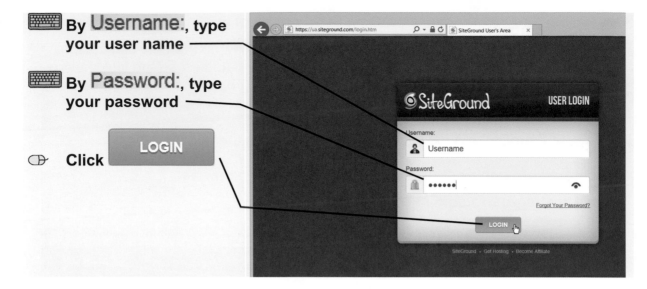

By **Username:**, type your user name

By **Password:**, type your password

Click **LOGIN**

In the next window:

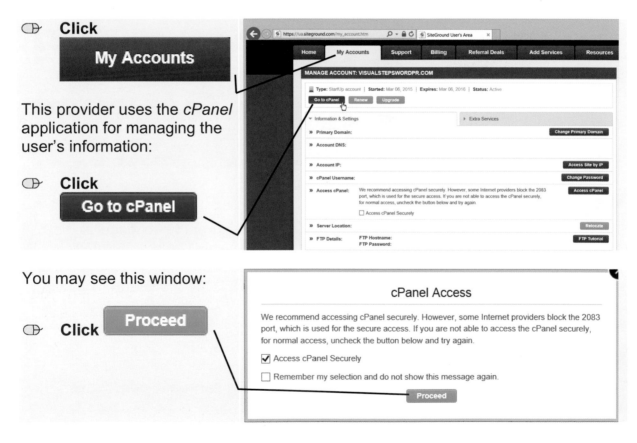

Click **My Accounts**

This provider uses the *cPanel* application for managing the user's information:

Click **Go to cPanel**

You may see this window:

Click **Proceed**

Now you see the *cPanel* control panel or another type of hosting manager. Here you will find a menu item or button that you can click directly to install *WordPress*:

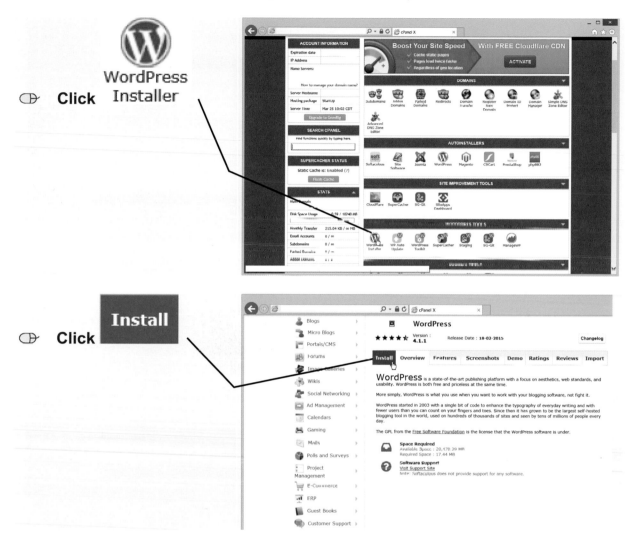

A wizard for the installation procedure will be opened. You will see a form where you need to enter the data for installing *WordPress*. Some of the data has already been filled in.

🢒 Please note:

The names of the various settings and the order in which they appear on the *WordPress* installation form on your own screen may differ slightly from what is shown here. If you are not sure about a certain setting, you can read the description that goes along with it to see what it is used for.

By default, the **Choose Protocol** is set to http://, do not change this:

The **Choose Domain** box has already been filled in:

The **In Directory** box needs to be blank:

The name of the *WordPress* database will be generated automatically:

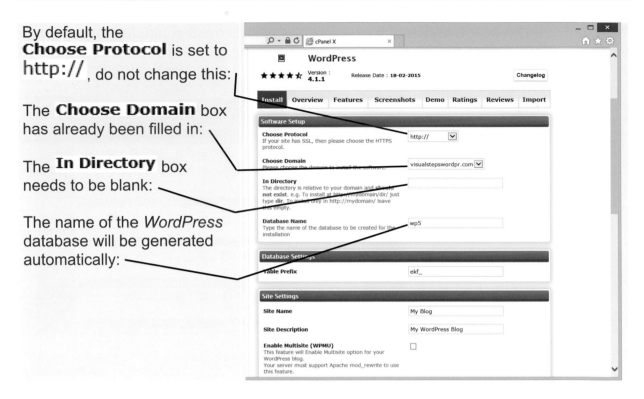

Now you will need to enter some additional information about the website. You can always change the name and/or description of the website later on:

The **Table Prefix** has been correctly filled in right away:

By **Site Name**, type the title of your website

This title will be displayed on the website itself, and can be changed later on.

By **Site Description** you can type a different description for your website, if you wish

Leave the box ☐ by **Enable Multisite (WPMU)** blank:

Now you can enter the data needed to log into the *WordPress* control panel of your website. You can make up your own user name and password, if you wish. The admin email address is used by *WordPress* to send you messages regarding your website. By default, the email address known to your hosting provider has been filled in here, but you can use another email address if you prefer.

➥Please note:
Do not use the default user name 'admin' as a user name. This name can easily be guessed by persons who want to log in without permission.

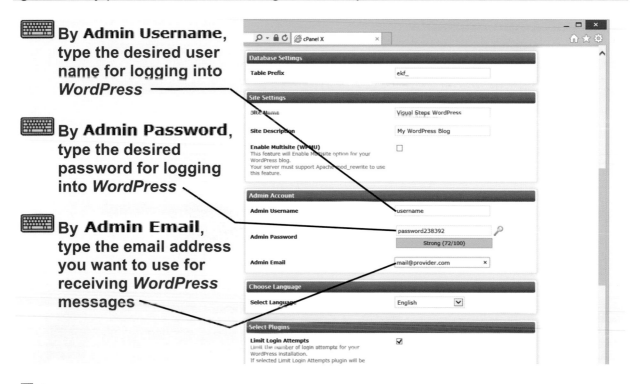

By **Admin Username**, type the desired user name for logging into *WordPress*

By **Admin Password**, type the desired password for logging into *WordPress*

By **Admin Email**, type the email address you want to use for receiving *WordPress* messages

➥ Please note:
Make sure to remember your login information. Write it down and store it in a safe place.

💡 Tip
Strong passwords
Use a strong password. Make sure the password is difficult to guess. Use at least six characters. Use both lower case and upper case letters, and also numbers, if you wish. It is best not to use existing names, since they can easily be guessed. An example of a strong password is "Krae68Ti". Sometimes the website will display the requirements that a password needs to meet, such as the minimal length required. And you may also see an indication of the strength of the password.

Finally, you can set a language for *WordPress*. You can also choose to limit the number of login attempts on your website. This is useful in case visitors are allowed to post comments on your website, and if you want to deter spammers. You can always disable this option later on:

☞ **If necessary, by Select Language, select** English

☞ **Check the box ☑ by Limit Login Attempts**

☞ **Check the data you have filled in**

☞ **Click** **Install**

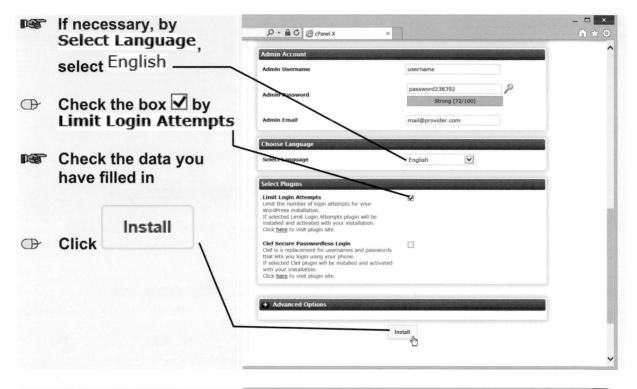

WordPress will now be installed on your web space:

This operation may take a few minutes.

When you see the notice that the installation is successively installed, you can leave the hosting manager by logging out:

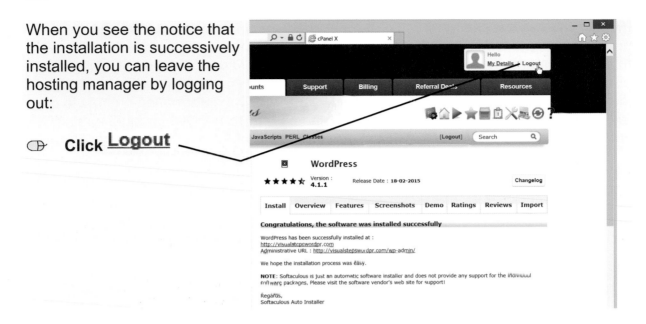

☞ **Click** **Logout**

Now you can take a look at the basic *WordPress* website:

In the address bar:

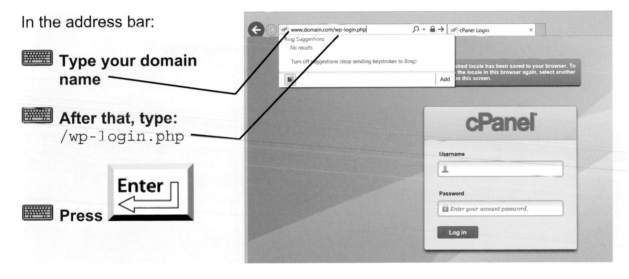

⌨ **Type your domain name**

⌨ **After that, type:** `/wp-login.php`

⌨ **Press** **Enter**

☞ **Continue with** *section 1.12 Viewing the Basic WordPress Website*

1.5 Setting Up Your Web Space with a Regular Provider

The first step for working with a *WordPress* website is setting up your web space so that it can run *WordPress*. Among other things, you will need to setup a database. Here you have two options: either the provider offers special support for *WordPress*, or they do not.

If your provider does not offer support for *WordPress* and you need to install the program yourself, you can follow the instructions here and in the next few sections. First, you are going to create a new database for *WordPress*. You do this using the control panel (user management panel) that comes with your web space.
If everything went well, your hosting provider has sent you information on how to use the control panel as well as the user name and password needed for logging in. If you have not received this information, you need to contact your hosting provider.

➥ Please note:

The control panel offered by your hosting provider will probably look different from this one. The images on your own screen will differ from the screenshots shown here and in the next few sections.

Usually you will find additional information on your provider's website, in the form of text or instructional videos, for example. You may need to follow the FAQ link first, in order to get to this information.

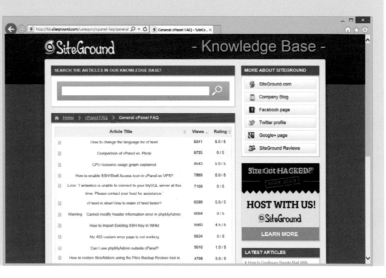

☞ **Go to the control panel of your web space** ✂²

⌨ **Type your login data**

☞ **Click the login button, for example**

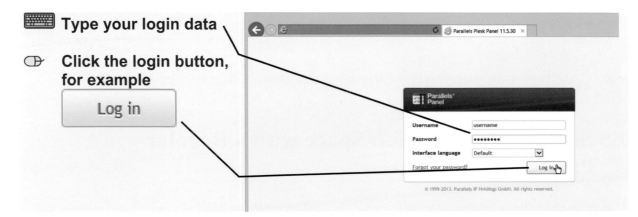

You will see the control panel:

☞ **Click**

Websites & Domain

☞ **Click**

Databases

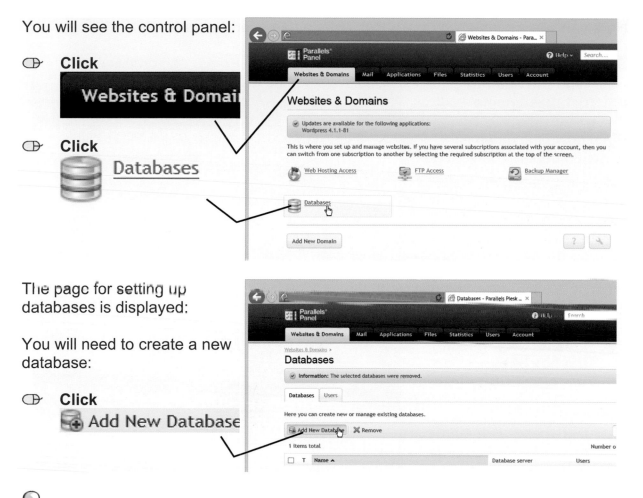

The page for setting up databases is displayed:

You will need to create a new database:

☞ **Click**

Add New Database

💡 Tip
Name for database
You can choose your own name for the new *WordPress* database. It is recommended to use an appropriate name for this database, such as the name of your website. For example, if your website's domain name is www.photoshop.com, you can name the database "photoshop". You can also add the letters db (database) if you wish, for instance, photoshopdb.

➥ Please note:
In this chapter we will be using the domain name visualstepswordpr. This name is derived from the domain name of the sample website: www.visualstepswordpr.com.

➥ Please note:
Sometimes, part of the database name has already been filled in, and you will only be allowed to add an extra portion of the name.

Here you see the page where you can enter a name for the database:

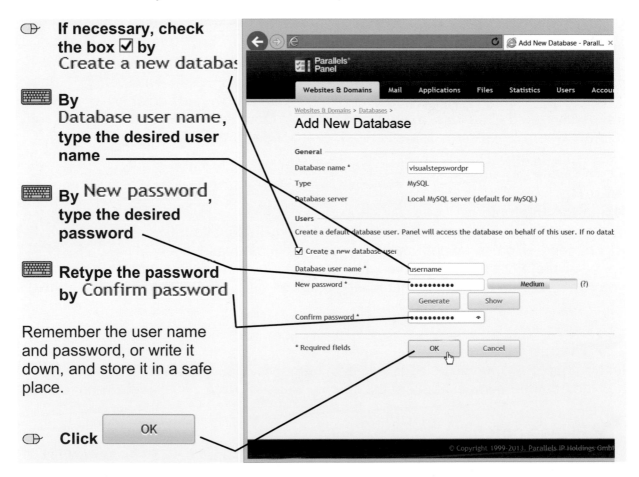

By Database name,
**type the desired
database name**

Write down the database
name on paper. You will need
it later on.

Now you will need to create a user for the new database. This is mainly a question of entering a user name and password that is linked to this database, in order to protect it. You can choose your own user name and password.

**If necessary, check
the box ☑ by**
Create a new databa:

By
Database user name,
**type the desired user
name**

By New password,
**type the desired
password**

**Retype the password
by** Confirm password

Remember the user name
and password, or write it
down, and store it in a safe
place.

Click OK

You will need to use the name of the database, and the accompanying user name and password later on, when you configure (set up) *WordPress*.

The new database has been created: ————

Now you have finished and can log out from the control panel:

☞ **Click your user name**

☞ **Click**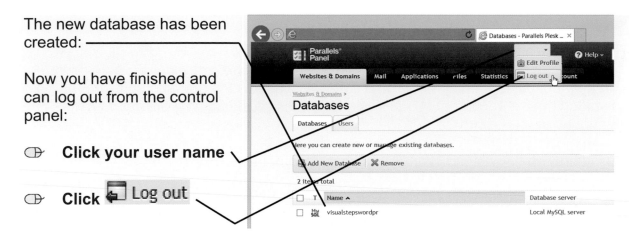

1.6 Downloading WordPress

You can download the *WordPress* program for free. On the wordpress.org website you will find a download option as well as other important information about *WordPress*. For instance, the most recent version of *WordPress*, and links to official themes, plugins, and other components you can use for your website. And you can view various sample websites that have been created with *WordPress*.
There are a lot of other resources available as well, such as how-to articles, frequently asked questions, manuals and other supportive documents. There is even a forum where *WordPress* users can ask questions and exchange information.

At wordpress.org you will find the main website for *WordPress*:

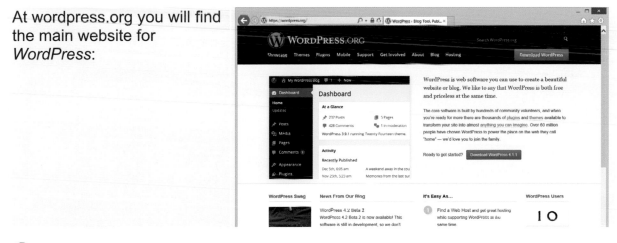

💡 **Tip**

Wordpress.com
There is also a site called wordpress.com. This is a hosting provider, specialized in offering web space for *WordPress* weblogs and websites. Here you can easily create a free *WordPress* weblog. If you want to have more options you will need to pay a monthly fee.

➥ **Please note:**

There are also some non-official websites that pose as official *WordPress* websites. Here you can download the program as well, with optional extras. Do not do this! You might expose yourself to harmful software, such as viruses and spyware, by downloading this version of *WordPress*. Only use the official *WordPress* websites mentioned in this book.

This is how you download *WordPress* to your computer:

☞ **Open the www.wordpress.org website** ✇¹

You will see the *WordPress* website:

☞ **Click**

Download WordPr

☞ **Click**

Download WordPr

➥ **Please note:**

You may see a more recent version of *WordPress*. In that case, just download the newest version. In general, this will not affect the way you work with this book. If a new version does affect the actions described in this book, you will find additional information on the website accompanying this book, **www.visualsteps.com/wordpress**. Look for the menu item *News and errata*.

First, save the file onto your computer:

Click Save

Once the download has finished:

☞ **Close the Internet browser** ✎³

1.7 Unzipping WordPress

The actual *WordPress* program consists of multiple programs and files that comprise the Content Management System. All these files are contained into a single ZIP file, after you have downloaded it. This is a file in which the data has been compressed (zipped), so that it does not take up so much space.
You will need to extract or unzip the ZIP file before you can use *WordPress*. This means that the files in the ZIP file will be placed in a folder. You can easily do this in *Windows* with the folder window, that is to say, *File Explorer*.

➡ **Please note:**
If you have another compression application installed on your computer, such as *WinZIP* or *WinRAR*, you can use these programs to unzip the ZIP file. In this section we will use the *Windows* folder window to unzip the file.

☞ **Open the folder window** ✎⁴

Open the *wordpress* folder that contains the ZIP file you just downloaded:

Click Downloads

You will see the compressed folder:

Right-click
wordpress-4.1.1

Click Extract All...

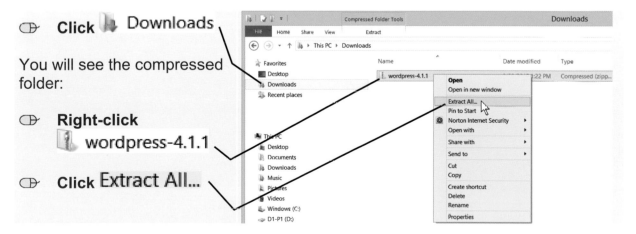

Save the files in the
wordpress folder:

☞   **Select the text to the
     right of** wordpress

⌨ **Press** **Delete**

In order to unzip the files:

☞   **Click** Extract

The content of the ZIP file is
extracted:

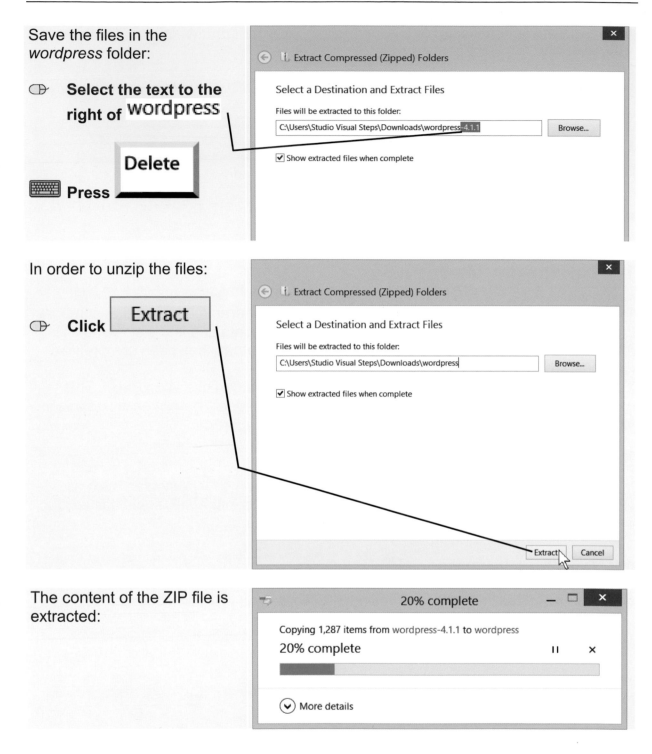

After the file has been unzipped, you will see the folder that has been extracted in a window:

In order to delete the compressed folder:

☞ **Go to the other *Downloads* folder window**

🖰 **Click the folder named with the number, for example** 📁 **wordpress-4.1.1**

⌨ **Press** **Delete**

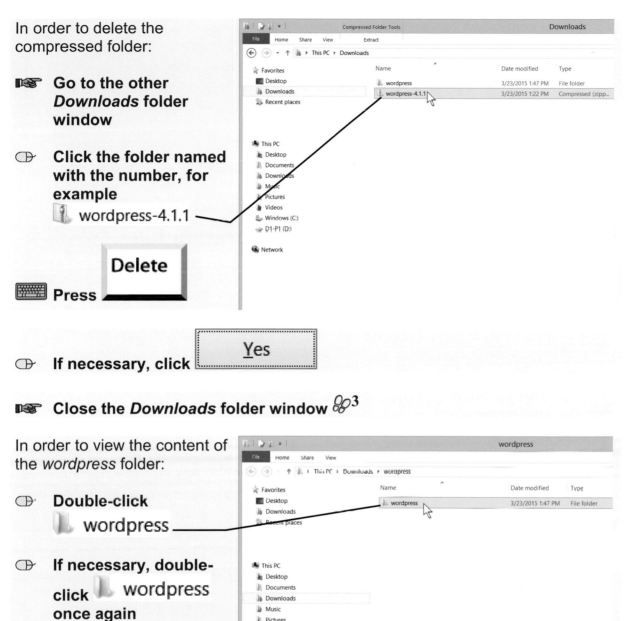

🖰 **If necessary, click** **Yes**

☞ **Close the *Downloads* folder window** 👣³

In order to view the content of the *wordpress* folder:

🖰 **Double-click** 📁 **wordpress**

🖰 **If necessary, double-click** 📁 **wordpress once again**

All the files of the *WordPress*
ZIP file have been placed in
the *wordpress* folder:

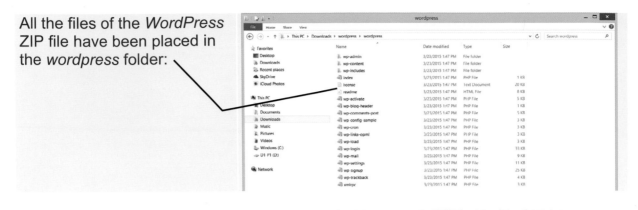

👉 **Close the folder window** ⚙️³

1.8 Adjusting the WordPress Configuration File

One of the main files in *WordPress* is the *configuration file*. This configuration file
contains important settings such as the database settings for *WordPress*. And the
settings for saving the website.
You can adjust this configuration file yourself, to ensure that *WordPress* has the
correct settings for using the program. This is done with a text editor, such as
WordPad or *Notepad*.

➥ **Please note:**

More advanced text editing programs, such as *Word* are not suited for directly
editing this type of file. If you use an advanced text editor, there is a risk of incorrect
text coding being used when you save the file, and the file may not be correctly
saved as a genuine PHP file.

➥ **Please note:**

If you want to adjust the configuration file, you will need to use the data you have set
for the database, in *section 1.5 Setting Up Your Web Space with a Regular Provider*.

This is how you open the *WordPad* program in *Windows 10*. On the taskbar:

⊕ **Click the search box**

⌨️ **Type:** `wordpad`

⊕ **Click** [A≡ **WordPad**]

This is how you open the *WordPad* program in *Windows 8.1*:

☞ **Click**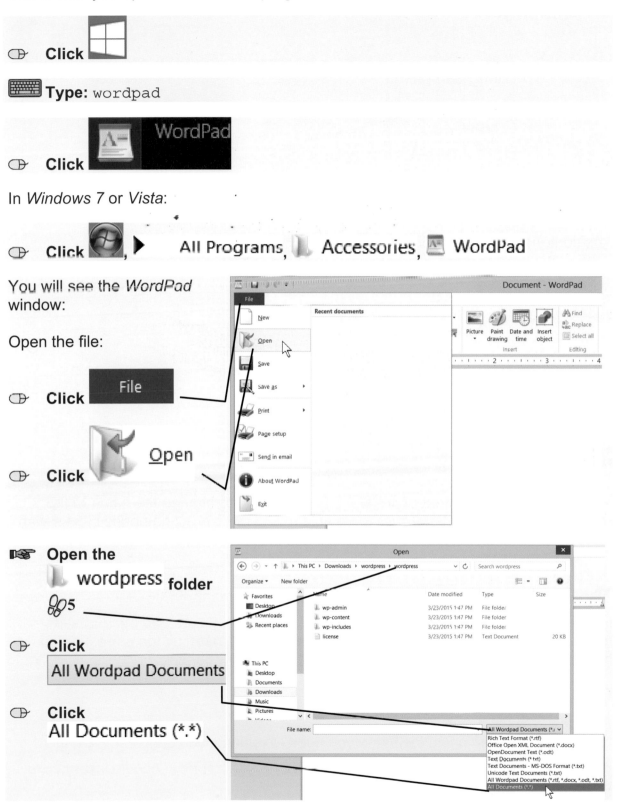

Type: wordpad

☞ **Click**

In *Windows 7* or *Vista*:

☞ **Click** , ▶ All Programs, Accessories, WordPad

You will see the *WordPad* window:

Open the file:

☞ **Click** File

☞ **Click** Open

☞ **Open the** wordpress **folder**

☞ **Click** All Wordpad Documents

☞ **Click** All Documents (*.*)

You will see all the files in

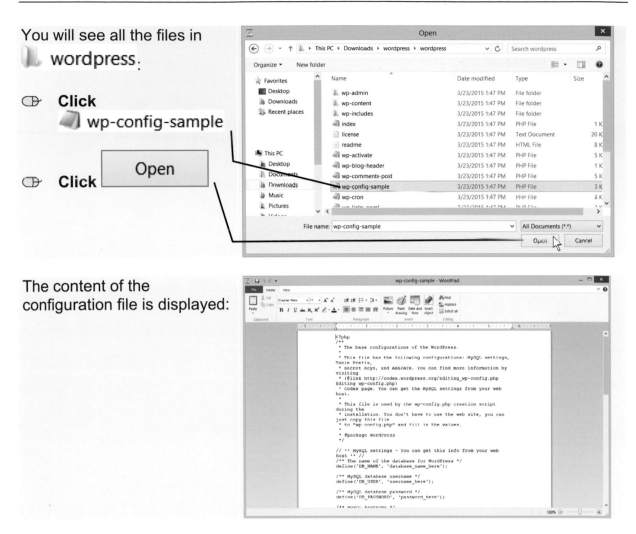

wordpress.

☞ **Click**

      wp-config-sample

☞ **Click**   Open

The content of the
configuration file is displayed:

You can adjust the content of this file. First, you need to change the name of the
database, in order for *WordPress* to be able to find the correct database in your web
space.
You will need to replace the text *database_name_here*.

Please note:

Only change the text between the quotation marks. Do not remove the quotation
marks. For example, replace the text *'database_name_here'* by the correct database
name of your own website. In this example this is *'visualstepswordpr'*.

💡 **Tip**

Find the correct name
If you have trouble finding the name you need to replace, you can search for this
name with the 🔍 Find option. The name you need to replace, occurs just once in
the configuration file.

⊕ **By** `define('DB_NAME',`
select the text
`database_name_here`

Please note: do not select
the quotation marks.

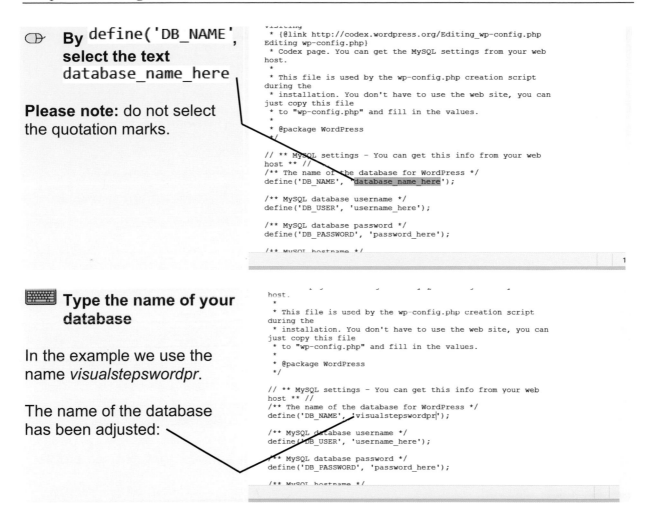

⌨ **Type the name of your
database**

In the example we use the
name *visualstepswordpr*.

The name of the database
has been adjusted:

In the same way, you can adjust the other data. In the following example we have
used the words *user name* and *password*. You need to fill in your own data instead:

☞ **By** `define('DB_USER',`
replace the text
`username_here` **by the
user name of the
database**

☞ **By**
`define('DB_PASSWORD',`
replace the text
`password_here` **by
the password of the
database**

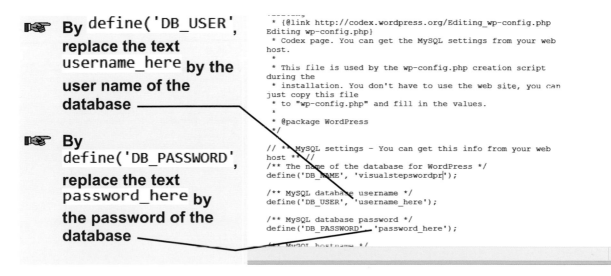

You see that the data has been adjusted:

The setting by `define('DB_HOST'` is almost always `localhost`:

You do not need to change the other settings.

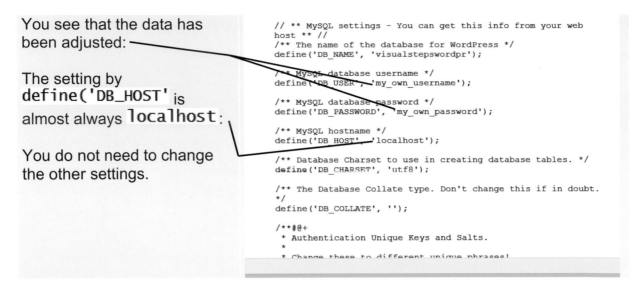

```
// ** MySQL settings - You can get this info from your web
host ** //
/** The name of the database for WordPress */
define('DB_NAME', 'visualstepswordpr');

/** MySQL database username */
define('DB_USER', 'my_own_username');

/** MySQL database password */
define('DB_PASSWORD', 'my_own_password');

/** MySQL hostname */
define('DB_HOST', 'localhost');

/** Database Charset to use in creating database tables. */
define('DB_CHARSET', 'utf8');

/** The Database Collate type. Don't change this if in doubt.
*/
define('DB_COLLATE', '');

/**#@+
 * Authentication Unique Keys and Salts.
 *
 * Change these to different unique phrases!
```

Tip

Incorrect data

If *WordPress* does not seem to be working after you have installed the program, you may have filled in the wrong data in the configuration file. In that case you should check the configuration file once more and see if you have entered the correct database name, user name, and password. Also make sure that you have not removed the quotation marks.

The problem may also lie in the hostname: this may not be *localhost*, but some other name. You will find the correct name in the data sent to you by your hosting provider. If it still does not work, you can check with your hosting provider.

Save the configuration file. You do that like this:

☞ **Click** 💾

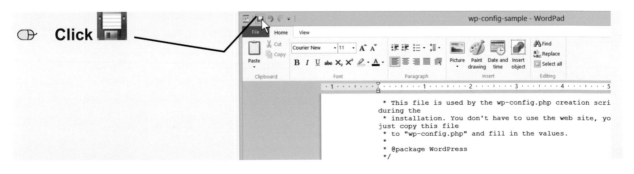

You have saved the configuration file.

☞ **Close WordPad** &⅔ **3**

Now you will need to adjust the name of the configuration file. The original file name is *wp-config-sample.php*. The name of this file needs to be changed to: *wp-config.php*. This is the official name of the configuration file.

At first, the file is named differently, in order to distinguish between the configuration file with the default (or blank) settings, and the settings you have changed or filled in.

Please note:

If your version of *Windows* has been set not to display file extensions, you will not see the .PHP extension after the file name.

☞ **Open the folder window** ᵂ4

☞ **Open the** 📁 **wordpress folder** ᵂ5

🖰 **Click** 📄 **wp-config-sample**

🖰 **Click** 📄 **wp-config-sample once again**

⌨ **Type:** `wp-config`

⌨ **Press** Enter

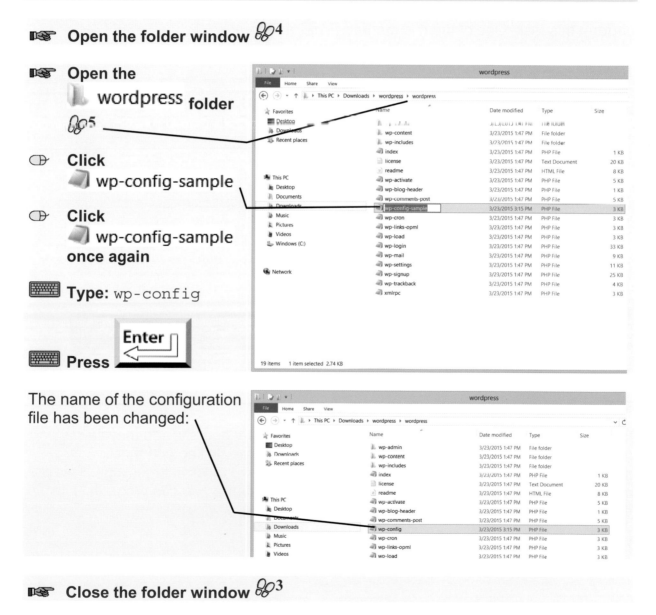

The name of the configuration file has been changed:

☞ **Close the folder window** ᵂ3

1.9 Installing and Setting Up FileZilla

If you have set up the web space and adjusted the configuration file, you can now upload the *WordPress* files to your Internet web space. You will need to use an *FTP program* in order to do that.

FTP stands for *File Transfer Protocol*. The word protocol stands for the way files are moved. In practice, this means that the program is suited for transferring files from your computer to an Internet computer (owned by your hosting provider), and vice versa, from the Internet to your own computer. There are various programs that can perform this task. One of them is the free *FileZilla* program.

You can download this program:

☞ **Open the http://filezilla-project.org website** 🦶[1]

You will see the *FileZilla* website:

☞ **Click**

Download FileZilla Client

All platforms

🔖 Please note:

If you use the download button to download the program directly, you may see a message generated by an overzealous antivirus program, telling you that this download is unsafe. This is a so-called false-positive and incorrect message. This is caused by the option to install other software along with the *FileZilla* program. This software is secure but wrongly triggers the message.

☞ **Click**
➨ **Show additional do**

Select the version for your own operating system:

For *Windows*:

☞ **By Windows (64bit)**
or Windows (32bit),
click the version with
(recommended)

It may take a while before you see the next window:

In *Internet Explorer*, you will see the message bar at the bottom of the window:

Save the download file:

☞ **Click** [Save]

➨ **Please note:**

If you are using another browser, this message may appear in a different location on your screen. In that case, just follow the instructions on the screen.

Your screen may turn dark, and you will be asked for permission to continue:

☞ **If necessary, give permission to continue**

The file will be downloaded:

When the download has
finished:

☞ **Click** Open folder

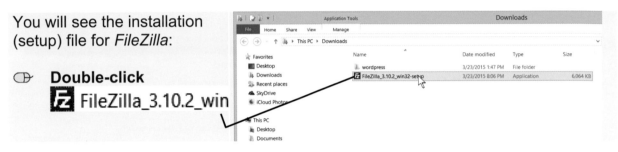

☞ **Close the Internet browser** 👣³

You will see the installation
(setup) file for *FileZilla*:

☞ **Double-click**
🗲 FileZilla_3.10.2_win

Your screen may turn dark again, and you will be asked for permission to continue:

☞ **If necessary, give permission to continue**

You will see this window:

☞ **Click** I Agree

FileZilla Client 3.10.2 Setup

License Agreement
Please review the license terms before installing FileZilla Client 3.10.2.

Press Page Down to see the rest of the agreement.

GNU GENERAL PUBLIC LICENSE
Version 2, June 1991

Copyright (C) 1989, 1991 Free Software Foundation, Inc.
 59 Temple Place, Suite 330, Boston, MA 02111-1307 USA
Everyone is permitted to copy and distribute verbatim copies
of this license document, but changing it is not allowed.

Preamble

 The licenses for most software are designed to take away your

If you accept the terms of the agreement, click I Agree to continue. You must accept the
agreement to install FileZilla Client 3.10.2.

Nullsoft Install System v2.46.5-Unicode

I Agree   Cancel

In this example we have selected the option to make *FileZilla* available to anyone who uses this computer:

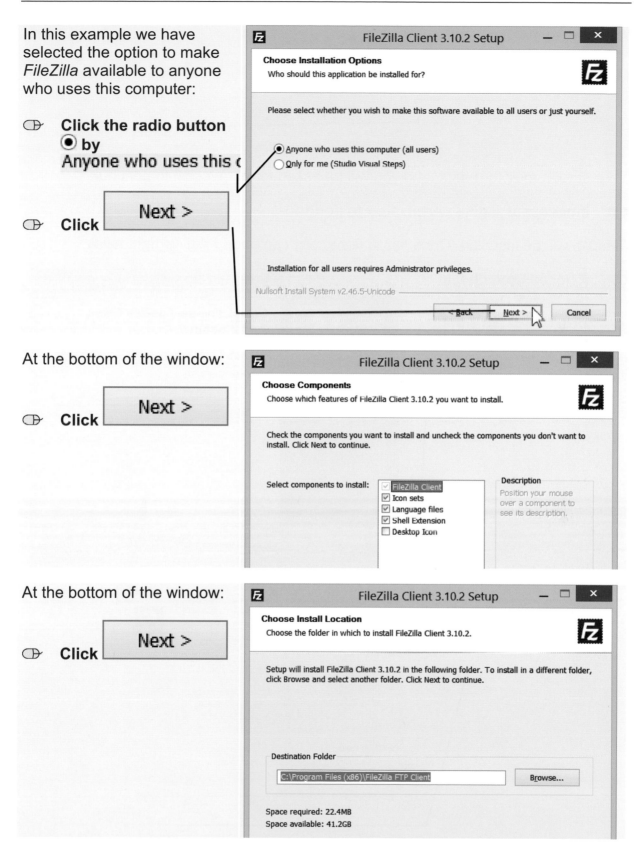

⊕ **Click the radio button
⦿ by
Anyone who uses this**

⊕ **Click** Next >

At the bottom of the window:

⊕ **Click** Next >

At the bottom of the window:

⊕ **Click** Next >

At the bottom of the window:

☞ **Click** Install

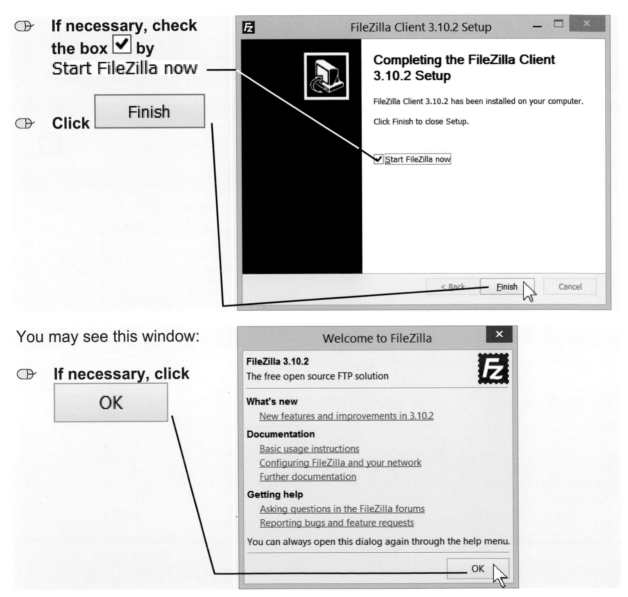

Your screen may turn dark, and you will be asked for permission to continue:

☞ **If necessary, give permission to continue**

FileZilla will be installed. Once this is done, you can open *FileZilla* right away:

☞ **If necessary, check the box ☑ by**
Start FileZilla now

☞ **Click** Finish

You may see this window:

☞ **If necessary, click**
OK

Before you can use *FileZilla* together with *WordPress*, you will need to set up the program first. In order to do this, you need to enter the data regarding your web space.

This data is the FTP data you received from your hosting provider. This information is usually included in the email you have received, or can be found at your hosting provider's website, along with the information about your user account. You will at least need to have the following data:

- the address of the ftp server (often recognizable by the 'ftp' text at the beginning)
- the user name for the ftp server
- the password for the ftp server

Please note:

The user name and password for the ftp server are often different from the user name and password for your user account with the hosting provider. Sometimes you need to enter this data in your account with your provider first, in order to use it later on.

This is how you enter the settings for the ftp server in *FileZilla*:

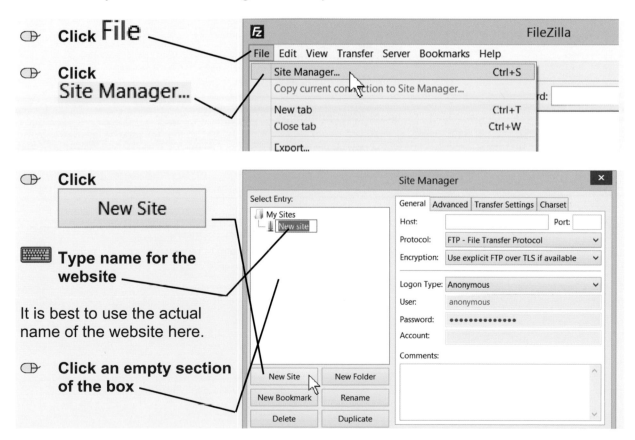

⊕ **Click File**

⊕ **Click Site Manager...**

⊕ **Click New Site**

⌨ **Type name for the website**

It is best to use the actual name of the website here.

⊕ **Click an empty section of the box**

The name has been filled in:

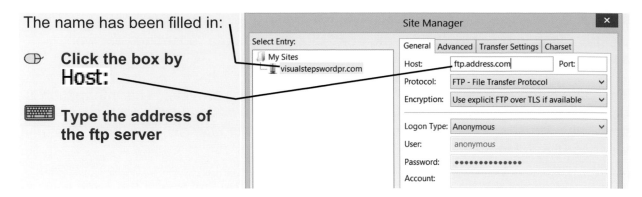

☞ **Click the box by Host:**

⌨ **Type the address of the ftp server**

Now you need to enter the user name and password:

☞ **By Logon Type:, select the Normal option**

⌨ **By User:, type the user name for the ftp server**

⌨ **By Password:, type the password for the ftp server**

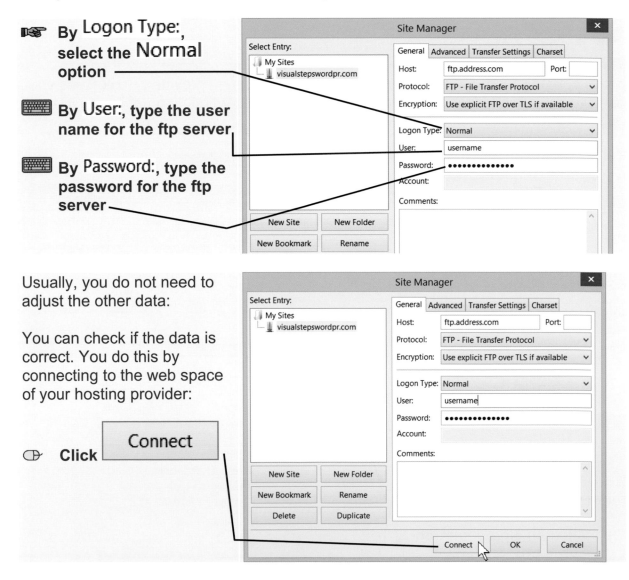

Usually, you do not need to adjust the other data:

You can check if the data is correct. You do this by connecting to the web space of your hosting provider:

☞ **Click [Connect]**

If the data is correct, you will be able to access your web space:

You can tell by the text *Directory listing of "/" successful*.

You will also see the content of your web space in this box:

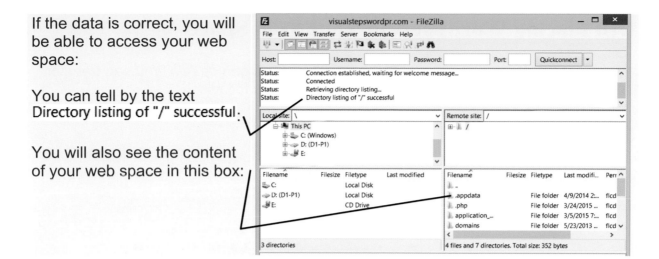

HELP! I cannot connect to my web space.

If you cannot connect to the web space at your hosting provider, you will see the message *Could not connect to server* in the *FileZilla* window. And you will not be able to see the folders in your web space. In that case, you can do the following:

☞ **Check whether the name of the ftp server and all the other login data has been correctly filled in**

If you have correctly filled in the data:

☞ **Use the information from your hosting provider to check if you need to fill in any additional data, such as** Port: **and** Protocol:

Once the data is added correctly:

☞ **In the *Site Manager*, by** Encryption: **, select Only use plain FTP (insecu**

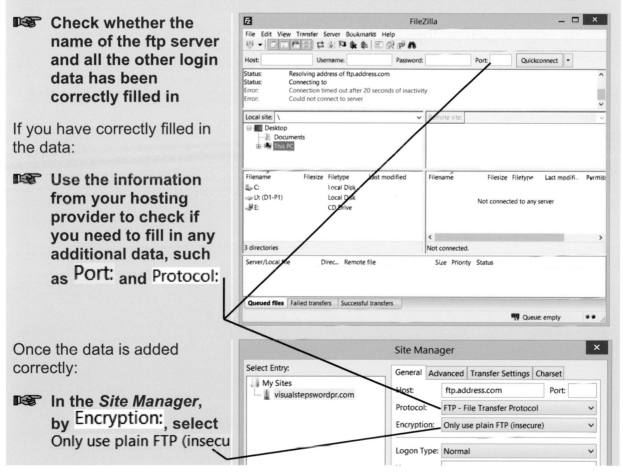

1.10 Placing WordPress in Your Web Space

If you have made a connection with the ftp server through *FileZilla*, you can transfer the *WordPress* files to your web space. You do that as follows:

HELP! The connection has been broken.

If you are inactive for too long while connected to the ftp server, the connection may have been closed down automatically. This is how you reconnect to the ftp server:

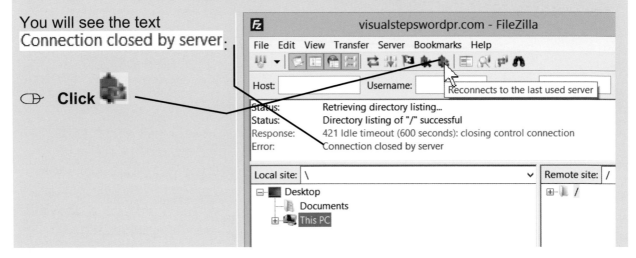

You will see the text
Connection closed by server:

☞ **Click**

First, find the folder with the *WordPress* files:

☞ **Click** Documents

By 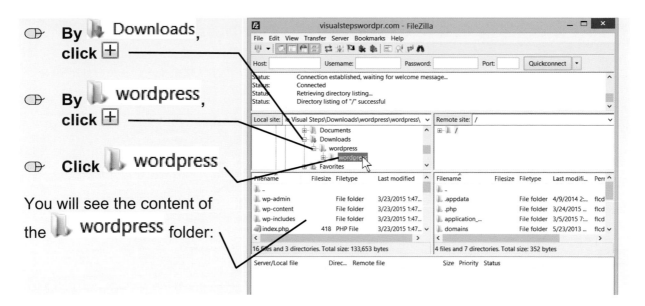 Downloads, click ⊞

By wordpress, click ⊞

Click wordpress

You will see the content of the wordpress folder:

Now you need to open the correct folder where you want to transfer the *WordPress* files. There are various folders already present in your web space, for example, for working with email, or for storing images. These folders will vary according to each hosting provider.

Usually, there is a special folder designated for placing the files that have to do with displaying the website. This folder may have names such as: html, public html, httpdocs, www, wwwroot, or something like that. You can find the name of this folder among the information sent to you by your hosting provider.

➡ Please note:

It is important to copy the files to the correct folder, otherwise you will not be able to create a website with *WordPress*. If you cannot find any of the folders mentioned above in your web space, you will need to ask your hosting provider for the correct folder.

In the box on the right-hand side:

Double-click the folder for the Internet files

In this example, the folder is called public_html.

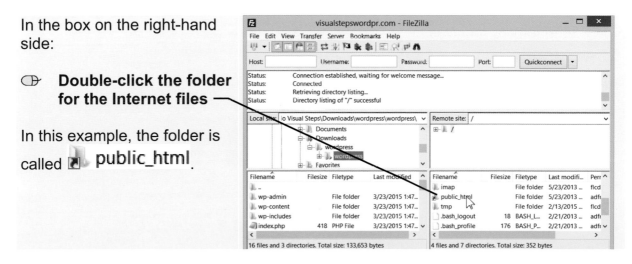

You will see the content of the folder:

You can copy all the files within the 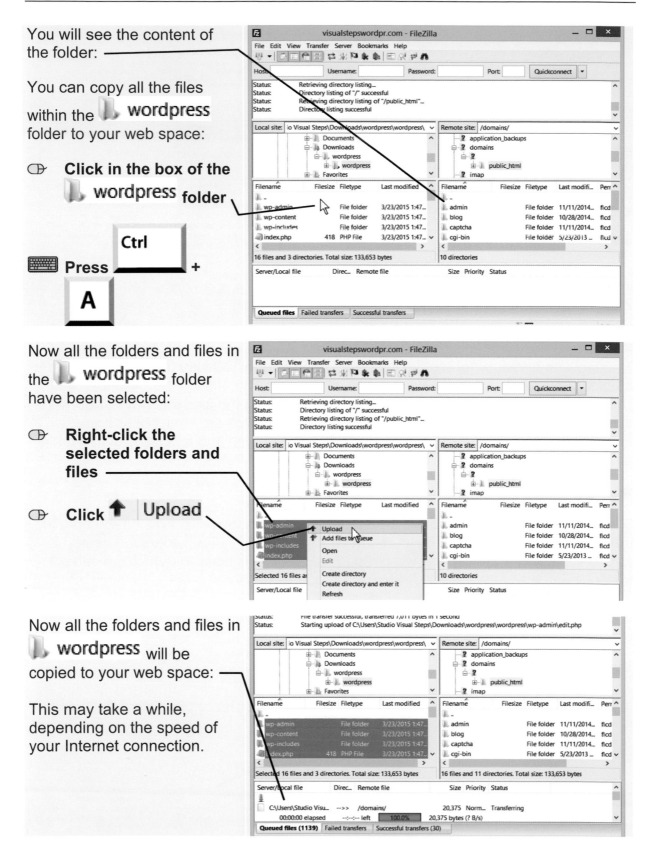 **wordpress** folder to your web space:

☞ **Click in the box of the wordpress folder**

⌨ **Press** Ctrl **+** A

Now all the folders and files in the **wordpress** folder have been selected:

☞ **Right-click the selected folders and files**

☞ **Click** ⬆ **Upload**

Now all the folders and files in **wordpress** will be copied to your web space:

This may take a while, depending on the speed of your Internet connection.

All the folders and files within

📁 **wordpress** have been

transferred:

The transfer was successful. This is the case if no failed transfers are reported:

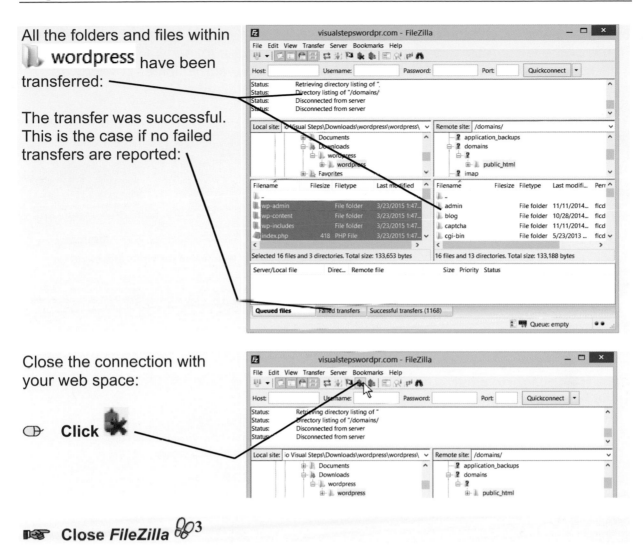

Close the connection with your web space:

☞ **Click** 🔌

☞ **Close** *FileZilla* 👣³

☞ **If necessary, close the folder window** 👣³

1.11 Installing WordPress

When the *WordPress* files have been copied to your web space, you can finish installing *WordPress* so that it can be used for your specific website. Since the *WordPress* package has already been installed on your web space, you only need to open the installation file in your Internet browser.

☞ **Open the Internet browser** 👣⁶

Now you need to type the web address of your website, that is to say, the domain name or the URL. After this name you type the text: */wp-admin/install.php*
This means that the installation file *install.php*, in the *wp-admin* folder in your web space, will be opened. An example of a *WordPress* installation file is *www.mydomain.com/wp-admin/install.php*.

Type your web address

Then type: `/wp-admin/install.php`

Press `Enter`

The installation file will be opened. If everything goes well, you will see the window below. In this window you can set the language used by *WordPress*:

If necessary, click English (United States)

Click `Continue`

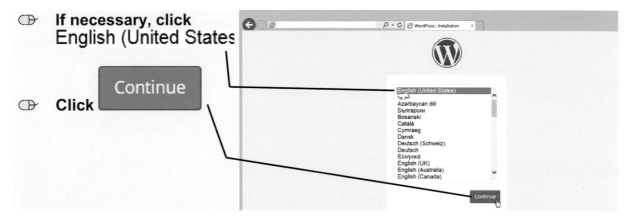

✂ HELP! I see an error message.

If you see an error message during the installation of *WordPress*, this may be caused by several reasons.

For example, if you see this message, you have typed an incorrect web address in the address bar:

☞ **Type the web address correctly and try again**

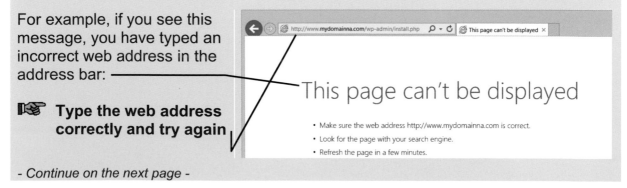

This page can't be displayed

- Make sure the web address http://www.mydomainna.com is correct.
- Look for the page with your search engine.
- Refresh the page in a few minutes.

- Continue on the next page -

If the installation file has been opened, but cannot connect to your database, you will see this window:

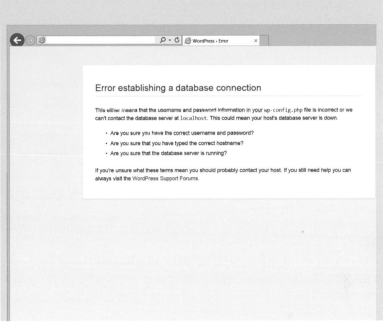

☞ **Check whether the data in the *wp-config.php* configuration file is correct**

You can read more about this topic in *section 1.8 Adjusting the WordPress Configuration File*.

If this does not work, then try again later. Sometimes, there is simply a temporary malfunction with your Internet connection.

Now you need to enter some other important data for *WordPress*, such as the login data for the website.

➥ **Please note:**

Do not use the default 'admin' name as a user name. This name can easily be guessed by people who want to log on without your permission.

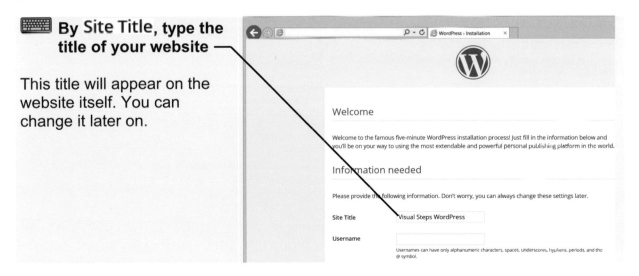

⌨ **By Site Title, type the title of your website**

This title will appear on the website itself. You can change it later on.

⌨ By **Username**, type the desired user name for logging on to *WordPress* ——

⌨ By **Password, twice**, type the desired password (twice) for logging on to *WordPress* ——

Note the rules for creating a password: ——

Information needed

Please provide the following information. Don't worry, you can always change these settings later.

Site Title   Visual Steps WordPress

Username   username
Usernames can have only alphanumeric characters, spaces, underscores, hyphens, periods, and the @ symbol.

Password, twice
A password will be automatically generated for you if you leave this blank.
●●●●●●●●●●
●●●●●●●●●●
Strong

Hint: The password should be at least seven characters long. To make it stronger, use upper and lower case letters, numbers, and symbols like ! " ? $ % ^ &).

✚ HELP! I see different windows.

WordPress is constantly being updated and improved; during installation you may see windows that are a little bit different. In that case, just follow the instructions in the windows and enter the required data.

⌨ By **Your E-mail**, type your email address ——

This email address is used by *WordPress*, to send you messages about your website.

☞ **Uncheck the box ☑ by** Allow search engines

☞ **Click**

Install WordPress

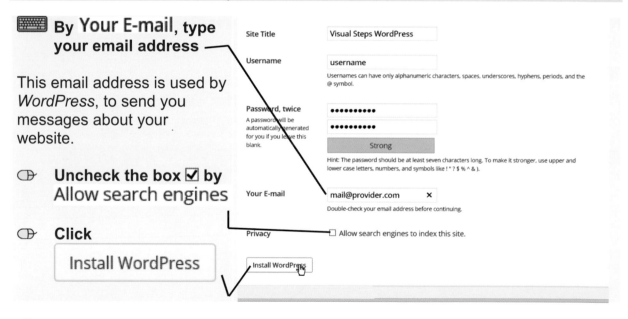

Site Title   Visual Steps WordPress

Username   username
Usernames can have only alphanumeric characters, spaces, underscores, hyphens, periods, and the @ symbol.

Password, twice
A password will be automatically generated for you if you leave this blank.
●●●●●●●●●●
●●●●●●●●●●
Strong

Hint: The password should be at least seven characters long. To make it stronger, use upper and lower case letters, numbers, and symbols like ! " ? $ % ^ &).

Your E-mail   mail@provider.com   ✕
Double-check your email address before continuing.

Privacy   ☐ Allow search engines to index this site.

Install WordPress

💡 Tip
Make your website visible to search engines
It is wise not to display your website to search engines such as *Google*, while you are still building the site. This will prevent visitors from finding your website when it is still in progress. You can change this setting later on, once you have finished building your website.

Click [Log In]

1.12 Viewing the Basic WordPress Website

After you have filled in the data in the installation window, the installation of *WordPress* will be complete. From then on, you can login to *WordPress* directly.

You will see the login window. Here you need to enter the user name and password you have previously set for *WordPress*. The login window may look a bit different by your own hosting provider.

➥ Please note:

You can use the Remember Me option on the login screen to remember your user name and password. This may seem very useful, but can also pose a security risk. If you check the box ☑ by Remember Me, the next time you log on, the user name will automatically be displayed after you have typed the first letter, and the password will automatically be filled in as well. This actually means that others can also log on to your website through your computer, and can edit your data. If you are using a public computer, it is recommended to never enable the Remember Me option.

By Username, **type your user name**

By Password, **type your password**

Click [Log In]

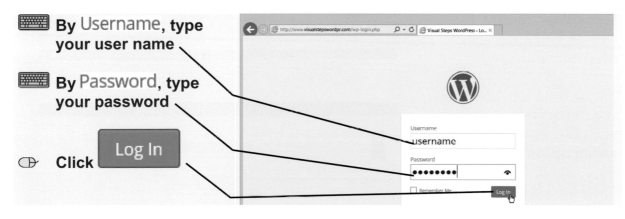

✗ HELP! I see the windows, but in a different order.

You may see these windows in a different order. In this case, enter the required data, and follow the instructions in the windows.

You may see a question regarding remembering the password:

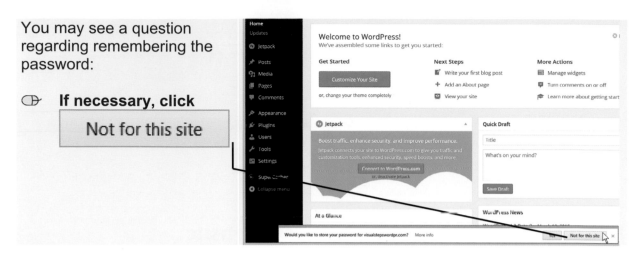

☞ **If necessary, click**

> **Not for this site**

Now you will see the *WordPress Dashboard.* In the Dashboard you can enter all the settings for *WordPress* and for your website. In the next few chapters you will read more about this feature.

You can also view the basic *WordPress* website through the Dashboard:

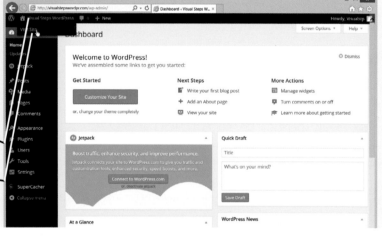

☞ **Place the pointer on the name of your website, for example** Visual Steps WordPress

☞ **Click** Visit Site

You will see the basic *WordPress* website:

The website has been filled with default text. This text may differ according to your hosting provider.

In the next few chapters you will learn how to replace this text and add images of your own.

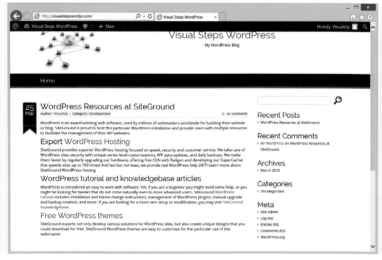

Now you can log out of *WordPress*:

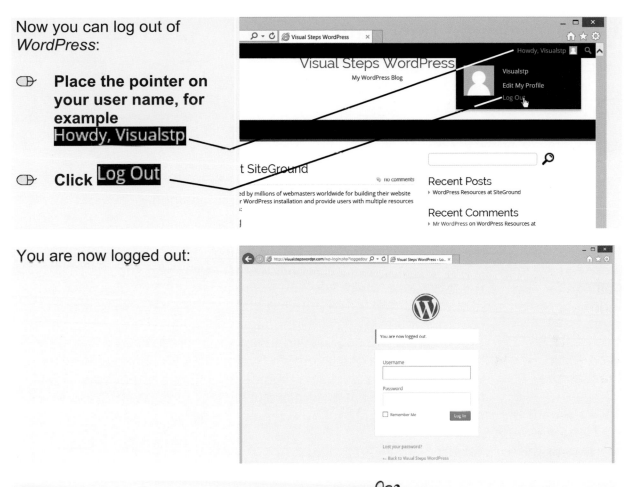

☞ **Place the pointer on your user name, for example Howdy, Visualstp**

☞ **Click Log Out**

You are now logged out:

☞ **Close the window of the Internet browser** 𝕲³

In this chapter you have learned how to set up your web space, and how to make the *WordPress* program ready for use. In the next chapter you will learn how to adjust the *WordPress* settings.

1.13 Background Information

Dictionary

CMS	Short for Content Management System.
Code	Text commands that tell the browser how the website should be displayed. PHP, JavaScript and HTML use code.
Configuration file	A *WordPress* file that contains the main settings, such as the database that *WordPress* needs to use.
Content Management System	A system with which you can manage the content of a website. The regular method of creating and maintaining a website requires you to work with languages such as HTML, JavaScript or PHP, and you need to manually enter all the lines of code by hand. A Content Management System lets you build and edit the website by using an online web editor without you having to edit the code yourself. It is a lot like filling in a form. *WordPress* is an example of a Content Management System.
Control panel	An area of your web space where you can edit various settings. Also called hosting manager.
Dashboard	The management panel of *WordPress*, where you can edit the *WordPress* settings and the website settings as well.
Database	A type of file in which you can store, edit, or delete data. *WordPress* uses a database to store the data that goes with a website.
Domain name	A domain name is the web address for your website, for example, www.visualsteps.com.
FileZilla	A free FTP program.
FTP program	An FTP program is used to upload or download files to and from a computer on the Internet, such as a hosting provider's server. The free *FileZilla* program is an example of an FTP program.

- Continue on the next page -

Hosting manager	An area of your web space where you can edit various settings. Also called control panel.
Hosting provider	A company that offers web space where you can place your website, usually for a fee. You can also register a domain name with a hosting provider.
HTML	A code that tells your Internet browser what and how the items on a website should be displayed.
MySQL database	A frequently used type of database that is required if you want to work with *WordPress*.
Open source	Software that can be used for free, and that is accessible to anyone who wants to add features to improve the software.
PHP	A programming language that tells your Internet browser what to display on a website, and how it should be displayed.
Server-sided	A server is just another name for a computer that is owned by a hosting provider. Server-sided means that a program runs on the provider's computer, and not on your own computer.
Theme	A ready-made template in *WordPress* that you can use to create a website. The layout and formatting have already been created. By using a theme, you do not need to build your website from scratch.
Unzip	Decompressing or restoring the files in a ZIP file to their original size and state (extracting), so you can use them.
Update	A new, improved version of a program.
Upload	Copying a file from your computer to a computer on the Internet, such as a hosting provider's computer.
URL	An abbreviation for 'Uniform Resource Locator', which means the web address for a specific website.
Web address	The address at which you can find a specific website. For example, www.visualsteps.com.
Weblog	A kind of Internet diary where users can share their adventures, thoughts, and feelings with others.

- Continue on the next page -

Web space	A space on the computer of a hosting provider, where you can place (upload) your website so that visitors will be able to view it.
WYSIWYG editor	WYSIWYG stands for: What You See Is What You Get. This type of program enables you to build a website without typing program code. You can add, edit and delete text and photos directly in the editor window. Once saved, the program will then generate the code needed to render the web page for the Internet.
ZIP file	A file that contains compressed files. The compression means the files take up less disk space than they would in their original (uncompressed) state. A compressed file needs to be extracted (unzipped). You can do this with *Windows*, and with other special compression programs, such as *WinZip*.

Source: WordPress Help

Choosing a hosting provider

In order to present a website on the Internet, you will need to have a web space. If you want to build a *WordPress* website, you will even need to have a web space for creating the website itself.

When you subscribe to an Internet Service Provider's service (ISP), you will often be offered free web space. This web space is often quite small, and you will not be able to use software such as *WordPress*. That is why you need to have a subscription with a hosting provider. Here you can also register a domain name for your website, while you are at it.

In the USA alone, there are thousands of hosting providers that offer all kinds of hosting packages. It is not easy to choose between them. That is why it is wise to reflect on the website you want to build. If this is a simple, small website, just for your personal use, and if you do not expect more than a few thousand visitors a month, a limited hosting package will suffice: these are often called *small*. This type of package offers around 10 GB (gigabyte) of space and up to 10,000 visitors a month, for example. If you want to build a company website with lots of pages and photos, and if you want to attract as many visitors as possible, you will need to use a more extensive package: medium, large or extra-large. Then you may get up to 30 GB of disk space or more, and you can handle up to 100,000 visitors a month.

- Continue on the next page -

When you are looking for a hosting package, there are some other requirements that you need to take into account as well, such as: do you want to use just one email address or multiple email addresses, do you need a single database or multiple databases, do you want to be able to use special software, such as *WordPress*, without too much trouble. Usually you can easily upgrade your package, from a simple one to a more extensive one, so it might be smart to start small. Apart from this, pricing and service are important too. It is worthwhile to look around a bit, and compare various hosting providers or even ask friends for their input.

Various hosting packages offered by SiteGround.com:

It is wise to register your domain name with the same provider where you host your website. In this case, you will not need to redirect your domain name to a web space that is hosted by another provider. And you can often get a discount when you purchase a hosting package along with a domain name all at once.

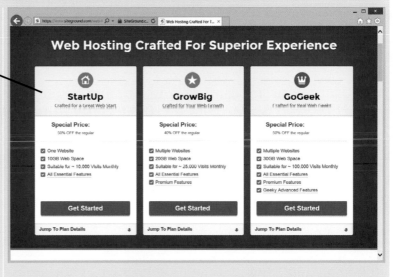

We recommend using a provider that offers special support for *WordPress*.

1.14 Tips

💡 Tip

Delete a website (*WordPress* is installed with a script)
Sometimes, you may no longer want to use a website you have created with *WordPress*. If you want to start all over again with another website, you can delete *WordPress*. If you reinstall *WordPress* again after the deletion, you will have a fresh start. You can also delete *WordPress* in case you want to use another type of CMS.

You need to delete *WordPress* through the control panel with your hosting provider. **Please note:** your own hosting provider may use a different procedure.

☞ **Go to your account at your hosting provider (see *section 1.4 Setting Up Your Web Space with a Provider that Supports WordPress*)**

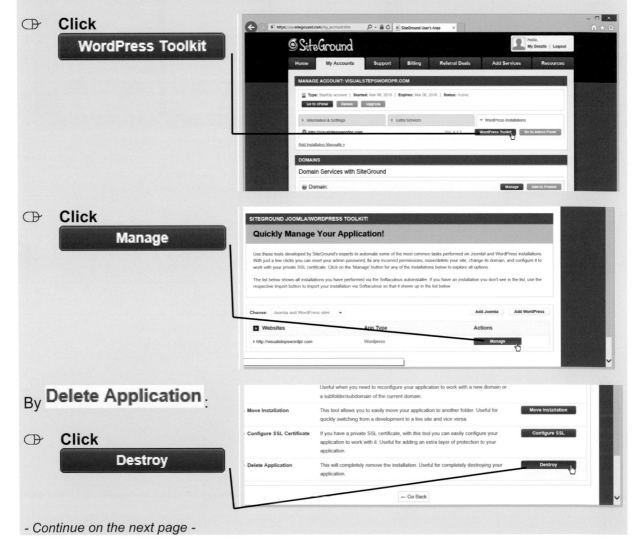

☞ Click **WordPress Toolkit**

☞ Click **Manage**

By **Delete Application**:

☞ Click **Destroy**

- Continue on the next page -

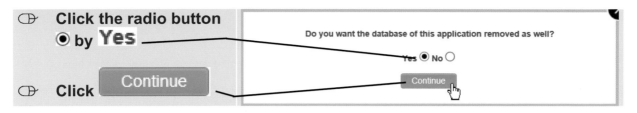

⬆ **Click the radio button ⊙ by Yes**

⬆ **Click** Continue

💡 Tip

Delete a website (if you have installed *WordPress* yourself)
Sometimes you will no longer want to use a website you have built with *WordPress*. If you want to start over again with a new website, you can remove *WordPress* and install it again to give you a fresh, a clean slate. Deleting *WordPress* is also useful if you decide to use a different CMS.

If you have installed *WordPress* yourself, you can manually delete *WordPress* through your FTP program, such as *FileZilla* (see also *section 1.10 Placing WordPress in Your Web Space*):

☞ **Open *FileZilla***

☞ **Connect to the ftp server**

☞ **If necessary, open the folder with the *WordPress* files**

⌨ **Press Ctrl and hold it down**

⬆ **Click the folders that begin with 'wp-'**

⬆ **Click all the files, except .htaccess**

⌨ **Press Delete**

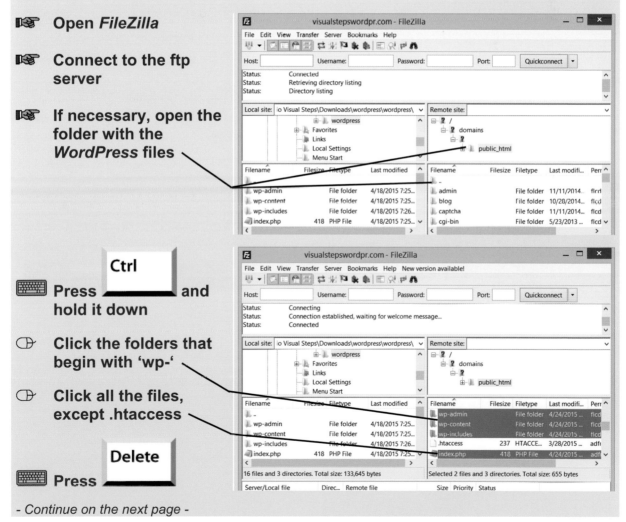

- Continue on the next page -

Click [Yes]

Now the selected folders and files will be deleted.

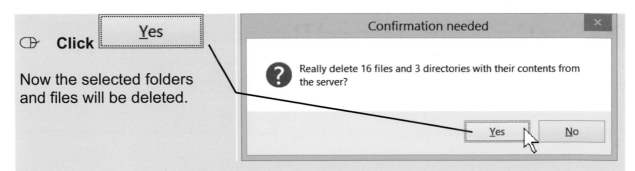

You will also need to delete the database that is used by *WordPress*. You can do this through the control panel of your hosting provider (**Please note:** Your own hosting provider may use a different procedure):

- 👉 **Go to the control panel of your web space** 👣²

- 👉 **Log in to the control panel**

- 👆 **Click**

  Websites & Domain

- 👆 **Click** Databases

- 👆 **Check the box ☑ by the database used by your WordPress website**

- 👆 **Click ✖ Remove**

- 👆 **Click** [Yes]

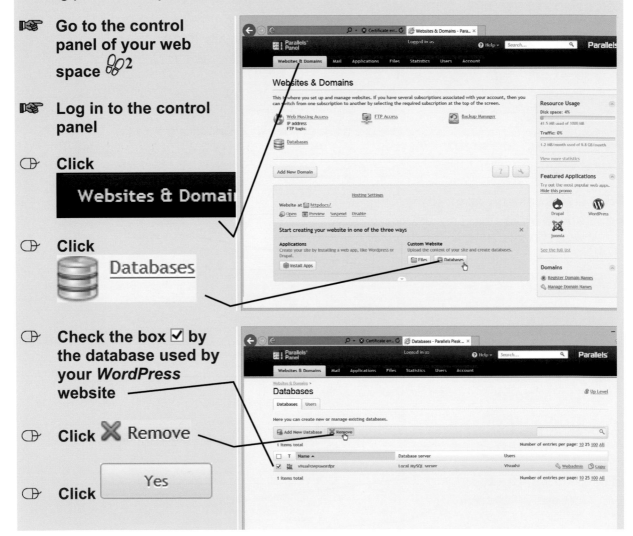

2. Setting Up WordPress

Once *WordPress* is installed, you can start building a website right away, if you want. But it is wiser to view the *WordPress* settings beforehand and adjust them, if necessary. All of the settings can be accessed through the Dashboard.

It is a good idea to become thoroughly acquainted with the Dashboard. You can view information about the kinds of settings that are possible. One of the main settings allows you to enter the title of your website, for example. You can also set the time zone for the time that is displayed on the website.

The write settings are especially important if you want to publish your website as a *blog*. Here you can determine how you would want to post your own messages on your blog, for instance.

The read settings determine how the messages on the website are displayed, and whether your website can be found by search engines such as *Google*. If you want your visitors to be able to post comments on your website, you can enable the necessary settings.

The media settings allow you to control how different types of media files, such as photos and videos, are displayed.

There are also settings for the so-called *permalinks*. These are the web addresses for the pages of your website. You can decide how these addresses are to be displayed. You will also find helpful advice about what the best options are.

Along with yourself, you can also add other users that will be authorized to edit your website. All of these things will be explained in this chapter.

In this chapter you will learn how to:

- log on to *WordPress*;
- work with the Dashboard;
- enter the general settings;
- enter the write and read settings;
- enter discussion settings;
- enter media settings;
- enter permalink settings;
- enter user settings;
- manage users.

2.1 Logging On to WordPress

At the end of the previous chapter you had a brief view of the Dashboard when you logged on to *WordPress.* The Dashboard is the place where you can edit your website and change the settings. To access it, you first need to log on:

☞ **Open** *Internet Explorer* 𝒪𝒪⁶

In the address bar:

⌨ **Type your domain name**

⌨ **Behind the domain name, type:** /wp-admin

⌨ **Press** Enter

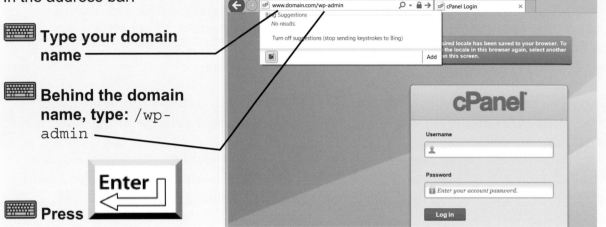

💡 **Tip**

Log on with wp-login.php
You can also log on by typing /wp-login.php after the domain name, instead of /wp-admin.

Now you will see the login window. Here you enter the user name and password you have previously set for *WordPress*:

⌨ **By** Username**, type your user name**

⌨ **By** Password**, type your password**

🖱 **Click** Log In

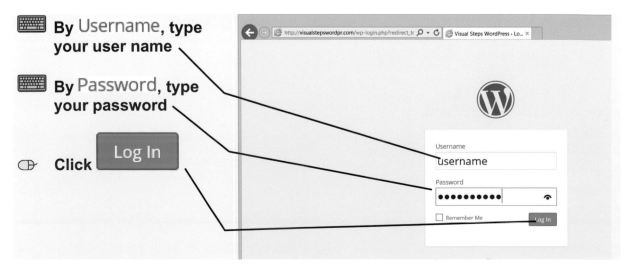

✖ HELP! I have forgotten my password.

You may have forgotten your login password for *WordPress*. If that is the case, you can request a new password:

⊂⊃ **Click**
     Lost your password?

☞ **Follow the
     instructions in the
     next few windows**

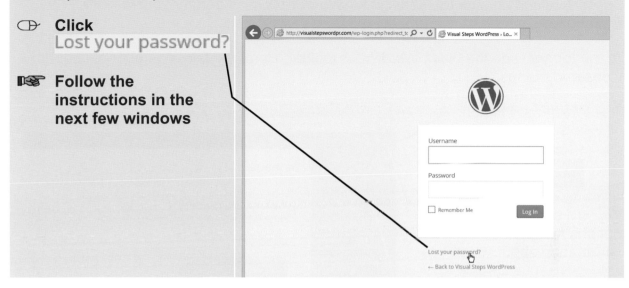

You will see the *WordPress* Dashboard:

If you are asked whether the system needs to remember the password:

⊂⊃ **Click**
     Not for this site

2.2 Getting Acquainted with the Dashboard

The Dashboard is the nerve center of *WordPress* and your website. You use it to set up, update and change the settings for *WordPress* itself and for your website. The Dashboard consists of different components.

At the top you see the black *WordPress* toolbar. Here you find a number of important icons and menus:

The *WordPress* toolbar:

☞   **Place the pointer on**

You will see a menu with options that provide information about *WordPress*:

☞   **Click** Documentation

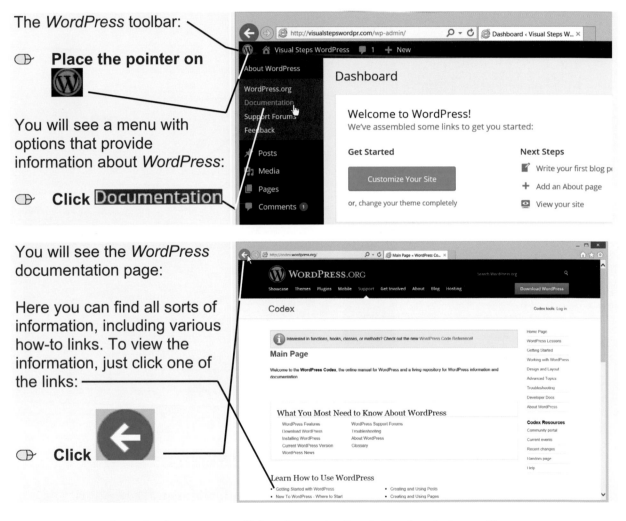

You will see the *WordPress* documentation page:

Here you can find all sorts of information, including various how-to links. To view the information, just click one of the links:

☞   **Click**

The other options in the menu will lead you to the following information:

About WordPress	Let's you view more information regarding this version of *WordPress*.
WordPress.org	Opens the main *WordPress* (organization) website.

- Continue on the next page -

Support Forums	Opens the web page with various user forums. Here you will find numerous subjects that have to do with working with *WordPress*.
Feedback	Opens the forum where you can add a request or submit a comment about *WordPress*.

There are other icons on the toolbar:

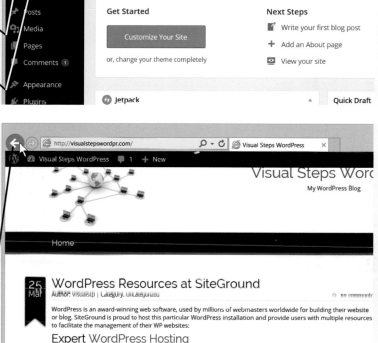

☞ **Place the pointer on the name of your website, for example**
🏠 **Visual Steps WordPres**

☞ **Click Visit Site**

The website will appear, in its current form:

This example may look different on your own screen.

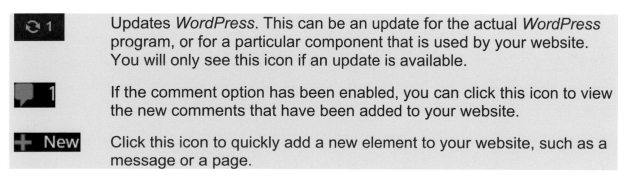

☞ **Click** ←

Here is what you can do with the other options on the toolbar:

🔄 1	Updates *WordPress*. This can be an update for the actual *WordPress* program, or for a particular component that is used by your website. You will only see this icon if an update is available.
💬 1	If the comment option has been enabled, you can click this icon to view the new comments that have been added to your website.
➕ New	Click this icon to quickly add a new element to your website, such as a message or a page.

The **Howdy, Visualstp** link will open the user menu:

☞ **Place the pointer on Howdy, Visualstp**

☞ **Click Edit My Profile**

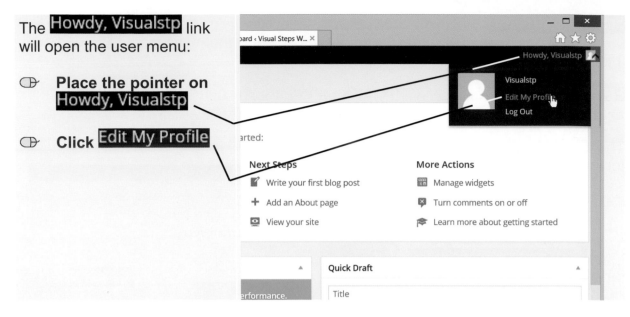

You will see your user profile in *WordPress*. Here you can enter and edit all kinds of personal information. To begin with, you can enter your personal preferences for the *WordPress* control panel. You can leave most settings as they are. In this example we have only selected a different color scheme:

By **Personal Options** you can find options for your Dashboard:

☞ **Click the radio button ◉ by Light**

By **Name** you can enter your first and last name, if you wish:

By **Contact Info** you will find options for entering contact information:

By **About Yourself** you can enter personal information, if you wish. Keep in mind that some themes will display this information automatically on the contact page of the website.

You can also set a new password for *WordPress* on this page:

In order to apply the changes, at the bottom of the window:

☞ **Click** Update Profile

Go back to the Dashboard:

☞ **Click** 🔵 Dashboard

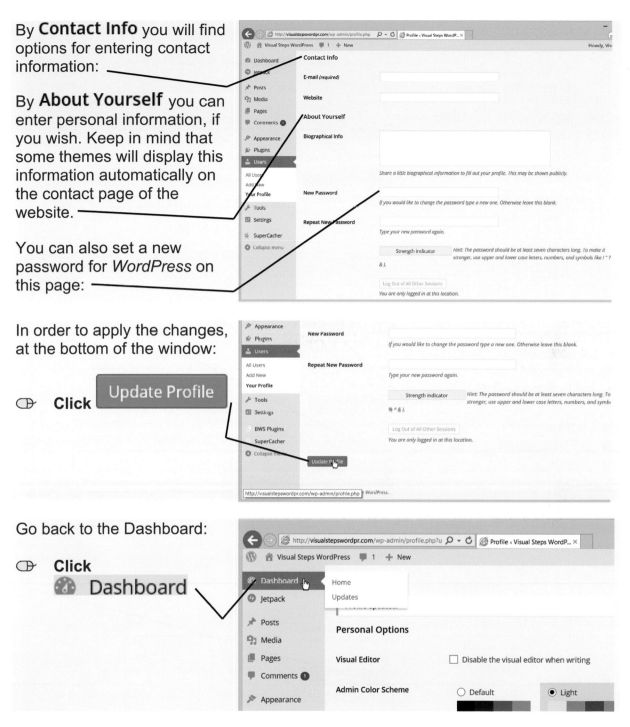

Now the *WordPress* color scheme has been adjusted.

Below the toolbar you will find two more menus with useful options:

The [Screen Options ▼] menu lets you determine what components can be shown on the Dashboard:

☞ **Click**
[Screen Options ▼]

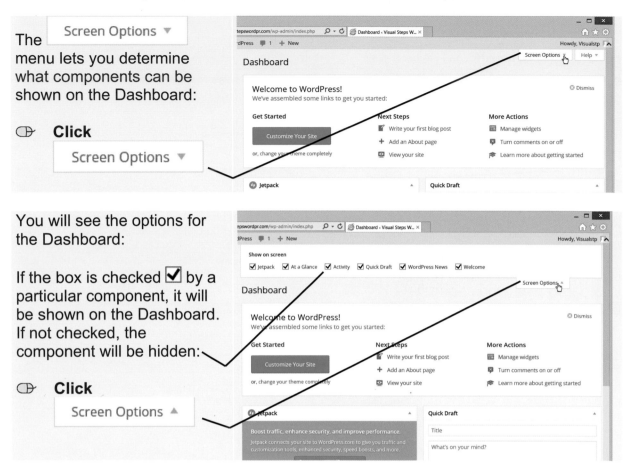

You will see the options for the Dashboard:

If the box is checked ☑ by a particular component, it will be shown on the Dashboard. If not checked, the component will be hidden:

☞ **Click**
[Screen Options ▲]

Now the *Screen Options* section will be closed.

The [Help ▼] menu gives you more information about working with the Dashboard:

☞ **Click** [Help ▼]

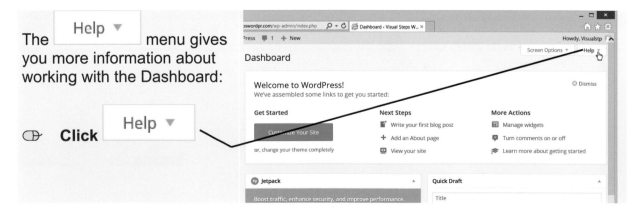

You will see a number of
options:

⊕ **Click** Content

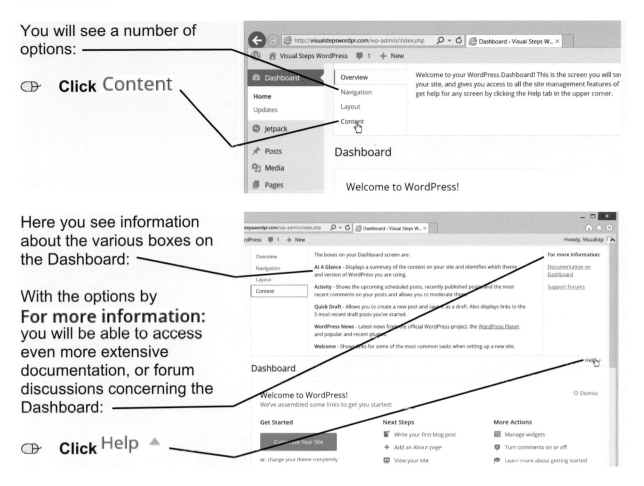

Here you see information
about the various boxes on
the Dashboard:

With the options by
For more information:
you will be able to access
even more extensive
documentation, or forum
discussions concerning the
Dashboard:

⊕ **Click** Help ▲

On the left side of the Dashboard you will find the main menu. The menu lets you
manage the various *WordPress* components and your website content. There are
several basic options. Additional options are provided by specific plugins that have
been installed (see *Chapter 6 Useful Plugins*).

Many of these menus contain
multiple options:

You can see them if you
place the pointer on the
option:

⊕ **Place the pointer on**
   Pages

You will see the options:

⊕ **Click** All Pages

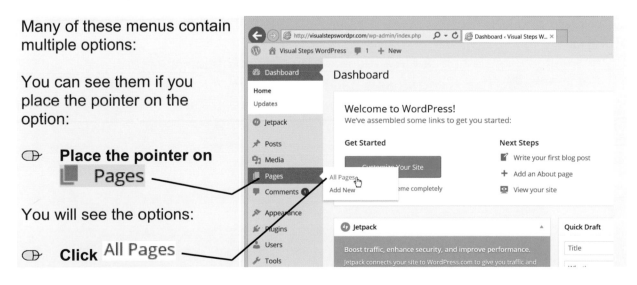

You will see your website's
pages:

☞ **Click**

   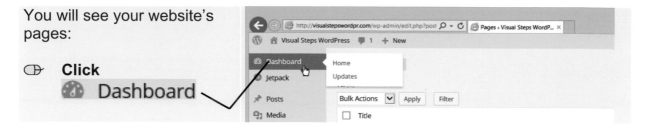

   Dashboard

In the next few sections and the following chapters you will find out more about the
various menu options.

The largest part of the Dashboard is taken up by the information screen. Here you
can find information about *WordPress* and its settings, and your own website
settings:

The Dashboard information
screen is divided into multiple
blocks, also called modules:

In this manner, the
information is presented in a
well-ordered fashion.

The type of information
shown will vary depending on
the menu item or the option
you have clicked.

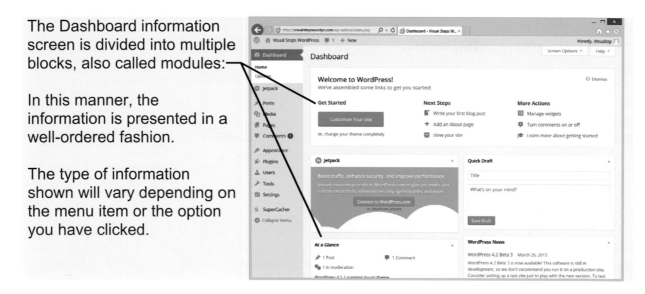

💡 **Tip**

Number by menu option
Sometimes you see a number in a red circle by a menu option, such as
💬 Comments ❶. This is known as a badge and is a way of alerting you that
something new has been posted, for example a new comment. A badge may also
indicate that an update is available in the *WordPress* program or one of its
components.

2.3 Entering General Settings

In the Dashboard you can adjust various settings for working with *WordPress* and your website. Some settings are entered only when you need to use them, but others can be set up right away.
In the general settings you can determine how you want to work with *WordPress*:

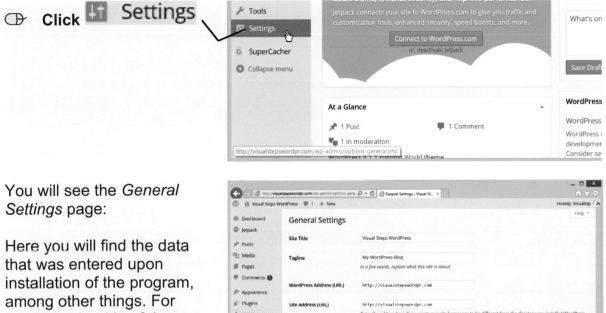

You will see the *General Settings* page:

Here you will find the data that was entered upon installation of the program, among other things. For example, the title of the website and your email address. You can adjust this data here, if you wish.

Here is a list of the settings and options you can edit on the *General Settings* page:

Site Title	The title of your website. This title will also be displayed on your website.
Tagline	The subtitle of the website. This can be a brief description, which may also be displayed on the website.
WordPress Address (URL)	The web address or domain name of your website.

- Continue on the next page -

Site Address (URL)	The web address or domain name of your website, in case it differs from the *WordPress* address. This name will be different if the *WordPress* software is installed in a different location from the address referred to by the domain name. For example: your *WordPress* software is installed at www.visualstepswordpr.com and your website is displayed at www.visualsteps.com.
E-mail Address	An email address to which *WordPress* can send messages.
Membership	Here you can indicate whether anyone can register with the website, for instance, if you allow visitors to comment on the messages you have posted on your website. See also *section 2.8 Entering User Settings* and *section 2.9 Managing Users*.
New User Default Role	Here you can determine the default role for new users, once they have registered. See also *section 2.8 Entering User Settings*.
Timezone	The time zone for the website. This is important for a correct display of the time on your website.
Date Format	The way in which the date is displayed on your website.
Time Format	The way in which the time is displayed on your website.
Week Starts On	The day on which the week starts. This affects the way in which a calendar is displayed on your website.
Site Language	The language in which *WordPress* is displayed.

For now you can enter a few settings for your website.

➥ Please note:

In this book we will build a sample website called Visual Steps WordPress. You can follow the steps to build this sample too, or start building your own website right away. If you decide to build your own website, you need to take into account that the screenshots in this book may differ from the screens of your own website.

If you want to change the title or tagline of your website:

⌨ **By Site Title, type the desired title**

⌨ **By Tagline, type the description for your website, for example:** Gardening as a hobby

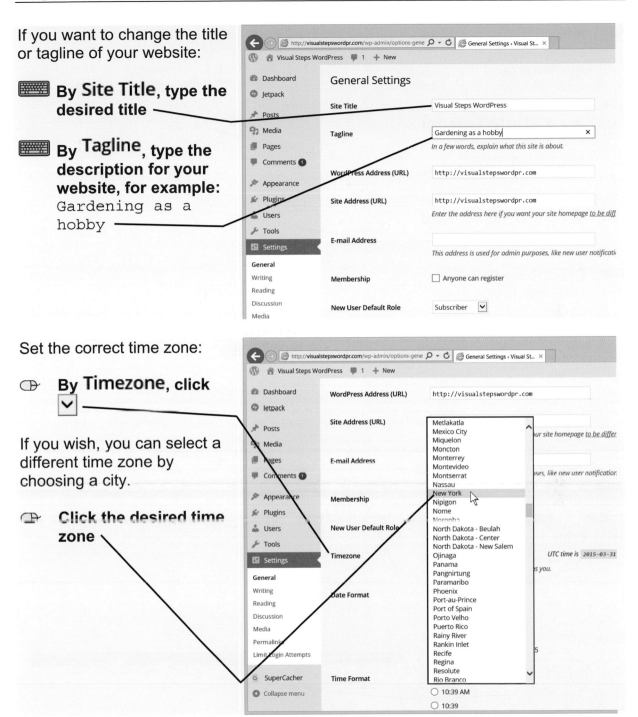

Set the correct time zone:

☞ **By Timezone, click ⌄**

If you wish, you can select a different time zone by choosing a city.

☞ **Click the desired time zone**

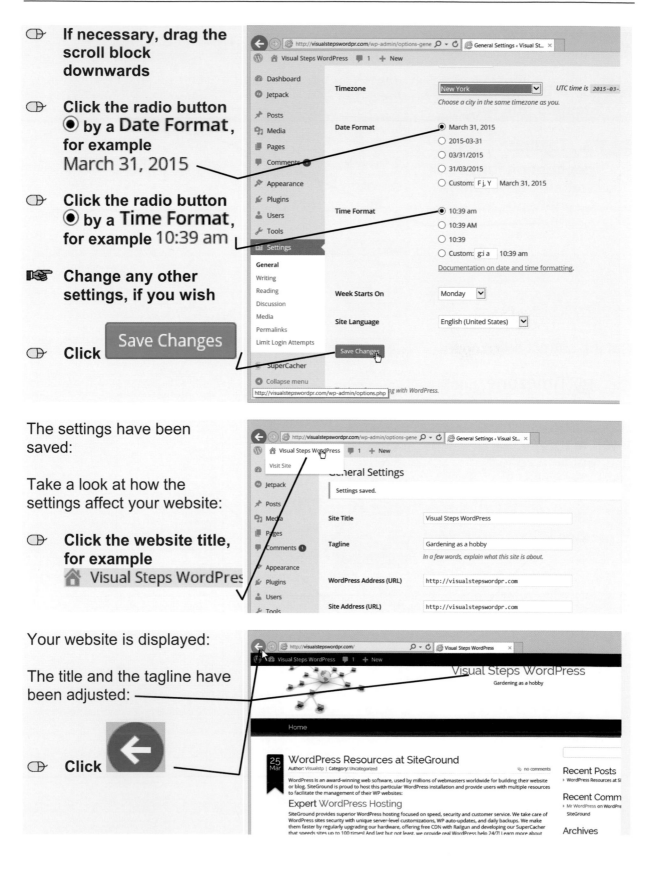

⊕ **If necessary, drag the scroll block downwards**

⊕ **Click the radio button ⊙ by a Date Format,** for example March 31, 2015

⊕ **Click the radio button ⊙ by a Time Format,** for example 10:39 am

☞ **Change any other settings, if you wish**

⊕ **Click** Save Changes

The settings have been saved:

Take a look at how the settings affect your website:

⊕ **Click the website title, for example** 🏠 Visual Steps WordPress

Your website is displayed:

The title and the tagline have been adjusted:

⊕ **Click** ←

2.4 Entering the Write and Read Settings

If you are building a website on which you want to post current messages, you need to set the appropriate write settings. Here you can determine how the messages on your website can be posted. These settings will often be used for a blog.

👉 **If necessary, click**
   ⬆ Settings

👉 **Click** Writing

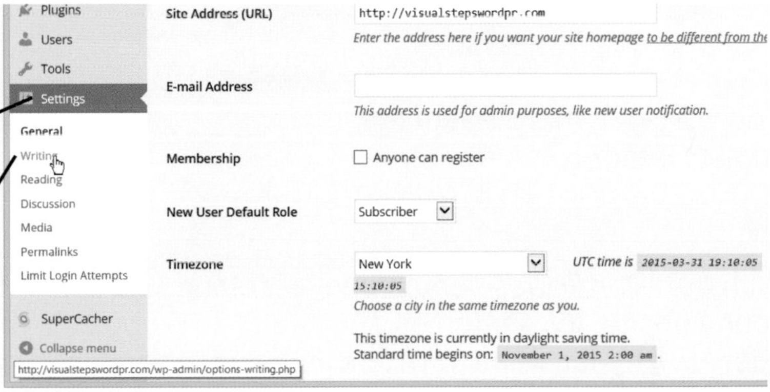

You will see the *Writing Settings* page:

Here you can set up the option for posting messages on your website via email, among other things:

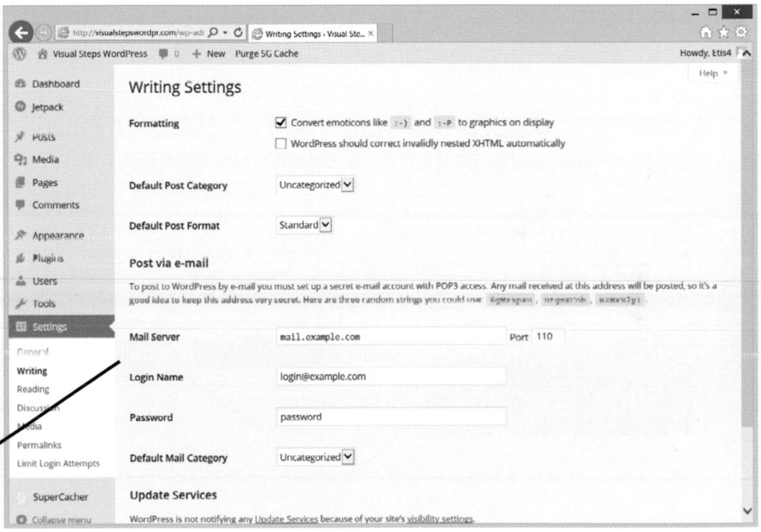

The read settings will determine how information is displayed on your website:

👉 **If necessary, click**
   ⬆ Settings

👉 **Click** Reading

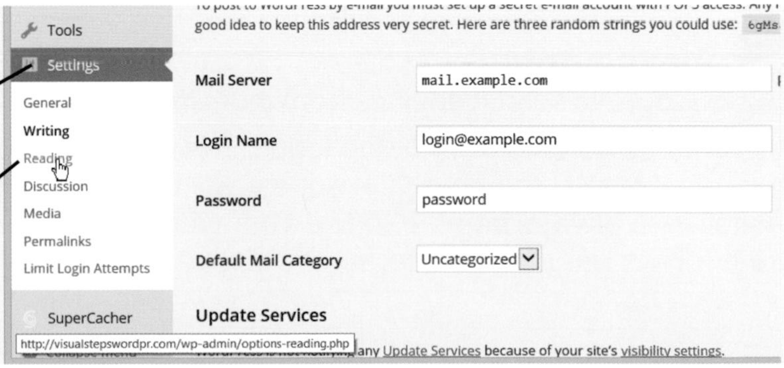

You will see the *Reading Settings* page:

On this page you can determine whether the home page is a page that contains messages, or a regular web page, among other things.

You will learn more about this subject later on.

With the *WordPress* search engine setting you can set the search engine visibility for your website, for search engines such as *Google*. If you enable this option, the web address of your website will be included in the *Google* search results, after a while.

While you are still building your website it is recommended that you disable this option. In this way you can quietly finish building and fine-tuning your site.

Once your website is finished, you can then enable this option, so visitors will be able to find your website through a search engine.

☞ **Check the box by ☑**
Discourage search engines

☞ **Click**

Save Changes

➥ **Please note:**

The Discourage search engines from indexing this site option will not automatically prevent the website from being found. It is simply a request directed at the search engines. Most of the time this request will be conceded.
Visitors will always be able to find your website by typing the web address directly in the address bar of their Internet browser.

2.5 Entering Discussion Settings

If you are building a website where visitors can comment on posts and messages, you need to set up the discussion settings. With these settings you can indicate when and how comments can be posted, and how they are to be managed.

Many regular or business websites do not offer any opportunities for visitors to post comments. But commenting is a common feature on many existing blogs.

☞ **If necessary, click Settings**

☞ **Click** Discussion

You will see the *Discussion Settings* page:

Here you can select an option for automatically receiving an email whenever a visitor has posted a comment, among other things.

2.6 Entering Media Settings

You can place various types of media files on your website, such as images and videos. For this you can enter a number of default settings:

☞ **If necessary, click**
  ⊞ **Settings**

☞ **Click** Media

You will see the *Media Settings* page:

Here you can enter the maximum size for images, among other things.

Here is a list of the settings and options you can edit on the *Media Settings* page:

Image sizes	Settings for the images that are displayed on the website. Images can be placed in a number of fixed sizes, for which you can set a maximum. All the images will be adjusted automatically to this size.
Thumbnail size	The maximum size for the smallest images, also called thumbnails. These are often used as miniature photos that refer to a larger photo.
Crop thumbnail	The thumbnail will be adjusted automatically to the size that is selected by **Thumbnail size**, and not displayed in its original format.

- Continue on the next page -

Medium size	The maximum width and height for medium-sized images.
Large size	The maximum width and height for large images.
Uploading Files	Settings for uploading media files to the website.
Organize my uploads	The media files you upload to your web space will automatically be saved in subfolders, arranged according to year and month. For example: a media file uploaded by you in April 2015, will be saved in a folder called *wp-content/uploads/2015/04*. *WordPress* will automatically remember where these images are located. The advantage of saving files this way is that you can maintain a better overview of all the files, better than if all the files would have been saved to a single folder.

For now you do not need to change these media settings.

2.7 Entering Permalink Settings

A website usually consists of multiple pages. Each page has its own web address, so visitors can also visit a specific web page right away. An example of such a web page address is www.visualstepswordpr.com/?127. This is called a *permalink*.

The name permalink is derived from the word permanent. The idea is, that the links to your web pages need to remain unchanged. If they keep changing, search engines will not be able to refer to your website, and hyperlinks on other websites will refer to the wrong pages on your web pages, or to non-existent pages. As a result, the Internet browsers of the people who want to visit your website will display an error message.

WordPress automatically creates these web addresses for your web pages, since they are often quite complicated to enter yourself, due to the numbers and other special characters they contain. If you want to help your visitors find a specific web page more easily, you can make sure that *WordPress* creates web addresses that are easy to type, such as www.visualstepswordpr.com/information.

It is important that you enter this setting before you have finished your website, and before you publish it on the Internet. In this way you will prevent search engines and other linking websites from using an incorrect web address for your web pages.

If necessary, click
⌖ **Settings**

Click Permalinks

You will see the *Permalink Settings* page:

These are the options for the permalinks:

If you are building a website that will be a blog or have a blog component, it can be useful to use the permalink setting that uses the date in the web address. This is because on a blog, you will probably post messages quite often, even several times a day. By including a date in the link, you can maintain a good overview of your website, and you can easily see when messages have been added.

On a regular website you will not be adding a new page or message as frequently. In this case you can select the option for creating permalinks that contain the title of the page.

➥ **Please note:**

Some hosting providers will display a message telling you to adjust the *htaccess* file when you have adjusted the permalink settings. If this is the case, you need to select the *Default* permalink setting.

☞ **Click the radio button ⦿ by Post name**

☞ **Click**

Save Changes

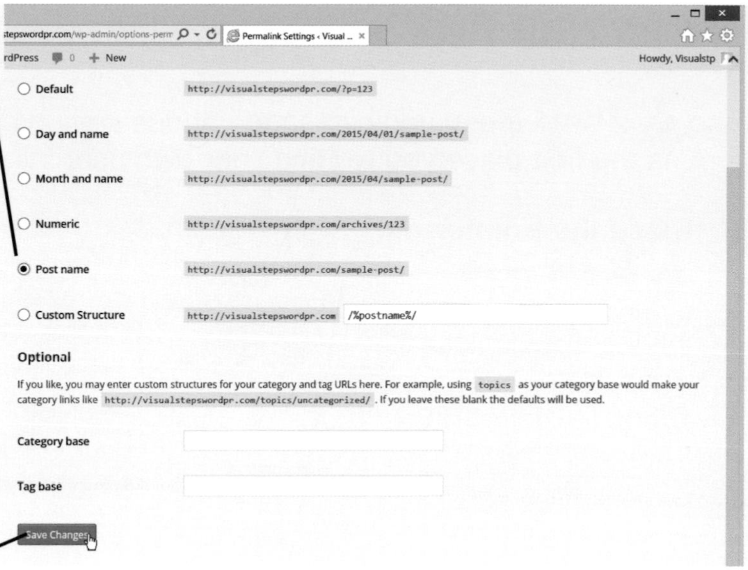

☞ **Tip**

Settings for a website that will be a blog or have a blog component

If you are building a website with a blog, it is best to use these settings:

☞ **Click the radio button ⦿ by Day and name or Month and name**

☞ **Click**

Save Changes

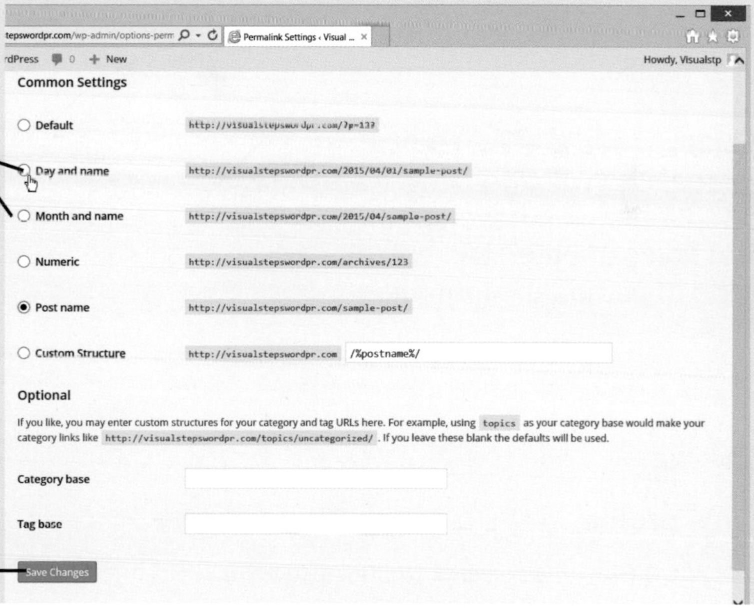

2.8 Entering User Settings

In the ![Users icon] Users menu you can enter various settings that concern the *WordPress* users. In the first place you will find your own user information here:

☞ **Place the pointer on**
       ![Users icon] Users

The options are displayed:

☞ **Click** Your Profile

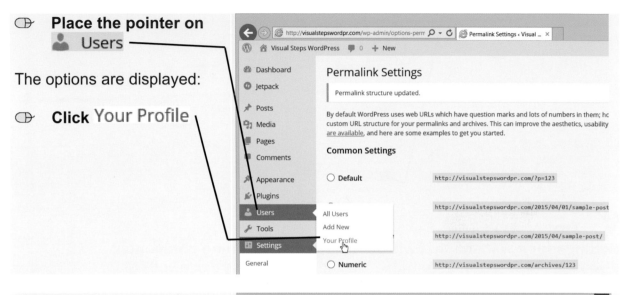

You will see your *WordPress* user profile:

Earlier in *section 2.2 Getting Acquainted with the Dashboard*, you have seen that you can enter and edit all sorts of personal information here.

💡 **Tip**

View profile

You can also view your profile through the Howdy, Visualstp ![avatar icon] link in the top right-hand corner of the window.

During the installation procedure you have already set yourself up as a *WordPress* user. This means you can automatically access *WordPress* and your website. But you may want to authorize others to access *WordPress* as well. For instance, if you manage the website together with somebody else, or post messages together with others, or if you want someone else to edit your website while you are on vacation.

For all these purposes you can add one or more extra users in *WordPress*. These users can independently log on and work with the website. You can determine what they can and cannot do:

You will see the options by
👤 Users:

☞ **Click** Add New

The page where you can add new users will be opened:

These are the options you can select when you add a new user:

Username	The name of the new user in *WordPress*. This field is mandatory, but you can think of a name yourself.
E-mail	The email address of the new user. This is also mandatory. You need to use a different email address for each user.
First Name	The first name of the user. Optional.
Last Name	The last name of the user. Optional.
- Continue on the next page -	

Website	The user's website. This does not need to be the website to which you add the user, but it may also be a personal website. Optional.
Password	The new user's password in *WordPress*. This is mandatory and you will need to enter it twice, for security reasons. You can make up this password, but be careful not to use the same password as before. Use a unique password, and not one that has been assigned to any other user.
Send Password?	Send the password to the new user via email? This can come in handy if you regularly add new users, for example, on a blog, and if you do not want to send these passwords manually.
Role	The role of the user determines the authorizations he has in *WordPress*, such as the ability to post messages.

By way of exercise, you can practice adding a new user. In the next section you will be able to delete this user, if you wish:

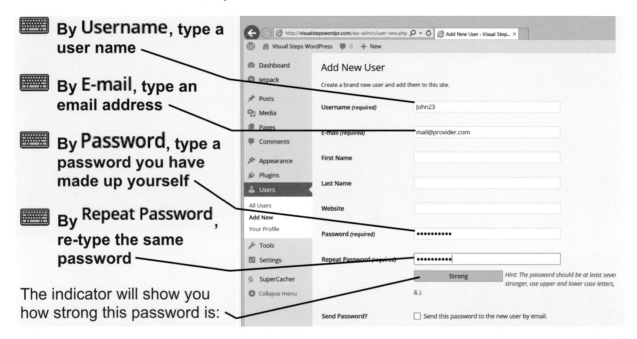

⌨ By **Username**, type a
user name

⌨ By **E-mail**, type an
email address

⌨ By **Password**, type a
password you have
made up yourself

⌨ By **Repeat Password**,
re-type the same
password

The indicator will show you
how strong this password is:

Now you are going to define the user's role. This is an important part of adding a new user, since it determines what the user's authorizations are. The user rights indicate what a user can do and cannot do in *WordPress* and on the website.

➥ **Please note:**

Most roles will not be used on regular websites, because you will rarely have options for posting messages and comments on such sites. But these roles will surely be used on a website that is a blog or which has a blog component.

You can choose from these roles:

Subscriber	A user who is only allowed to edit his or her own profile page.
Contributor	A user who is allowed to manage his or her own posts, but not allowed to publish them on the website. This needs to be done by the administrator or editor.
Author	A user who is allowed to manage his or her own posts, and publish them on the website.
Editor	A user who is allowed to manage and publish his or her own posts, and those of other users.
Administrator	A user who is allowed to manage all the settings and posts of *WordPress* and the website.

The user who has logged on or registered during the installation of *WordPress* has automatically been assigned the role of administrator.

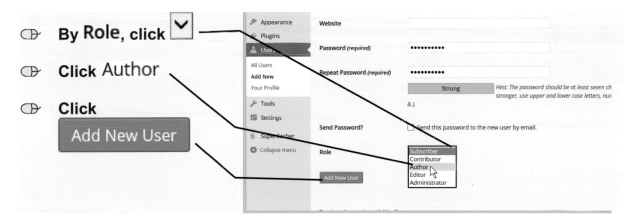

- ☞ **By Role, click** ☑
- ☞ **Click** Author
- ☞ **Click** Add New User

The new user will be added.

2.9 Managing Users

You can now see who is currently allowed to use *WordPress*. Normally, you will automatically see the user overview after you have added a new user.

If you do not see the *Users* page:

👆 By 👤 **Users**, click
All Users

On the *Users* page you will see the users who can access your website:

Currently there are two users.

The role of these users:

In this window you can view all users, and manage them as well. You will only be able to do this if you are the administrator. Here is how you edit the profiles:

👆 **Place the pointer on the name of the user you just added**

👆 **Click** Edit

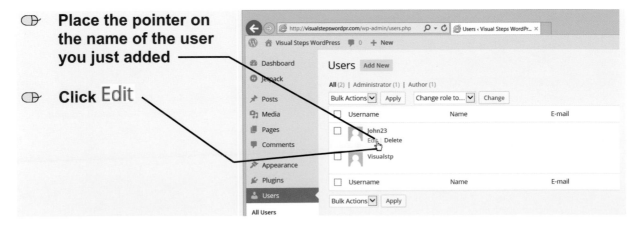

You will see the user profile in *WordPress*:

Here you can enter and edit all sorts of personal information (see *section 2.2 Getting Acquainted with the Dashboard*).

Click

You can also change the role of a user. In this way you can assign fewer or more access rights to a user:

Check the box ☑ by the name of the new user

By Change role to...,

click ☑

Click Editor

Click Change

You will see that the role of the user has been adjusted:

Please note: There will always need to be at least one *WordPress* administrator, so he or she can change the settings.

You can also delete a user:

⊕   **Place the pointer on**
     the name of the new
     user —————————

⊕   **Click** Delete

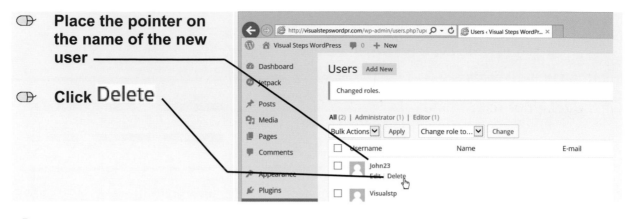

💡 Tip

Save messages and links
When you delete a user, you can decide whether to delete or keep the messages and links that have been posted by this user. Or you can transfer these messages and links to the administrator of the website. If the messages and links are transferred to the administrator, they will still be visible to the visitors of the website.

Now you can confirm the
deletion of the user:

⊕   **If necessary, click the**
     radio button ⦿ **by**
     Delete all content.

⊕   **Click**

     Confirm Deletion

You will see that the user has
been deleted:

2.10 Logging Out of WordPress

Now that you have finished viewing and editing the *WordPress* settings, you can log out. Any changes you have made to the settings are saved automatically in the *WordPress* database.

☞ **Click your user name**
   or Howdy, Visualstp

☞ **Click** Log Out

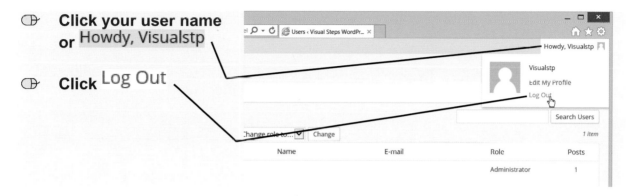

You have logged out.

☞ **Close the window** $\mathcal{QV}^3$

➥ **Please note:**

It is very important that you remember to log out once you have finished working with *WordPress*, or when you need to leave your computer unattended. This will prevent others from accessing *WordPress* or editing your website without your permission. It you are logged in as an administrator, an intruder may be able to change your password. This could mean that you will no longer be able to login to *WordPress* and maintain your *WordPress* website.
Ask the other administrators and users of your website to always log out as well.

2.11 Background Information

Dictionary

Admin	Another name for administrator or manager. This is the user who can set up all the *WordPress* options through the Dashboard.
Information screen	The part of the Dashboard where the information and settings of *WordPress* and of your website are displayed.
Permalink	The fixed web address of a web page, such as www.visualstepswordpr.com/?127.
Rights	The rights determine what a user can and cannot do in *WordPress* and on a website. For example, write messages.
Role	A title assigned to a user that determines what his or her rights are on a certain website.
Search engine	A website that collects data from lots of other websites and displays them as search results, in order to help you find them more quickly. For example, *Google*.
Thumbnail	A miniature image that usually refers to a larger image.

Source: WordPress Help

2.12 Tips

 Tip

Limit Login Attempts

The Limit Login Attempts setting by ⬛ Settings limits the number of times that someone can log on to *WordPress*. This is a measure to help fight against spammers.

💡 **Tip**

Update WordPress

New updates for *WordPress* and its components, such as themes and plugins, are released on a regular basis. Some hosting providers will automatically install these updates. In other cases you will need to do this yourself. But, you will always need to update themes and plugins yourself. It is recommended to install updates as soon as they have been released.

You will automatically be reminded that there are updates available:

When you open the Dashboard you will see the Updates ❶ notification:

In the menu you can see that this is a plugin update:

➲ **Click** Updates ❶

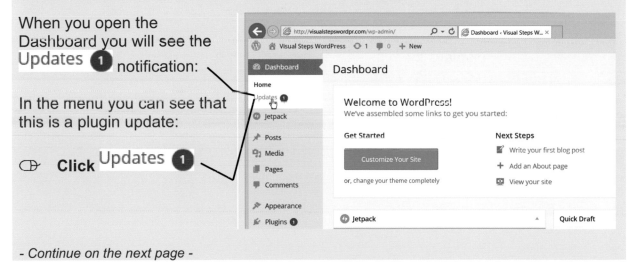

- Continue on the next page -

You will see the window with all the available updates:

☞ **Check the box ☑ by the update**

If you want to update all the components in a category, you check the box ☑ by Select All:

☞ **Click**

Update Plugins

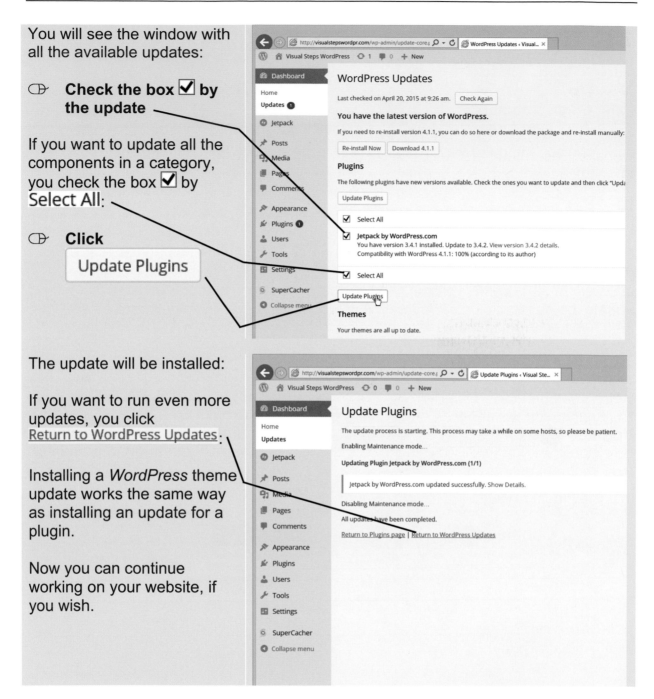

The update will be installed:

If you want to run even more updates, you click Return to WordPress Updates:

Installing a *WordPress* theme update works the same way as installing an update for a plugin.

Now you can continue working on your website, if you wish.

3. Working with Themes

Once you have *WordPress* correctly installed and set up, you can begin to build your website. The default method of building a website in *WordPress* is to use a *theme*. A theme is a ready-made template for a website. It contains all the information about the layout and formatting. If you use a theme, you will not need to build the website from scratch.

Usually a theme will already contain some sample text and images. You can easily replace these items with your own text and images.
There are many elements in a theme that can be changed according to your own preferences. For example, you can choose different colors and adjust the layout of the pages. The options may vary according to the theme selected. By using a theme as a basis, you can build your own website very quickly

WordPress makes it easy for you to find themes that match the category or type of website you want to build. By using the search function you can quickly find the appropriate themes. Then you can easily install a theme and use it for your website. You can also try out a new theme without too much trouble. In this way, you can quickly restyle your website and give it a whole new look without having to convert or transfer the content.

In this chapter you will learn how to:

- find a theme;
- install a theme;
- change a theme;
- delete a theme;
- set up a theme;
- edit the header.

➥ Please note:

In this book we will build a sample website called Visual Steps WordPress. You can follow the steps to build this sample too, or start building your own website right away. If you decide to build your own website, you need to take into account that the screenshots in this book may differ from the screens of your own website.

3.1 Viewing the Default Theme

In order to build your website, you need to log on to *WordPress* first:

☞ **Open the Internet browser** ⁶

☞ **Open the login window by *WordPress*** 🐾⁷

☞ **Log on with *WordPress*** 🐾⁸

You will see the *WordPress* Dashboard. By default, a basic theme has already been installed with the installation of the *WordPress* program. When we were writing this book, this default theme was called *Twenty Fifteen*.

Your hosting provider may also provide their own default theme as a basic theme. If this is the case, the theme will differ from the *Twenty Fifteen* theme. SiteGround, for example, the provider used for the examples in this book, uses their own basic theme.

By **At a Glance** you can see which theme has been installed:

On the Dashboard you can view the basic *WordPress* website:

⊕ **Click the name of your website, for example**
🏠 Visual Steps WordPress

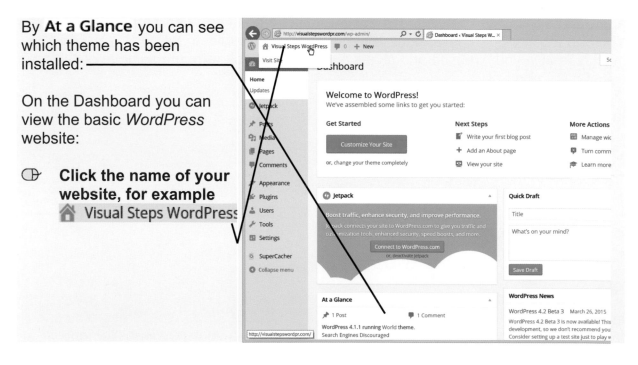

You will see the *WordPress* basic website created with the default theme:

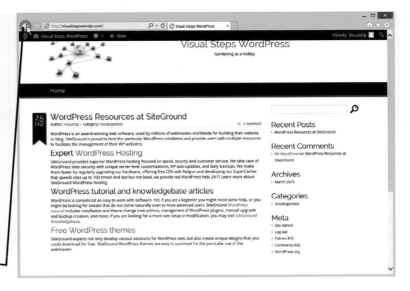

This website does not yet have any images and still uses default text. In the next few chapters you will be replacing these items with your own text and photos.

Click

3.2 Finding a Theme

You can use the default *WordPress* theme to build your website, if you wish. But there are lots of other themes you can install from the *WordPress* website.

Please note:
It is recommended that you download themes only from the official *WordPress* websites, or from websites that *WordPress* acknowledges. These websites usually offer professional themes at a fee. If you download themes from other, unknown websites, you may run the risk of infecting your computer with viruses or spyware.

The *WordPress* theme finder is very useful, when you are looking for a theme that goes with your website topic or purpose. With this tool you can enter your preferences and find the matching themes.

Tip
The right theme for your website
What the right theme for your website is also depends on your taste, among other things. Because of this, it is difficult to give you objective tips for finding the best suitable theme.
In the first place, it is wise to determine how much text and photos you want to place on the website. This can help you decide on a theme that meets the requirements. If your website contains a lot of photos, it is best to use a theme that has already reserved space for a lot of photos. For example, a theme with a photo gallery. This means you will not need to change so many things on your website.

- Continue on the next page -

If you already have a specific subject for your website, you can use the search function to look for this subject. You will often find multiple themes that suit your subject. For instance, a gardening theme.

If you have chosen some specific colors for your website, you can also look for these colors. If the default theme contains these colors, you will not need to change them later on. Although some themes offer a possibility of adapting the colors of various components according to your own taste.

You can also look for other properties of a website. For example, if you know that you want the layout of the website to span three columns, you can search for this property. If necessary, you can search for multiple properties at once. This way, you will limit the number of suitable themes, but you will surely find the themes that best suit your wishes.

This is how you find a theme:

⊕ **Place the pointer on**
   ⚒ Appearance

⊕ **Click** Themes

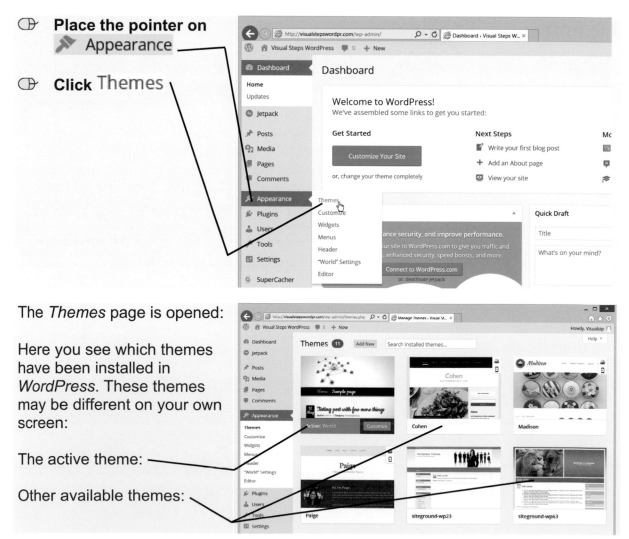

The *Themes* page is opened:

Here you see which themes have been installed in *WordPress*. These themes may be different on your own screen:

The active theme:

Other available themes:

You can install multiple themes in *WordPress*. Next, you can choose the theme you want to activate. This means that the activated theme will be applied to the website.

To look for another theme:

☞ **Click** Add New

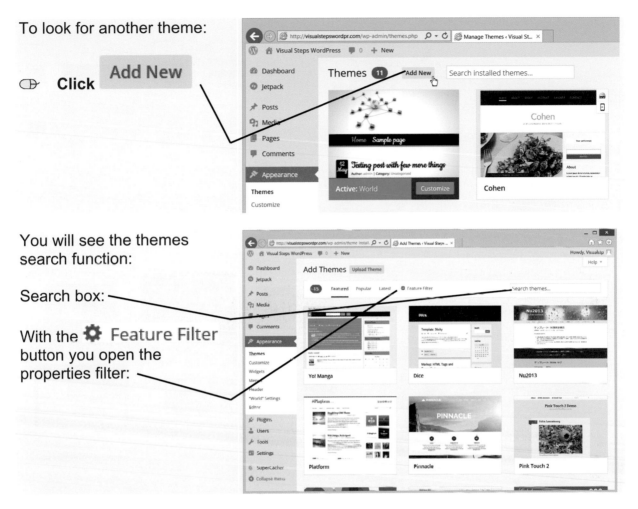

You will see the themes search function:

Search box:

With the ⚙ Feature Filter button you open the properties filter:

There are different ways of looking for themes with this search feature. The first method is by using the categories at the top of the window. You will see themes that have been featured (highlighted) by the *WordPress* editors, for example, or the latest themes.

🐦 **Please note:**

You may see a different feature theme or new theme. These themes are refreshed on a regular basis.

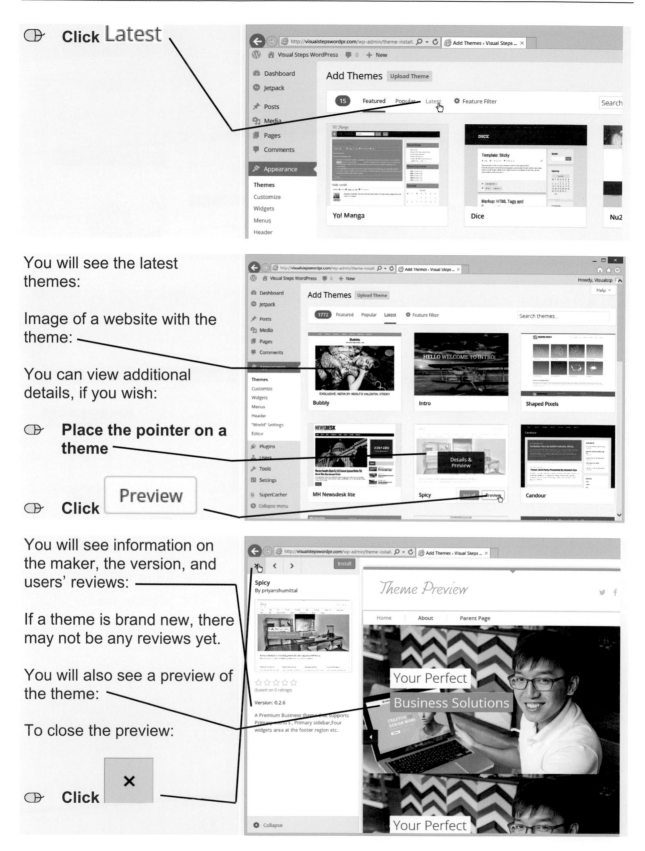

👉 **Click** Latest

You will see the latest themes:

Image of a website with the theme:

You can view additional details, if you wish:

👉 **Place the pointer on a theme**

👉 **Click** Preview

You will see information on the maker, the version, and users' reviews:

If a theme is brand new, there may not be any reviews yet.

You will also see a preview of the theme:

To close the preview:

👉 **Click** ×

➤ Please note:

Some previews cannot display an image. These will be displayed once you have installed the theme.

You can also find a theme by entering keywords. For example, the title or description of a theme.

By way of exercise, you can search for themes that have to do with shops:

⌨️ **In the search box, type:** shop

You will see themes that contain the keyword 'shop':

The preview of these themes can be viewed as well.

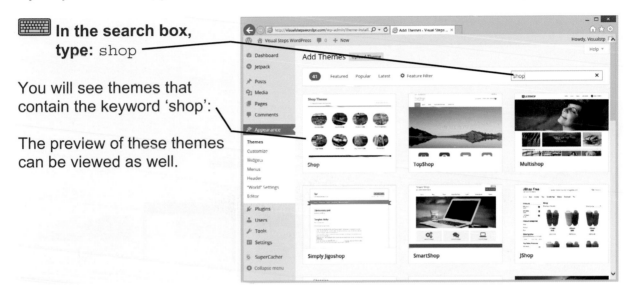

Furthermore, you can search by using *Property filters*. By applying one or multiple filters, you can limit the number of themes that are found, and narrow the search down to the type of theme you want to find.
You can filter on color, number of columns, and other technical properties, for example.

💡 Tip

Technical properties

The properties you can enter by the ⚙️ Feature Filter category are of a quite technical nature. They may contain special features or certain settings that can be adjusted in the theme. For instance, the option of adjusting a menu or the background color.

☞ **Click**

   ⚙ Feature Filter

☞ **By the Colors category, check the box ☑ by Blue**

☞ **Click**

   Apply Filters 1

You will see themes that contain a blue color:

If there are many themes, you can view them by dragging the scroll box down:

☞ **Click Edit**

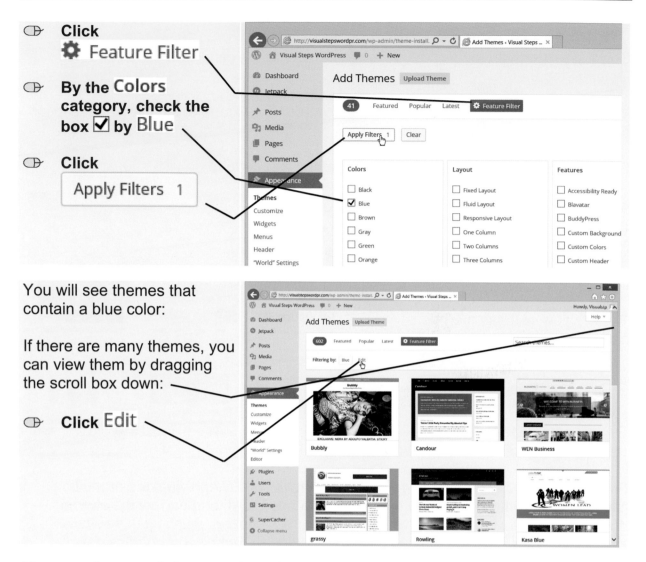

You can also search for a number of popular themes, such as vacation, photos, or themes that are linked to a specific season of the year:

☞ **Uncheck the box ☑ by Blue**

By the Subject category:

☞ **Check the box ☑ by Photoblogging**

☞ **Click**

   Apply Filters 1

You will see themes on the subject of photo blogging:

These themes are especially suited for posting photos.

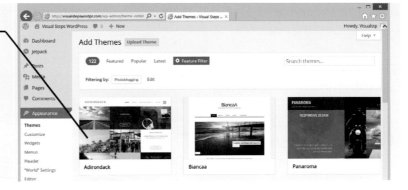

💡 Tip

Themes with a comment box
Some themes have a comment box that is displayed on one or multiple pages. Visitors can enter their comments in such a box. This is mostly the case with themes for blogs. If you do not need to use a comment box, it is better to choose a theme that does not have one. In some themes they cannot be deleted.

3.3 Installing a Theme

Once you have found a suitable theme, you can install it. *WordPress* installs a new theme to your web space very quickly.

In this example you will be installing a random theme. You will not be using this theme later on when you begin to build the sample website. If you have decided to create your own website instead of the sample website, you can install a suitable theme for your website at this point.

👉 **Place the pointer on a theme**

In this example we have used the Panorama theme:

👉 **Click** Install

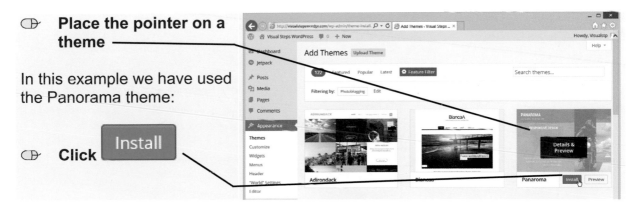

The theme will be installed.

After the theme is installed, you will see this window:

<u>Live Preview</u> allows you to view an example of the website:

If you want to install more themes, click <u>Return to Theme Installer</u>

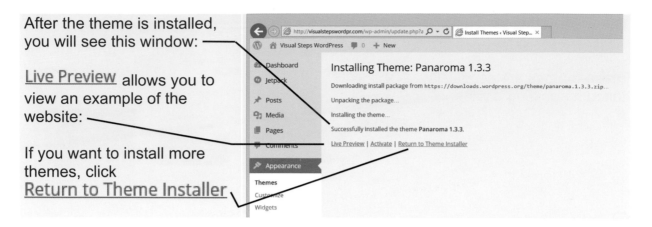

Now the theme has been installed to your web space, but you cannot use it yet to create a website. The theme must be activated first.

➥ **Please note:**

If you activate a theme, the current theme will automatically be deactivated. If you have already built a full website with that theme, this website will be displayed with the new theme, after you have activated it.

Some of the elements may not be correctly represented with the new theme. In such a case, it is wise to create a backup of the old theme first, before using a new theme for your entire website.

The method for creating a backup can vary per hosting provider. Most hosting providers provide software with which you can create backups. On your provider's website you can usually find information on this topic. If you cannot find any info, then contact your provider to find out how they support the creation of backups. *WordPress* itself also has options for creating a backup. You can create backups with various plugins such as *Duplicator*. You can read more about plugins in *Chapter 5 Adding Extra Components*.

☞ **Click** <u>Activate</u>

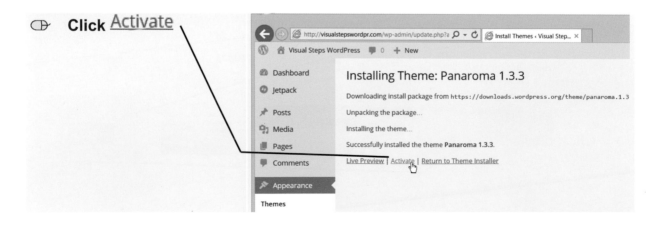

After the activation procedure is finished, you will see this window:

The activated theme:

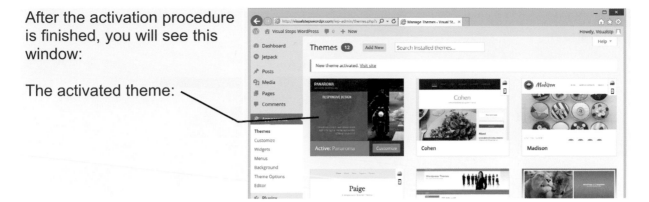

💡 **Tip**

Settings for widgets and plugins
Some themes are accompanied by extra components, such as *widgets* and *plugins* that will be installed along with the theme. After the theme has been installed, you might see a message telling you that the theme contains support for widgets or plugins. In this case, you can immediately adjust the settings for these widgets or plugins. You can read more about this in *Chapter 5 Adding Extra Components* and *Chapter 6 Useful plugins*.

☞ **Click the name of your website**

You will see the website with the new theme:

The title you had previously entered for your website will now be displayed in this theme:

☞ **Click** ←

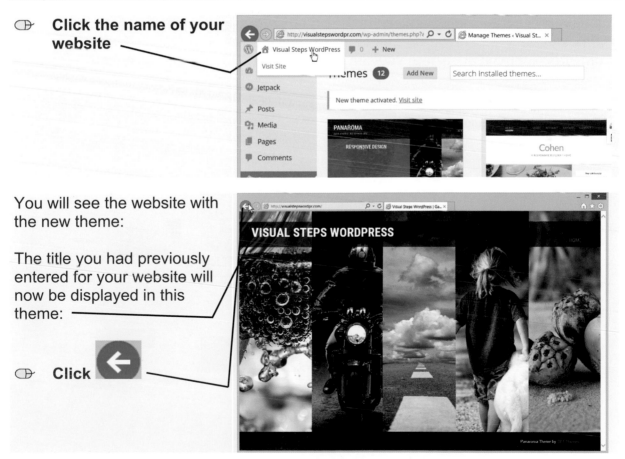

You will see the *Themes* page again:

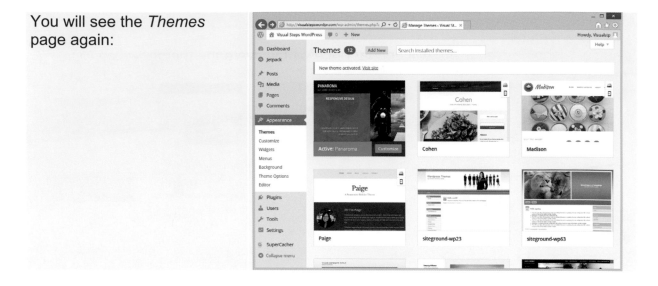

3.4 Changing a Theme

After you installed the new theme, the theme for the website is changed by activating the new theme. You can change a theme very quickly without finding and downloading a new theme first, if the theme has already been installed. On the *Themes* page you can find all the themes that have been pre-installed with your *WordPress* installation. There you can simply select a theme and activate it:

☞ **Place the pointer on an inactive theme**

☞ **Click** `Activate`

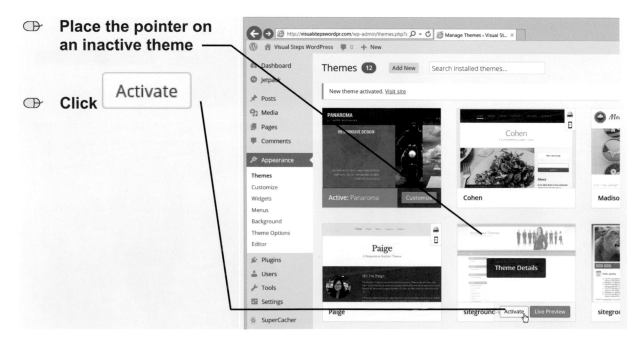

🩹 HELP! I see a wizard.

With some themes, a wizard will appear once you activate the theme, which will guide you through the theme settings. If you do not want this, just go back to the *Themes* page:

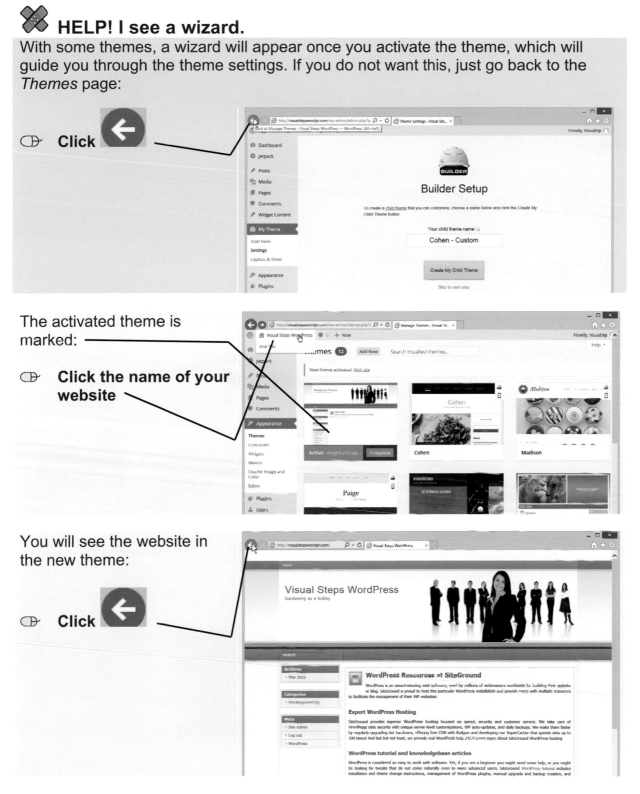

☞ **Click** ⬅

The activated theme is marked: ──────

☞ **Click the name of your website**

You will see the website in the new theme:

☞ **Click** ⬅

Go back to the *Themes* page.

3.5 Deleting a Theme

The themes you have installed are saved to your web space. If you do not want to use a theme, it is a good idea to delete it. This way, the theme will not take up any extra space in your web space and you can maintain a good overview of the *Themes* page. You can always find a new theme or install a previously deleted one again.

➤ Please note:

Themes are sometimes deleted from the *WordPress* database because they contain errors, or because the manufacturer does not want to offer the theme for free anymore. Seasonal themes may also be available for installation for just a short while.

This is how you delete a theme:

☞ **Click the desired theme, for example, the theme previously installed**

You will see the details of the theme:

☞ **Click Delete**

If you really want to delete the theme:

☞ **Click** | OK |

If you do not want to delete the theme:

☞ **Click** | Cancel |

You are back on the *Themes* page:

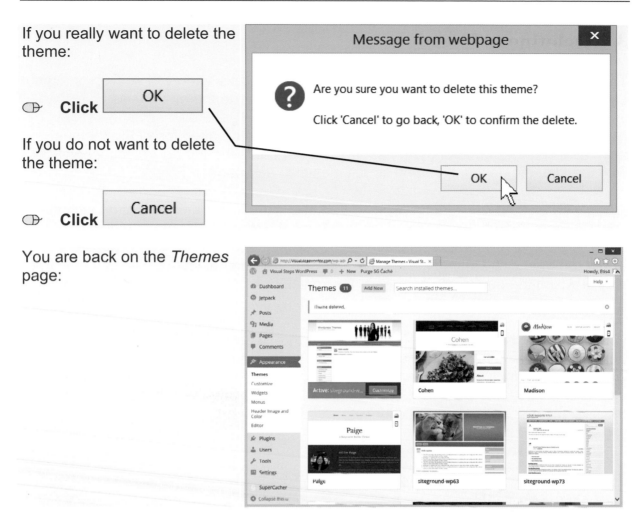

💡 **Tip**

Filter for installed themes
If you have lots of installed themes on the *Themes* page, you can search for them in the same way you search for new themes on the *WordPress* website:

⌨ **Type keyword by**
    Search installed then

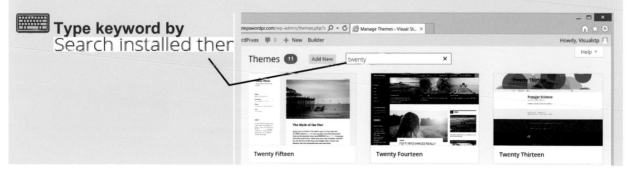

3.6 Setting Up a Theme

The theme is the basis of your website. Each theme has a variety of settings that you can adjust. The actual number of settings depends on the theme you use.

Some settings can be set through *WordPress* and can be used for all the themes, such as the background and the header. The header is the top part of the website, with the title, the description, and sometimes also an image.

Along with these basic settings, you can enter a number of settings that go with the specific theme you have chosen. Depending on the theme, you may be able to set extra options for the header, such as a logo, or the colors of many other elements within the theme. All of these elements will form the general *layout*. The layout is the way in which the pages are arranged. These settings help you determine to a large degree what your entire website will look like.

In this book we have used the *Twenty Eleven* theme as a sample theme. This is a default *WordPress* theme that is very suitable for building a simple, straightforward website. You can select another theme for your website, if you prefer. If you do decide to do this, take into account that not all of the examples in this book, such as the settings, will be identical to your own website.

First you need to install *Twenty Eleven*:

☞ **Click** **Add New**

⌨ In the search box, type: `Twenty`

You will see the default *WordPress* themes from the past few years:

⊕ Place the pointer on the Twenty Eleven **theme**

⊕ Click Install

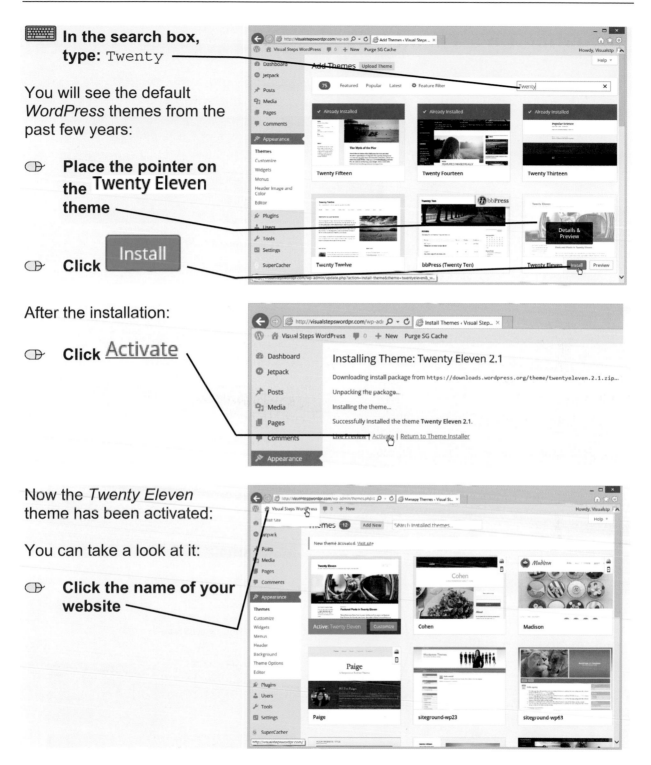

After the installation:

⊕ Click Activate

Now the *Twenty Eleven* theme has been activated:

You can take a look at it:

⊕ Click the name of your website

You will see the website with the theme:

☞ **Place the pointer on the name of your website**

☞ **Click** Themes

➥ **Please note:**

You may see a different default photo on the website. The default image of the *Twenty Eleven* theme is changed regularly. It is a part of the theme.

To display the theme settings:

☞ **Click** Customize

You will see a variety of settings:

You can close the settings panel by clicking ☒ :

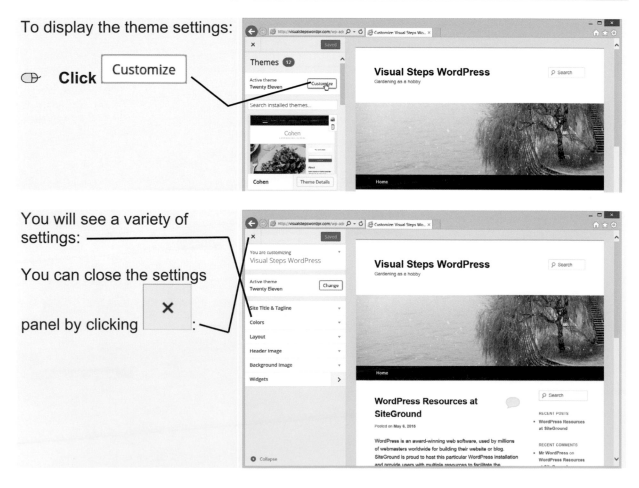

HELP! I do not see the preview page.

If you see the Dashboard instead of the preview page, you can view the theme settings in this way:

☞ **By** Twenty Eleven,

click Customize

You can also click Customize in the menu:

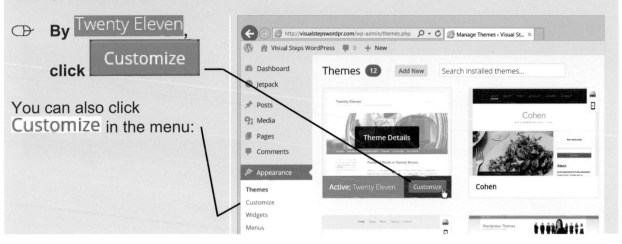

The settings of a theme are ordered by category. For example, you can view and adjust the settings for part of the *Twenty Eleven* header. These are the settings for the website's title and tagline.

Please note:

When you installed and set up *WordPress*, you may have entered a title and caption or tagline for your website. With some themes, these titles will not be displayed by default. You will need to enter them separately within the theme settings.

☞ **Click**
Site Title & Tagline

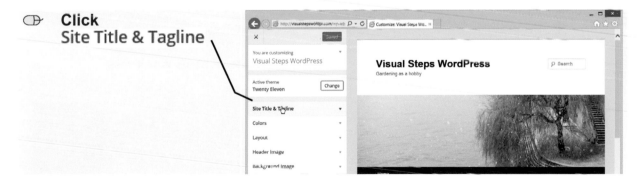

Element to which these
settings refer: ——————

Title and tagline: ——————

Display header text (or not): ——

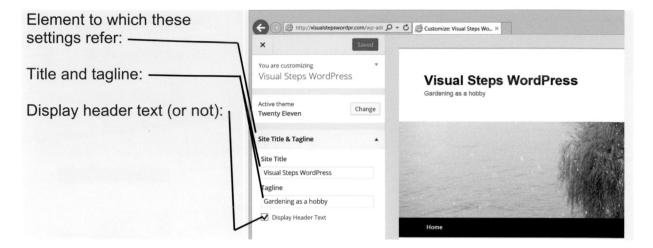

💡 Tip

Close a category
You can close an open category by clicking the header once more, for example, by clicking **Site Title & Tagline** ▲.

It is usually a good idea to display the title and tagline of the website on the website itself. For this you can use the name and the text you previously entered when you were setting up *WordPress*.

If your website title is already displayed in the header image, for example, it is better not to display the title and tagline in the text.

To hide the website title and tagline:

☞ **Uncheck the box ☑ by**
Display Header Text

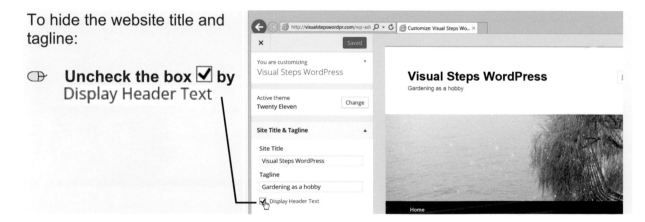

Now the title and tagline are not visible anymore:

To display the title and tagline again:

☞ **Check the box ☑ by** Display Header Text

If you do want to display the website title and tagline, you can still enter a different name and other text for the tagline:

⌨ **Type a different title by** Site Title**, if you wish**

⌨ **Type a different tagline by** Tagline**, if you wish**

In order to apply the changes:

☞ **Click**

Save & Publish

You can see the changes in the preview window:

Please note: small changes may not be immediately visible in the preview window. But they will be visible on the actual website.

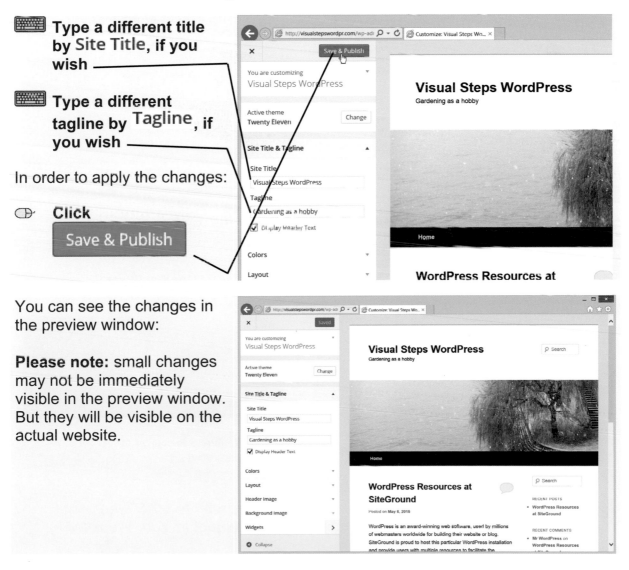

3.7 Setting Colors

It is important to choose suitable colors for your website. You have already made a choice while you were picking a theme, but with most themes you can also change the colors afterwards. There are a few themes where you can adjust the colors of almost every element. But with other themes, such as the *Twenty Eleven* theme, you can only choose between a number of schemes that have fixed colors for some of the elements.

This is how you set the colors for a theme such as *Twenty Eleven*:

☞ **Click Colors**

You will see the color settings:

The view of the color scheme:

The color of the header text:

Background color of the website:

The link color:

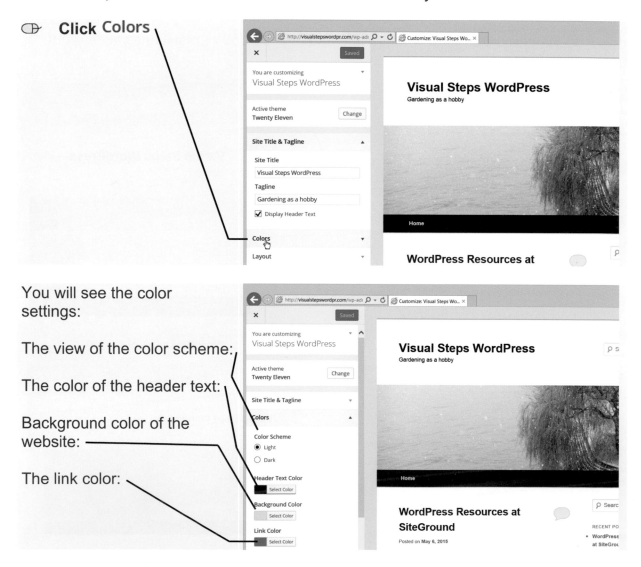

Hyperlinks are pieces of text that you can click and that refer to other web pages. You can read more about them in *Chapter 4 Adding Content to Your Website*.

💡 Tip

Color of the hyperlinks

It is important that the hyperlinks on the website stand out. This will make it clear to the visitor that this is a hyperlink, and not ordinary text. That is why you need to select a different color for hyperlinks, other than the color of the regular text.
Also make sure that the color of the hyperlink is sufficiently in contrast with the background. Yellow hyperlinks on a white background, for example, are not conspicuous enough.

You can select a different color scheme:

☞ **By Color Scheme,
   click the radio button
   ⦿ by Dark**

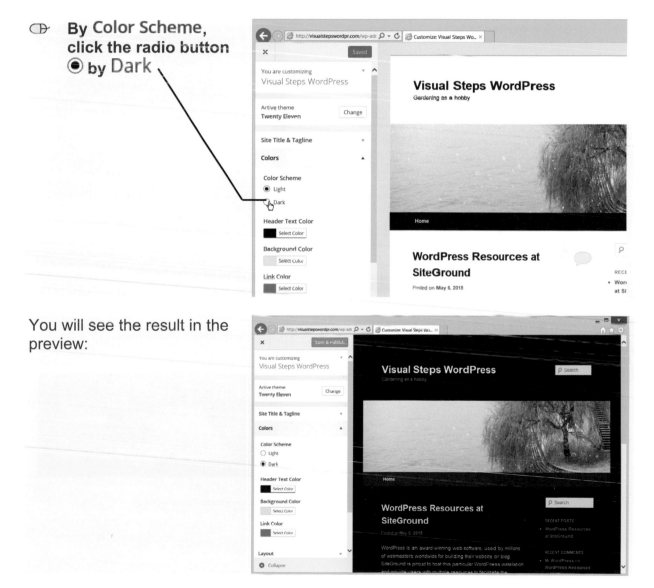

You will see the result in the preview:

☺ Tip

Black background color
Sometimes, a black background color will look very pretty on a website. Nevertheless, black is not often recommended as a background color. Especially in the case of a website that contains a lot of text. Reading the text will become tiresome if you use a black background. It is better to choose white, or another, lighter and less bright color.

You can remove the color scheme with the black background:

**By Color Scheme,
click the radio button
⦿ by Light**

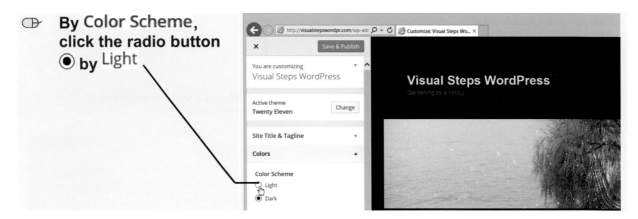

There are various elements for which you can set a specific color. For example, the color of the text in the header:

**By
Header Text Color,
click** Select Color

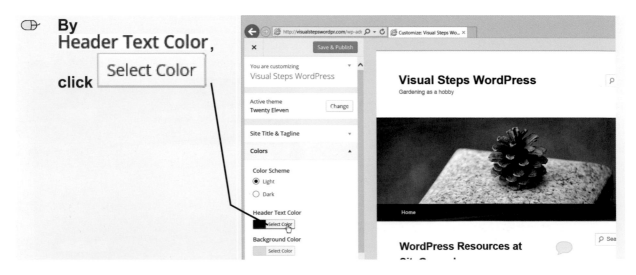

You will see the current color settings for this element:

Color code: ————————

Color table: ————————

Color intensity: ————————

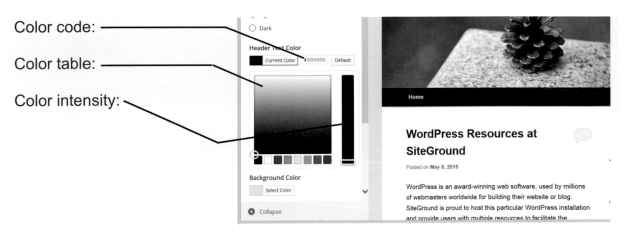

There are several ways of setting a color. Each color has its own universal numeric code. This is the *hexadecimal* code, a counting system based on 16 digits (0 to 9 for the values zero to nine, and A, B, C, D, E and F to represent the numbers ten to fifteen). In *WordPress,* the color code is always preceded by a hash tag: #.

For example, if you already know what the color code is, because your photo editing program displays this code, you can enter it right away:

If you want to set the color blue by entering a code:

⌨ **In the color code box, type:** `#1e73be` ————

The text in the header will now turn bright blue: ————

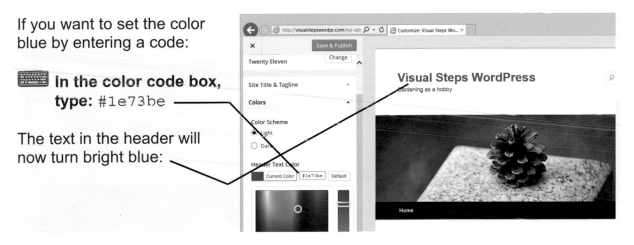

The advantage of using a color code is that you can exactly determine the color you want to use. This comes in handy if you want to use the same color for different elements.

You can also set the color by using the color table. This is done step by step. First, you select the basic color:

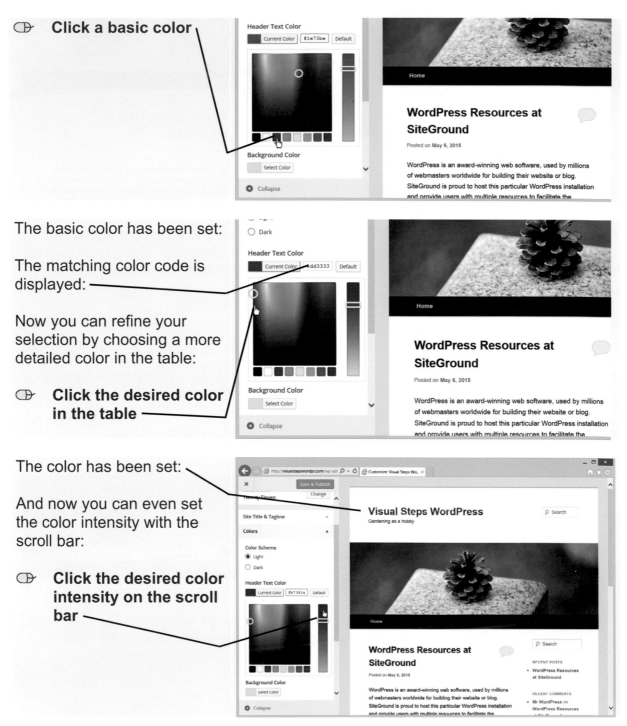

☞ **Click a basic color**

The basic color has been set:

The matching color code is displayed:

Now you can refine your selection by choosing a more detailed color in the table:

☞ **Click the desired color in the table**

The color has been set:

And now you can even set the color intensity with the scroll bar:

☞ **Click the desired color intensity on the scroll bar**

You have set the color of the
title and tagline through the
color table:

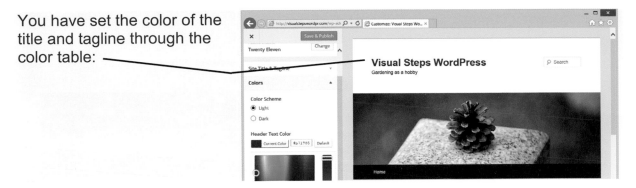

If you want to restore the original color of an element:

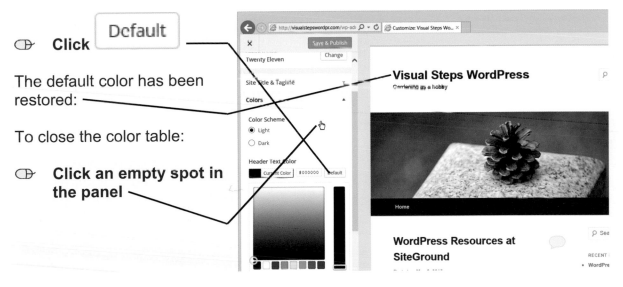

☞ **Click** [Default]

The default color has been
restored:

To close the color table:

☞ **Click an empty spot in
the panel**

In this way you can set the desired color for various elements. You can try out
different colors, and see which combinations work best. If you find that a color is not
quite suitable, you can always change it later on.

💡 **Tip**

Copy a color code
If you want to use the same code for multiple elements, you can copy the color code:

☞ **Select the color code**

⌨ **Press** [**Ctrl**] + [**C**]

- Continue on the next page -

By the desired element:

⊕ **Select the color code**

⌨ **Press Ctrl + V**

The color code has been copied.

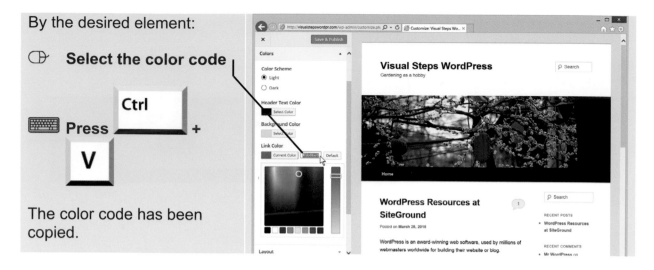

3.8 Defining the Layout

The *layout* is the way the page is arranged. For example, many themes have an option to select a different layout for the columns that display the text. You can almost always choose the number of columns, but you can also indicate where the sidebars and the content are placed. Sidebars are used to display special texts and components, such as menus and lists. You can read more about them in *Chapter 5 Adding Extra Components*.

⊕ **Click Layout**

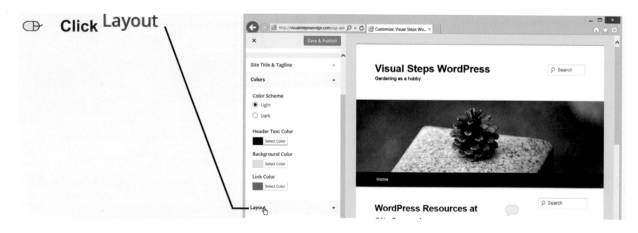

Content on the left, sidebar
on the right: ————————

Content on the right, sidebar
on the left: ————————

Only content, no sidebars: ————

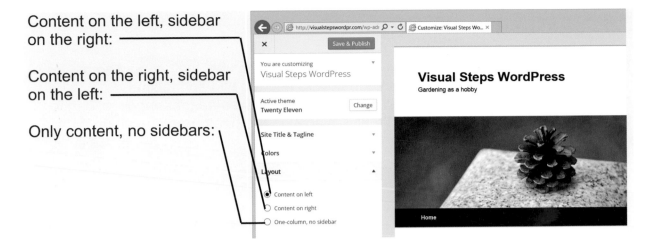

You can choose to display the sidebar on the left-hand side and the content on the
right-hand side, for example:

☞ **Click the radio button**
⦿ by Content on right

Now the sidebar is on the left-
hand side: ————————

The content is on the right-
hand side: ————————

☞ **Click the radio button**
⦿ by Content on left

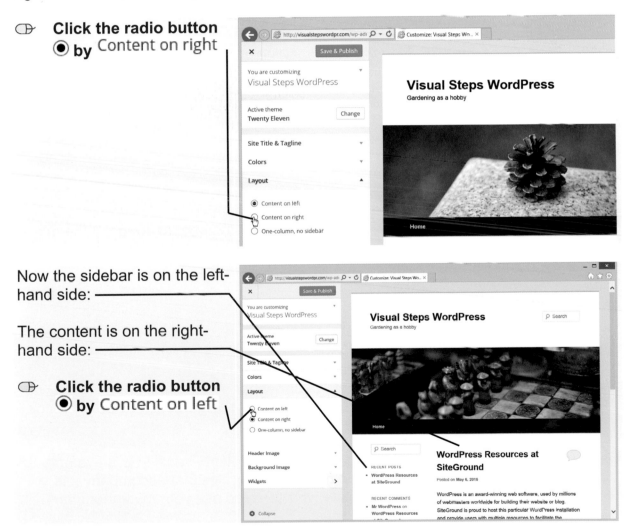

3.9 Adjusting the Header

The header is the top part of the website. It contains the title, tagline, and sometimes an image too. You have previously seen how to edit the title and tagline.
Although it is not strictly necessary, many websites have a *header image* or *banner*. This is usually an image or a photo that is placed in the header and takes up the full width of the website.

The header image in the
Twenty Eleven theme:

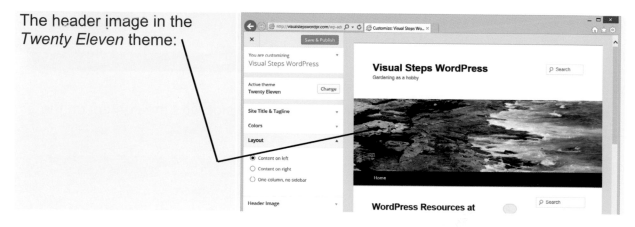

A header image often enhances the appearance of a website. The image provides variation with regard to the text, and can also serve as an introduction.
Almost every theme contains one or more images you can use on your website. You can also use your own, unique image as a banner. This makes your website stand out more.

If your own image is the wrong size, you can resize the image in *WordPress*. Just remember to keep the height-width ratio in balance for the header image. If the ratio is not correct, the image can look slightly skewed or otherwise distorted and your website will not look pretty.

💡 **Tip**

Correct size of image
You can crop and resize your image in *WordPress*. But it is better to make sure the image fits the header as well as possible, before uploading it to your website. You can usually find the correct size of the image or banner by the header settings; if you use an image of this size you will not need to resize it. You can also resize an image in a photo editing program, such as *Adobe Photoshop Elements*.

You can upload the image for the header or banner to *WordPress*. In this example we have used a practice photo from one of the practice files that accompany this book. If you are creating your own website, you can also use your own photo, of course.

🐦 **Please note:**

You can find the practice file that is used in this book on the companion website. In *Appendix B Downloading the Practice Files* at the end of this book, we explain how to copy the practice files to your computer.

👆 **Click** Header Image

🩹 **HELP! There is no option for a header image.**

If the theme settings do not include an option for adding a header image, or if the image cannot be added in one way or another, you can also add a header image through the *WordPress* settings:

In the Dashboard:

👆 **Hover the pointer over** 🖌 Appearance

👆 **Click** Header

👉 **Follow the following instructions on the next page for adding a header image**

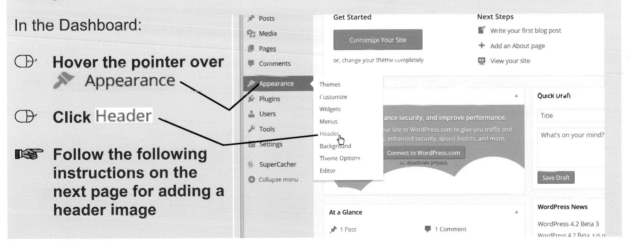

The settings for the header image are displayed:

The best size is indicated:

☞ **Click**

Add new image

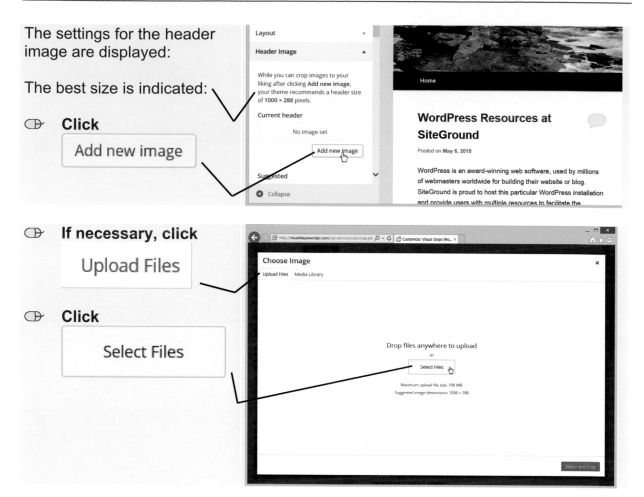

☞ **If necessary, click**

Upload Files

☞ **Click**

Select Files

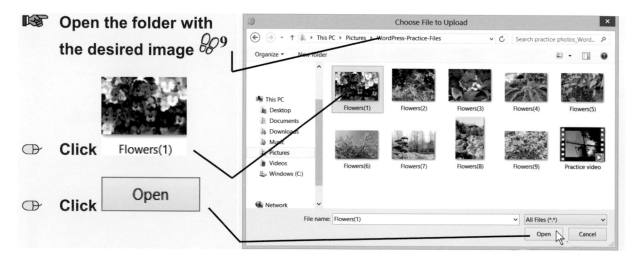

The *Choose File to Upload* window is opened:

👉 **Open the folder with the desired image** 👣⁹

☞ **Click** Flowers(1)

☞ **Click** Open

 **HELP! I see an error message.**

If the file you want to upload is too big (regarding the size in kilobytes), you will see an error message. In this case you will need to make the image smaller, or convert it to another file format, such as JPG or PNG.

☞ **Click** ◀

🖝 **Adapt the file**

🖝 **Upload the file again**

The header image will be uploaded. It will appear in the *WordPress Media Library*. This is where all the uploaded media files are saved.

It necessary, you can adjust the size of the selection. This may result in some extra space being displayed around the image in the banner. And the image may also be distorted a bit. This depends on the theme.

☞ **Click the desired media file**

☞ **Click**
Select and Crop

The *Media Library* may already contain a few images:

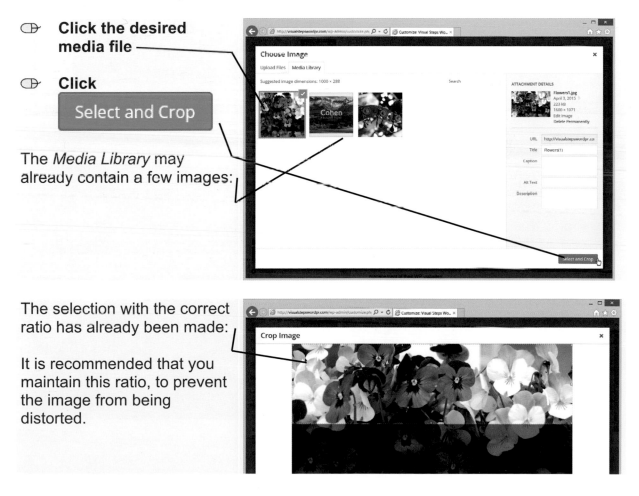

The selection with the correct ratio has already been made:

It is recommended that you maintain this ratio, to prevent the image from being distorted.

You can select a different part of the image, if you wish:

☞ **Place the pointer on the selection**

☞ **Drag the selection upwards or downwards**

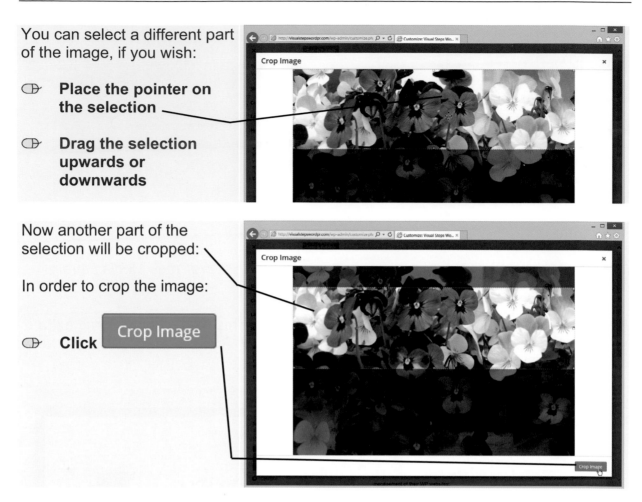

Now another part of the selection will be cropped:

In order to crop the image:

☞ **Click** Crop Image

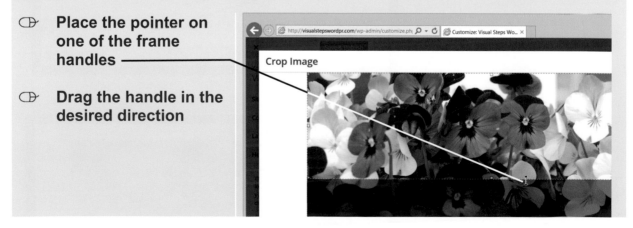

💡 Tip

Enlarge or decrease the selection
You can enlarge or decrease a selection by adjusting the selection frame:

☞ **Place the pointer on one of the frame handles**

☞ **Drag the handle in the desired direction**

👆 **Click**

Save & Publish

You can close the settings panel:

👆 **Click** ✕

The image has been placed in your website's header:

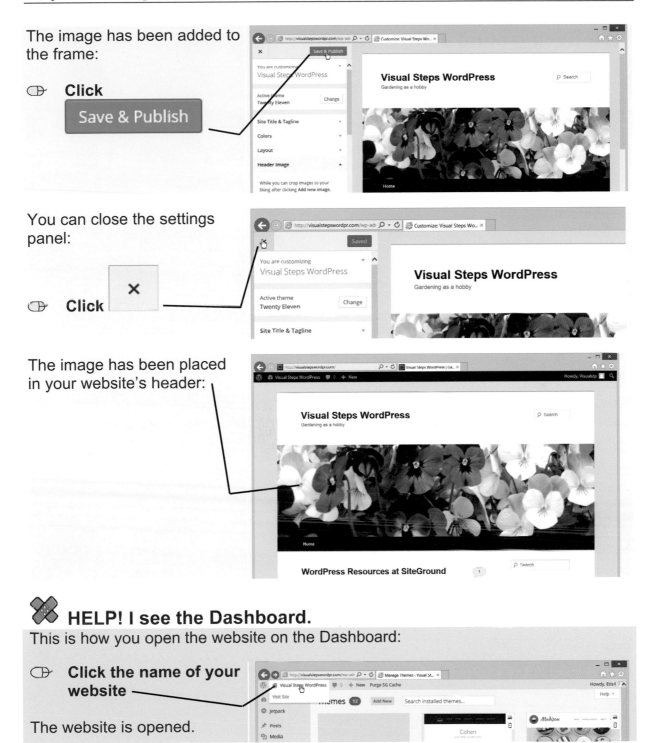

![bandage icon] **HELP! I see the Dashboard.**

This is how you open the website on the Dashboard:

👆 **Click the name of your website**

The website is opened.

👉 **Log out of *WordPress*** 👣¹⁰

In this chapter you have read about working with themes in *WordPress*. In the next chapter you will read how to use the theme to build your own website.

3.10 Background Information

Dictionary

Activate	Selecting an installed theme to be the theme for your website.
Header	The top part of the website, containing the title, tagline, and sometimes also an image.
Hyperlink	A clickable text or image that refers to other web pages.
Layout	The arrangement of the pages.
Plugin	A component that is installed separately and which adds extra functions to your website. There are plugins for security, for example, as well as those that allow you to add an entire webshop to your website. Some plugins are included in certain themes.
Sidebar	The sidebar is a column at the top, bottom, left or right-hand side of a web page. Which sidebars are available for your website, depends on the theme you use.
Tag	A keyword that is used to describe the theme.
Theme search function	A function in *WordPress*, used to quickly find a certain theme.
Twenty Eleven	One of the default themes in *WordPress*.
Widget	An extra function that can be added to the *sidebar* of your website.

Source: WordPress Help

3.11 Tips

Tip
An image as a background
You can use an image as a background for a website, instead of a color. You do that like this:

☞ **Click** 📌 **Appearance**

☞ **Click** Background

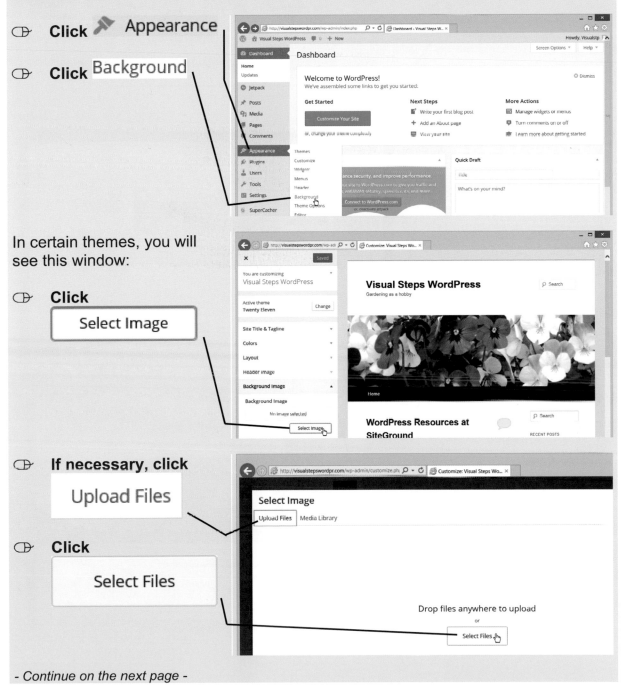

In certain themes, you will see this window:

☞ **Click**

Select Image

☞ **If necessary, click**

Upload Files

☞ **Click**

Select Files

- Continue on the next page -

You will see the folders on
your computer:

☞ **Open the desired**
    folder

☞ **Click the image**

☞ **Click** | Open |

☞ **Click**

    | Choose Image |

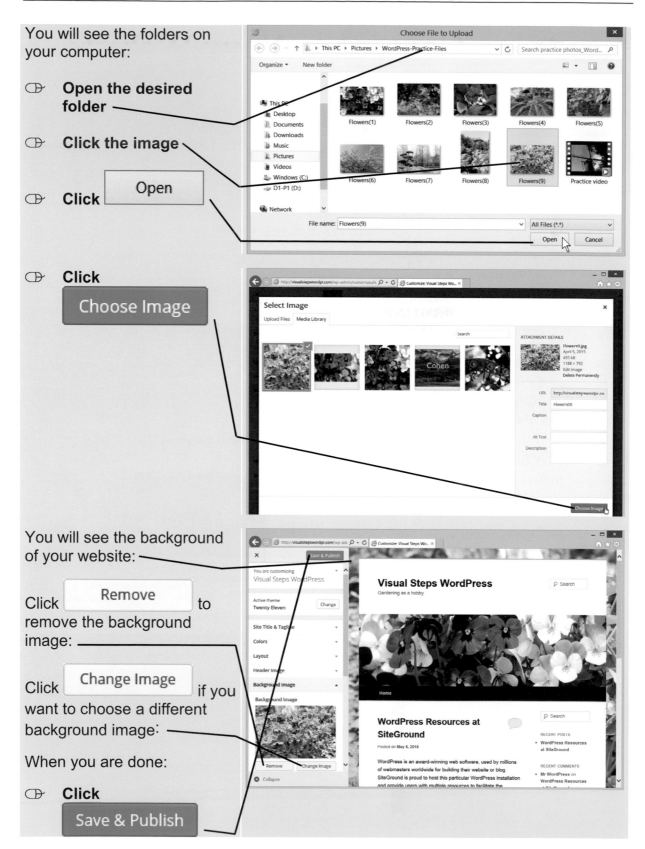

You will see the background
of your website:

Click | Remove | to
remove the background
image:

Click | Change Image | if you
want to choose a different
background image:

When you are done:

☞ **Click**

    | Save & Publish |

4. Adding Content to Your Website

If you have installed a theme, some of the elements have already been filled in with sample text or images. Along with the header, the website that uses this theme may also display sample text, images, hyperlinks, and sometimes even other elements. Some themes only use a single sample page, but other themes may have multiple pages.

The good thing about these sample pages is, that you can immediately see what the web page will look like, with regard to the layout and formatting. On the other hand, when you are building a regular website, it is a disadvantage that *WordPress* is primarily directed at building blogs. This is demonstrated for instance, by the fact that a few of the default themes have a sample page with a message on which visitors can add comments. You will usually just want to place your own text on a regular web page.

To do this you can convert the sample page to a *static page.* This will create a welcome page or starting page for your website. Then you can add text, images, and hyperlinks to this page. Once you have done this, you can add additional new pages and extend your website further. You can add and edit text and images, and insert hyperlinks. By filling in the boxes (or fields) within the *WordPress* editor you can determine how the various elements on a web page are displayed.

In order to connect all the web pages together in a logical way, you can use a menu. This menu contains all the pages of your website, and enables a visitor to quickly reach the page he or she wants to visit.

In this chapter you will learn how to:

- create and publish a new page;
- add and edit text;
- add a hyperlink to a text;
- set the home page;
- edit and delete a page;
- add and edit an image;
- work with menus.

Please note:

In this chapter you can use the practice files that go with this book. In *Appendix B Downloading the Practice Files* at the end of this book, we explain how to copy the practice files to your computer.

4.1 Creating a New Page

In order to build your website, first, you need to log on to *WordPress*:

☞ **Open the login window by *WordPress*** 🦶⁷

☞ **Log on with *WordPress*** 🦶⁸

You will see the *WordPress* Dashboard.

💡 **Tip**

Preparation for a website
Before you start building your own website, it is wise to determine what exactly you want to present on you website, and for which target group the website is intended. In this way you can already start collecting text and images beforehand for the content of your website. It is also useful to know in advance which pages you want to include in your website. You can take all of these things into account as you start building the website.

The first thing you probably want to get started with is building the *home page* or *start page*. This is the first page the visitor gets to see when he or she visits your website. It is also the page that is the starting point for the rest of the website. Normally, you will use the home page as a brief introduction to your site. You welcome your visitors by telling them what your website is about and what they can expect to find there. The *Twenty Eleven* theme offers at first glance a home page that is focused on maintaining a blog. You will see a list of current messages that visitors can comment on.

But you can replace this default format showing the latest posts with a static page. A static page in *WordPress* is a page where new messages are not continuously posted. The text on this page usually remains unchanged for longer periods of time. This is why it is called a static page.

⊕ **Place the pointer on**
   ⬆ Settings

⊕ **Click Discussion**

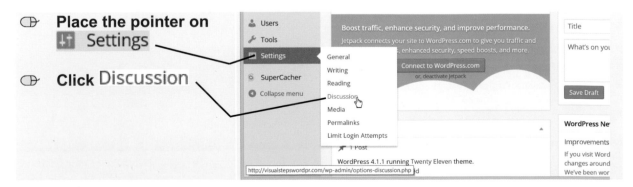

The *Discussion Settings* window appears:

☞ **Uncheck the box ☑ by**
   Allow people to post co...

☞ **Drag the scroll box**
   downwards

At the bottom of the page:

☞ **Click**

   Save Changes

Now you can create a new home page. The sample website already has a home page, although this page currently shows a list of messages and comments. You can disable this page later on, and replace it with the new home page.

🖝 **Please note:**

With some themes, the home page that is presented is already a welcome or introduction page, and not a messages page. This is often the case with themes that are specifically intended for building a website. With many of the paid themes there are various website themes and not as many blogs.
If you use one of these themes, you will not need to create a new home page. Instead, you can simply adapt the one provided by default and edit it the way you want. You can read through the instructions below to find out how to create new pages for your website.

This is how you create a new page:

☞ **Place the pointer on**
   + New

☞ **Click** Page

You may see a message:

☞ **If necessary, click**
  ⊗ **Dismiss**

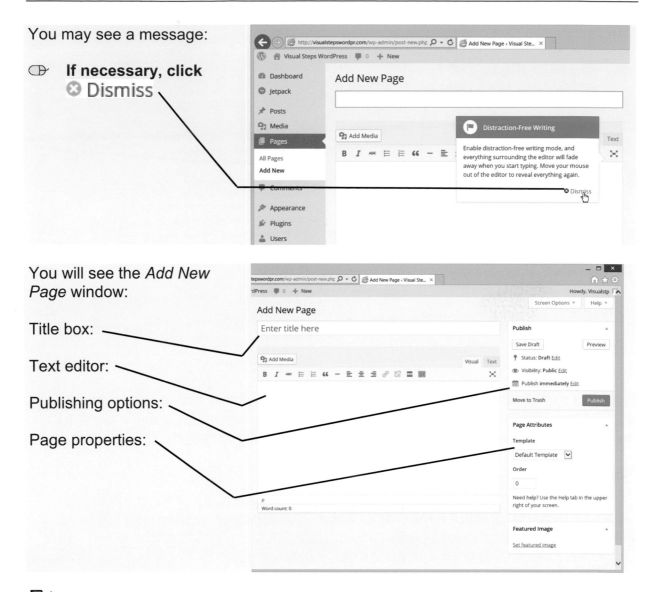

You will see the *Add New Page* window:

Title box:

Text editor:

Publishing options:

Page properties:

🐦 **Please note:**

You can use the [📇 Add Media] button to add media, such as images, to the page from your computer. Sometimes this procedure does not function properly at first, because a certain folder is missing from the web space. If that is the case, you can add media to your website in another way. You can read more about this in *section 4.11 Adding an Image to the Media Library*.

4.2 Adding a Title

First you need to enter the title for the page. It is wise to keep the title short. This is especially important if you want to place the title in a menu.
In that case you need to make sure that the menu option that refers to the page is not impossibly long. It is best to use a title that consists of no more than two words. The title will also be displayed on the web page.

You can start off simply by calling the home page Home:

By Enter title here, **type:** Home

☞ **Click in the text editor**

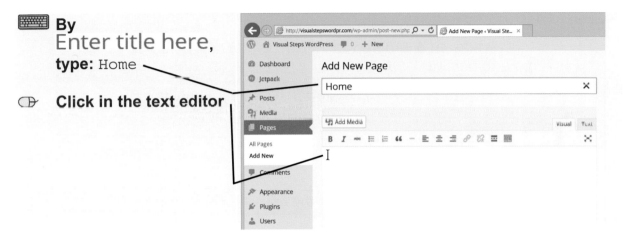

4.3 Adding Text

The next step is placing text on the web page. For this you use the *Visual Editor,* the text editor from *WordPress*, which works pretty much like a regular text editor such as *Word*:

Tabs:

Toolbar:

Text box:

Status bar:

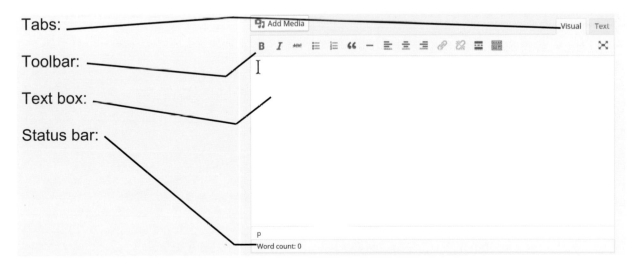

In the text editor you can choose between the *Visual* (What You See Is What You Get) and *Text* (HTML) views. The *Visual* view is used to type the text as it will be displayed on the website. You will see exactly how the text will look like on the web page.
The *Text* view is intended for entering text in HTML code. This can be useful if you want to define more precisely how the page should look. But to use this view you will need to have some basic knowledge of HTML.

You can edit the text using the icons shown on the toolbar:

B *I* ᴬᴮᴱ	Display text in bold, italics, or strike through.
	Display an unordered list (bullet points) or an ordered list (numbered).
"	Display text as a quote, between quotation marks.
—	Horizontal line.
	Align text to the left, center, or right.
🔗	Insert or edit a hyperlink in the text.
	Delete a hyperlink from the text.
	Add the hyperlink *Read more* to the text. This type of link allows the reader to read an excerpt and then *jump* to the remainder of the text elsewhere on the page.
	Toolbar with additional options.
	Display the editor in full screen mode.

You can also display an additional toolbar:

☞ **Click** ▦ ────

The extra toolbar will appear:

Please note: This is a toolbar that can be toggled on/off by clicking it.

The second toolbar contains the following options:

Paragraph ▼	Characteristics for text formatting (see *section 4.4 Formatting Text*).
U	Underline text.
≡	Justify text.
A ▼	Select text color.
📋	Paste text without formatting.
⊘	Delete formatting from text.
Ω	Insert special symbols.
⇤	Decrease indentation of text.
⇥	Increase indentation of text
↰	Undo edit.
↱	Redo edit.
❓	Help information.

💡 Tip

Display name of function

If you let the pointer hover over an icon in one of the toolbars, the name of the function or what it does will appear in a small tooltip.

👆 **Click** B

⌨ **In the large text box, type:** `Welcome to the Visual Steps practice website.`

You will see that the text is rendered in bold.

Some words are underlined in red due to the automatic spellchecker:

This does not affect how the text is displayed on the website.

Type the second sentence:

👆 **Click** B

⌨ **Press** Enter ⏎

⌨ **In the text box, type:** `This website is intended as a practice site where you can practice working with WordPress.`

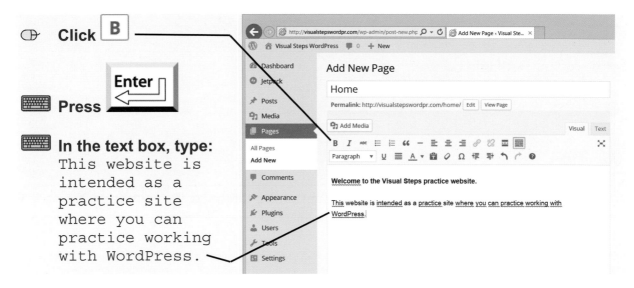

Now you can see immediately how the text you have entered is displayed on your website:

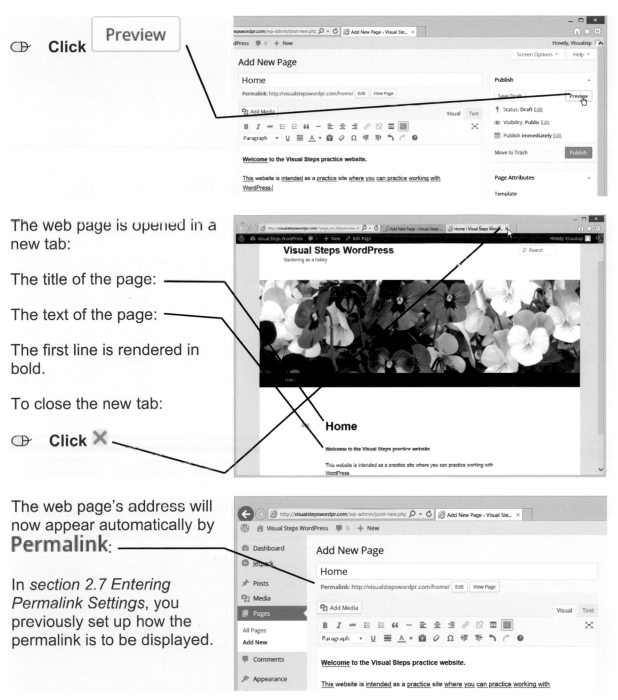

☞ **Click** Preview

The web page is opened in a new tab:

The title of the page: ———

The text of the page: ———

The first line is rendered in bold.

To close the new tab:

☞ **Click** ✖

The web page's address will now appear automatically by **Permalink**: ———

In *section 2.7 Entering Permalink Settings*, you previously set up how the permalink is to be displayed.

💡 **Tip**

Edit a permalink

You can change the automatic permalink by clicking [Edit]. Then you can adjust the text that follows the domain name. This can be useful if you use a longer title for your web page. You can shorten this title for the permalink. Keep in mind that you cannot use blank spaces or other special characters in the permalink. Only use letters and numbers.

Now you can fill in the page with additional text:

☞ **Click in between the last sentence**

⌨ **Type a blank space**

⌨ **In the text box, type:**
The subject is
gardening as a
hobby: a popular
subject on many
websites.

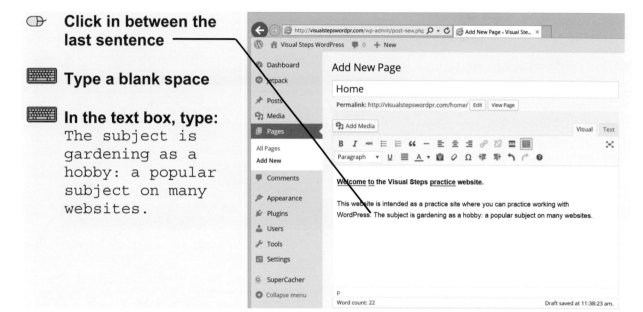

You can type the text first and later add some formatting. To do this, you need to select the text to be formatted first. In this way you can display some of the text as a quote, for example. This is often used on websites as a way of quoting someone:

☞ **Select the text in the last paragraph**

☞ **Click** 66

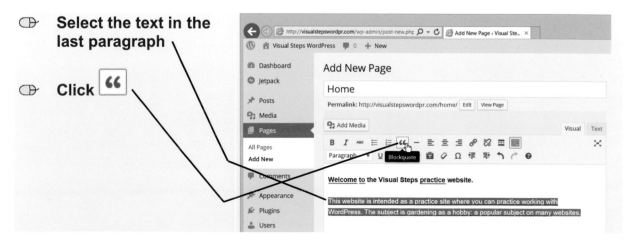

You see that the text is
displayed differently: ——

You can easily undo this edit:

☞ **Click**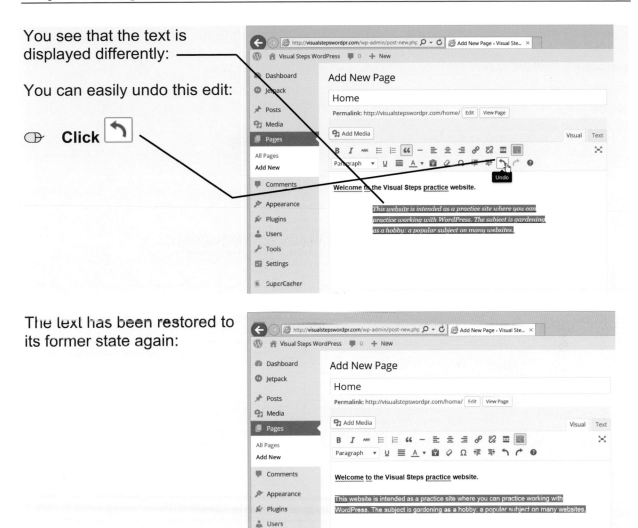

The text has been restored to
its former state again:

4.4 Formatting Text

You can reposition the text by using the ![Enter] key and then select another
formatting option such as bold.

A better way of formatting text is by using *styles*. You can enter a style for any part of
the text. For example, you can define the text as a header, or as a paragraph. This
type of formatting has been used by websites for quite a long time. It ensures that the
text blocks on each page have the same properties. In this way, the text such as a
header will look the same on every page.

For instance, you can select the *Header* (or *Heading)* style for all the headers on all the pages. The headers are numbered from 1 to 6. Number 1 stands for the largest header, and number 6 stands for the smallest header. Just set *Heading 5* for each identical header on each page, and these headers will be displayed in exactly the same way. The choice of header also affects the space that is displayed above and below the text.

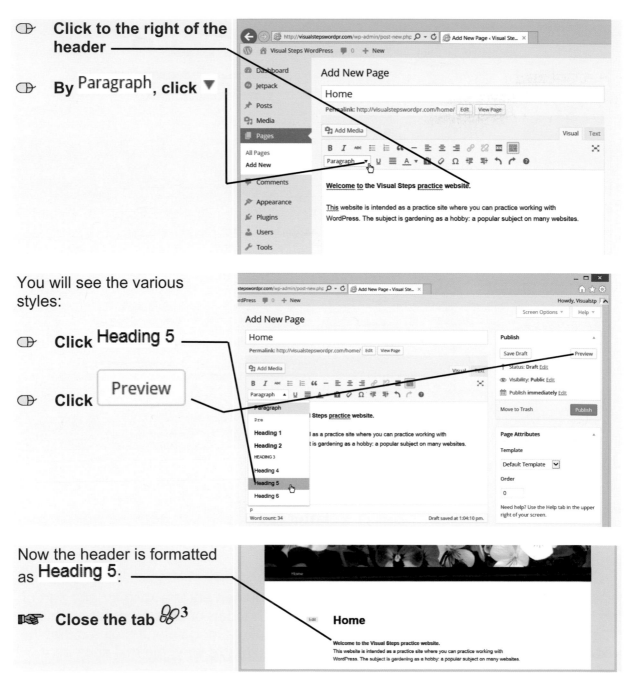

☞ **Click to the right of the header** ⎯⎯⎯⎯⎯⎯

☞ **By** Paragraph **, click ▼**

You will see the various styles:

☞ **Click** Heading 5 ⎯⎯⎯⎯⎯⎯

☞ **Click** Preview

Now the header is formatted as Heading 5. ⎯⎯⎯⎯⎯⎯

☞ **Close the tab** 👣³

Tip

Do not make the header too big
Try to make sure that a header does not cover up or diminish the title of a page.

For headers you will normally use one of the *Heading* styles. You can select the *Paragraph* style for the regular text on the page.

Tip

Combining styles with formatting
You can also combine a text with a certain style, such as *Heading*, with a type of formatting, such as bold or italic. But be sure not to render too much text in italics. Italicized text is often harder to read and less clear on a website.

4.5 Adding a Hyperlink to Text

You can also format a bit of text as a hyperlink. You select the portion of the text for the hyperlink that will refer to another web page or an external website, for example:

☞ **Select the text 'Visual Steps' in the first sentence**

☞ **Click** 🔗

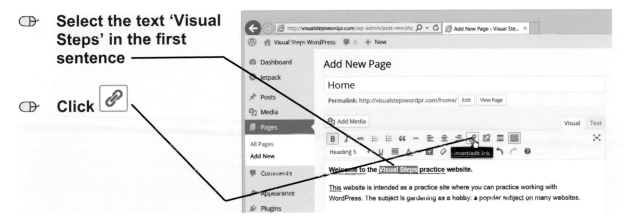

Now the *Insert/Edit link* window is opened. In this window you can enter the web address of the website to which this link needs to refer:

⌨ **By URL, type:**
`http://www.visual steps.com`

Please note: make sure you always type "http://" at the beginning of a web address.

By Title you see the text you have selected:

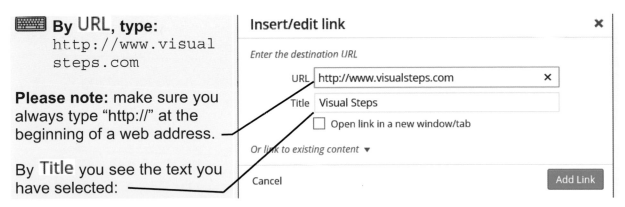

You can have the website open in a separate window, or on a new tab:

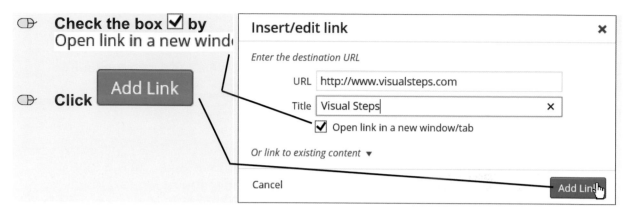

☞ **Check the box ☑ by**
Open link in a new wind

☞ **Click** [Add Link]

Insert/edit link   ✕

Enter the destination URL

URL http://www.visualsteps.com

Title Visual Steps   ✕

☑ Open link in a new window/tab

Or link to existing content ▼

Cancel   Add Link

💡 **Tip**

Open the website in a separate window
It is often best to open a website to which you have created a link in another window, or new tab of the Internet browser. In this way you ensure that your own web page is still open and can be easily reached.
If your web page is replaced by the website you have linked to when the visitor clicks the hyperlink, there is always a chance your visitor will not return to your website anymore.

You can see that the link has been added to the text:

The link has acquired the color that was set by the theme settings (see *section 3.7 Setting Colors*).

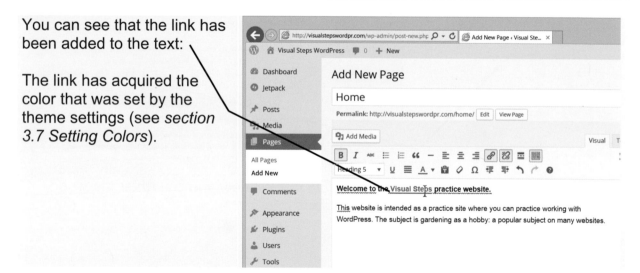

You can fill the entire web page with additional text and add more formatting.

When you are done filling the page you can preview it:

Click Preview

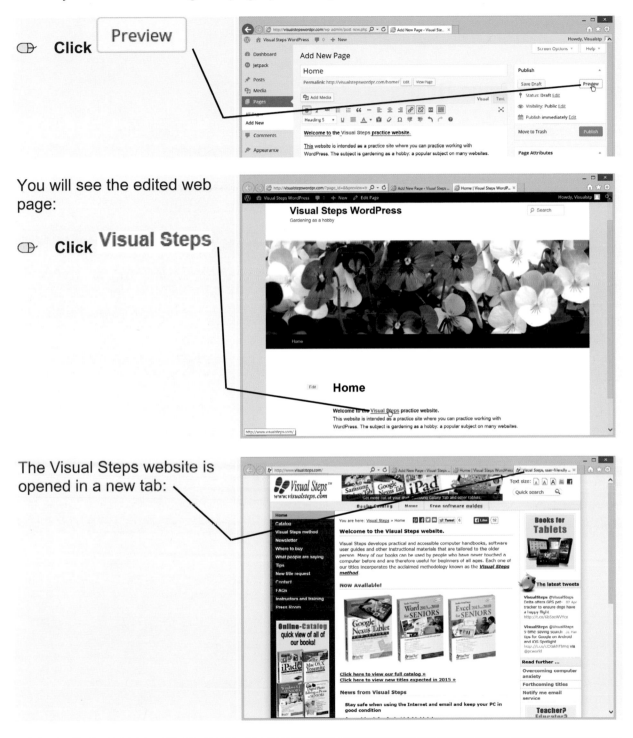

You will see the edited web page:

Click Visual Steps

The Visual Steps website is opened in a new tab:

☞ **Close the tab with the Visual Steps website** ✂³

☞ **Close the tab with the website preview** | Home | Visual Steps WordP... ✕
 ❧3

4.6 Saving Page Drafts

Now you can save the new web page. One of the options is to save this page as a *draft*. This option saves a copy of the page while you are working. The page will not yet be added to your website and is not visible to others.

💡 **Tip**

Temporary saving
It is recommended to regularly save your page as a draft, while you are working. Then you will always have an older version if you were to lose your work for some reason or other. Once you have saved a draft page, you can also stop working with *WordPress*. You can log in later another time and continue working on this page.

This is how you save a draft page:

☞ **Click** `Save Draft`

The draft page has been saved:

In the *Tips* at the end of this chapter you can read how to open a draft page and continue working.

4.7 Entering Page Attributes

Now you can enter *page attributes*. These are some of the properties of a page:

The *Page Attributes* pane can be found on the right-hand side of the window:

Type of page:

Location of the page between the other pages:

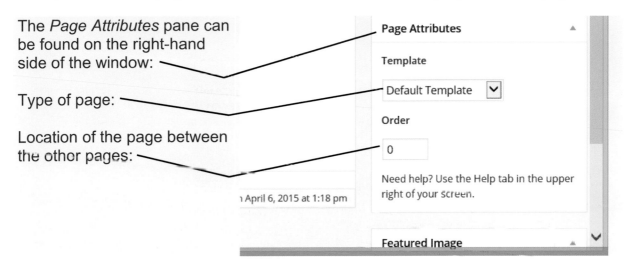

Themes often come with multiple types of page layouts. If that is the case, you can select one of these layouts by *Template*. The *Twenty Eleven* theme, for example, has a default layout with a text column (*Showcase Template*) and a template with a sidebar (*Sidebar Template*).
In this example you will be using the default layout.

The **Order** page attribute lets you determine the order of the web pages. This is the position in the menu where the page is displayed. In this way you can insert a new page between existing pages. The higher the number, the lower in the row the page will be presented.

But you need to take into account that the way this option works depends on the theme you use. With some themes, the order of pages in the menu is determined by the menu settings.

💡 **Tip**

A different image in the header
Usually, each page has the same header at the top. If you wish, you can also use a different header image on each page:

In order to use another image in the header, you click
<u>Set featured image</u>:

You can read more about uploading images in *section 4.11 Adding an Image to the Media Library*.

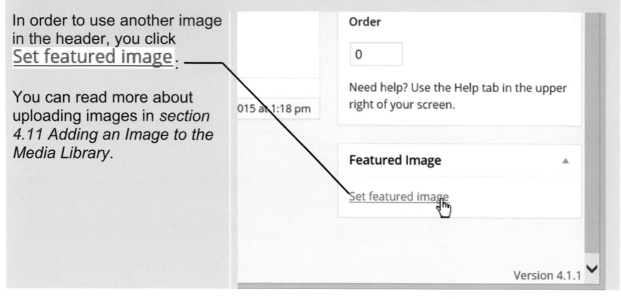

After you have entered all the settings, you can publish the page:

In the top right corner you see the *Publish* pane:

Save draft page:

Status of the page:

Who is allowed to view the page:

Previous versions of the page:

Publish now or later on:

Delete page:

By default, a page is visible to all visitors. But you can set a page to be visible only to yourself (*Private*), or only to visitors who know the correct password (*Password Protected*). For a regular website, you can select *Public*:

☞ **By 👁 Visibility:, click** **Edit**

If you want to enter another visibility setting, you click the radio button ⦿ by the desired option, and then click OK :

In this example we will close these options:

☞ **Click Cancel**

You can decide to publish the page right away, or set a date and time for publication. It may be useful to publish the page later on; in the case that the page contains information about something that will happen in the future. For example, an offer or a discount in a webshop. But usually, you can publish a page immediately:

☞ **By 📅 Publish immediately, click Edit**

If you want to enter a date and time of publication for the page, you need to select the date and time, and then click OK :

In this example we will close these options:

☞ **Click** Cancel

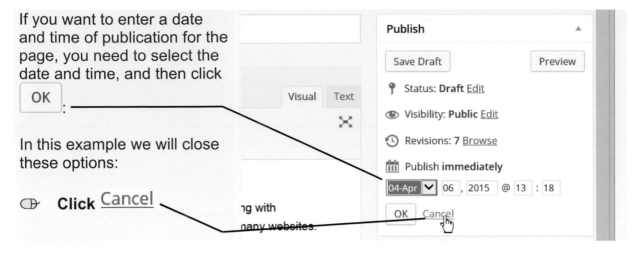

💡 **Tip**

Delete a page

If, upon reflection, you decide not to use the new page, you can delete it. All the data and settings for the page will be deleted. The page will also be removed from the page list. This will happen even if you have previously saved the page as a draft.

This is how you delete a new page:

☞ **Click** Move to Trash

💡 **Tip**

More page options

You can install various widgets and plugins with which you can add extra settings to the pages of your website. With some themes, these widgets and plugins have already been installed. You can enter the name of the page's author, for example, or set *metatags*. Metatags are keywords that enable search engines to find a website. You can read more about working with widgets and plugins in *Chapter 5 Adding Extra Components*.

4.8 Publishing a Page

After you have entered all the settings, you can publish the new web page. This means that the page will be officially added to the website, and will also be saved in the database as part of the website. The page will also become visible to all visitors. That is to say, if the visibility of the page is set to *Public*. This is how you publish your new page:

In the *Publish* pane:

☞ **Click** Publish

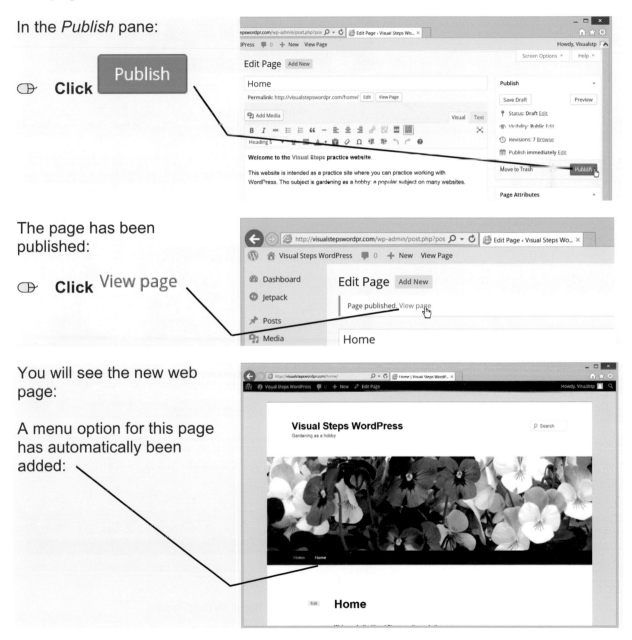

The page has been published:

☞ **Click** View page

You will see the new web page:

A menu option for this page has automatically been added:

In the same way you can add more new web pages to the website.

4.9 Setting the Home Page

Currently, the website now has two pages called *Home*. This is because the theme comes with a default home page. This default homepage is often a page showing the latest posts and not a static page:

Click left **Home** menu option

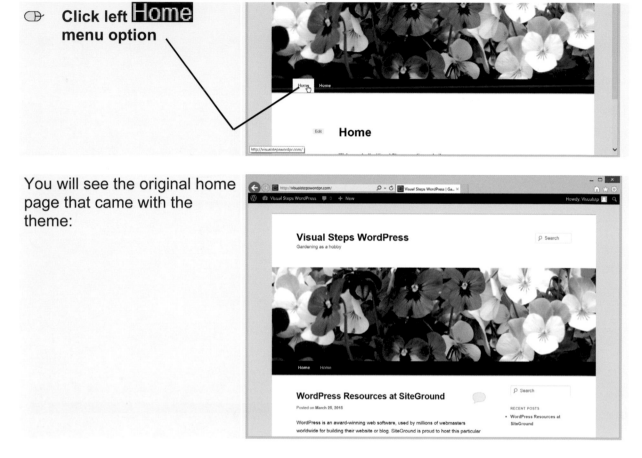

You will see the original home page that came with the theme:

Of course, it is confusing to have two home pages on your website. But you can easily disable the default home page from this theme. You do this by setting the new home page you have just created as the home page:

Place the pointer on the name of your website

Click **Dashboard**

☞ **Place the pointer on** Settings

☞ **Click** Reading

The *Reading Settings* window appears:

☞ **Click the radio button** ⦿ **by** A static page

☞ **By** Front page: **, click** ⌄

☞ **Click** Home

☞ **Click** Save Changes

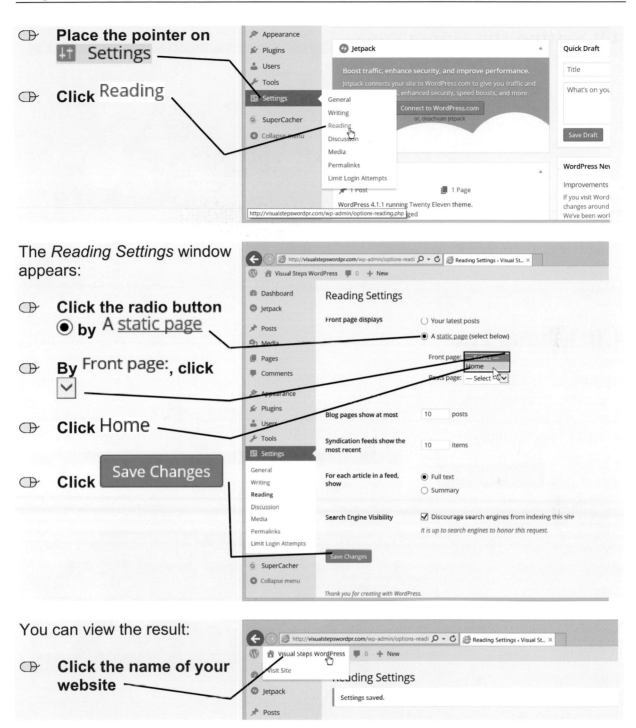

You can view the result:

☞ **Click the name of your website**

Now you will only see one
Home page:

This is the new *static* page
you just created. The page
with the current posts called
Home has been disabled.

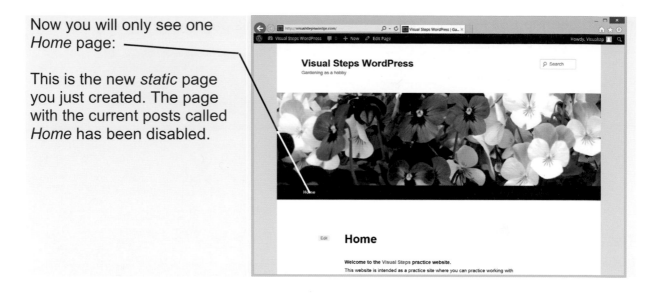

4.10 Editing Text

Besides creating new text pages, you can also edit text on existing pages. You can
add, edit, or delete text:

In order to edit the page:

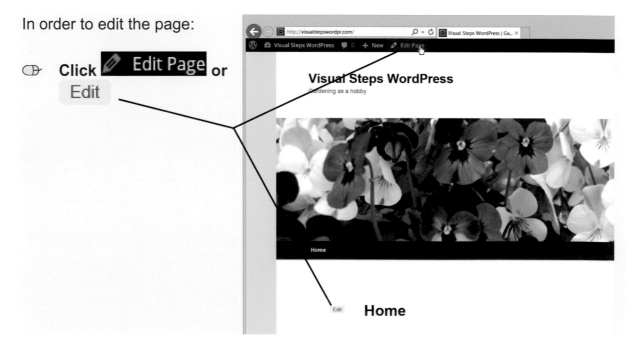

Click [Edit Page] or
[Edit]

You will see the *Edit Page* window. The functions on this page work in pretty much the same way as when you were creating a new page:

☞ **Replace 'Welcome' with:** `Hello! Welcome`

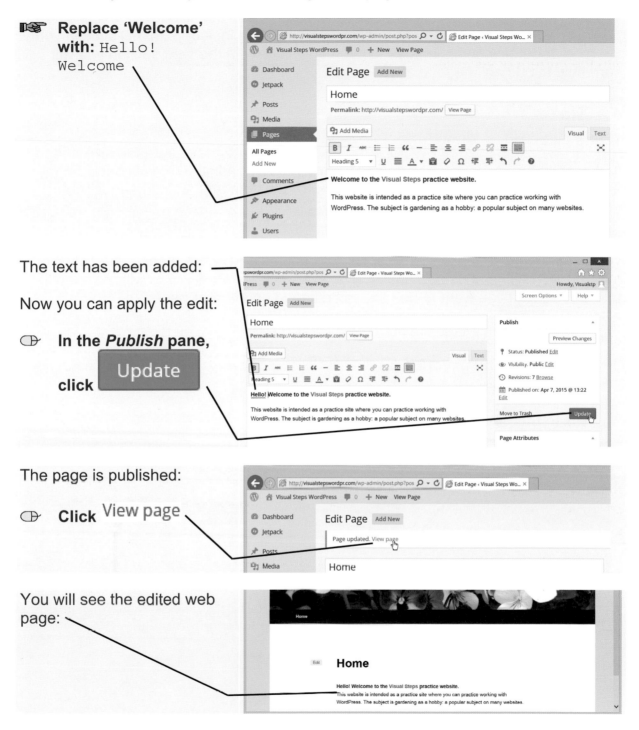

The text has been added:

Now you can apply the edit:

☞ **In the *Publish* pane, click** **Update**

The page is published:

☞ **Click** View page

You will see the edited web page:

You can also edit a page through the page management window. You can read more about this in the *Tips* at the end of this chapter.

4.11 Adding an Image to the Media Library

Nowadays you hardly see a web page any longer that is just filled with text. Most of the time there is at least one or more images or photos included. In this section you can read about uploading images to the media library. In the next section you will learn how to add an image to a web page.

💡 Tip

Quality and size of images
You can resize an image in *WordPress*. But it is better to make sure the size and quality of the image is as good as possible, before uploading it. This is because the editing options in *WordPress* are rather limited. You can edit an image in a photo editing program, such as *Adobe Photoshop Elements*.

There are several ways of adding images. One of the methods is by using the *media library*. All the uploaded media files, such as photos and other images, are collected in this library. Once an image has been uploaded to the library, you will not need to upload it again if you want to use the same image on another page.

This is how you add images to the media library:

☞ **Click the name of your website**

☞ **Place the pointer on**
   📷 Media

☞ **Click Add New**

Now you need to select the files from your computer:

☞ **Click** Select Files

The window called *Choose File to Upload* is opened:

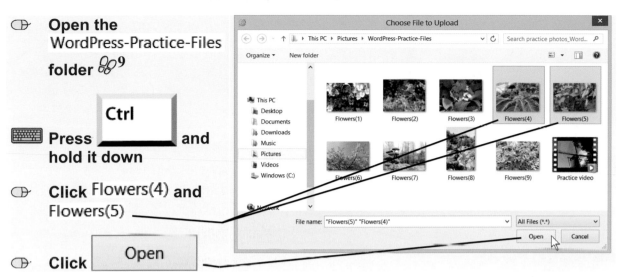

☞ **Open the WordPress-Practice-Files folder** ✂️⁹

⌨️ **Press** **Ctrl** **and hold it down**

☞ **Click** Flowers(4) **and** Flowers(5)

☞ **Click** Open

The files will be uploaded. When the upload has finished, you can add a description and adjust some settings for each image:

You will see both files:

☞ **By** Flowers(4), **click** Edit

 HELP! I see an error message.

If the file you want to upload is too big (expressed in kilobytes), you will see an error message. In this case, you need to reduce the size of the image first, or convert it to a different file format, such as JPG or PNG.

☞ **Click** ⬅️

☞ **Adapt the image to a smaller size**

☞ **Upload the file once again**

⊗ HELP! Error message while uploading images.

You may see an error message while you are uploading images from your computer to *WordPress*. This may happen because the upload program used by *WordPress* does not work in accordance with the properties of your web space. If that is the case, you can try an alternate method of uploading:

☞ **Click** browser uploader

You will see another uploader:

☞ **Click** Browse...

☞ **Select the desired images**

☞ **Click** Upload

If this does not work either, then take a look at the error message and contact your hosting provider.

A window is opened showing various image settings for this image:

Title of the image:

Data for this image:

Edit image:

Caption by image:

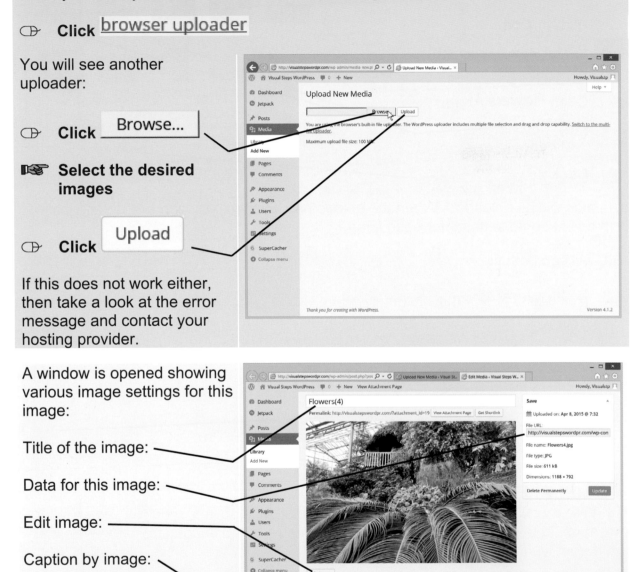

☞ Drag the scroll box downwards

Alternative text for the image:

Description of the image:

You can edit an image directly within the *WordPress Attachment Details* pane. This can be handy in the case where an image is shown in the wrong orientation. You can rotate the image and crop it if you need to. You can take a quick look at some of the options for editing:

☞ Click Edit Image

Crop or rescale the image:

Tools:

Image:

To which image sizes do the edits apply:

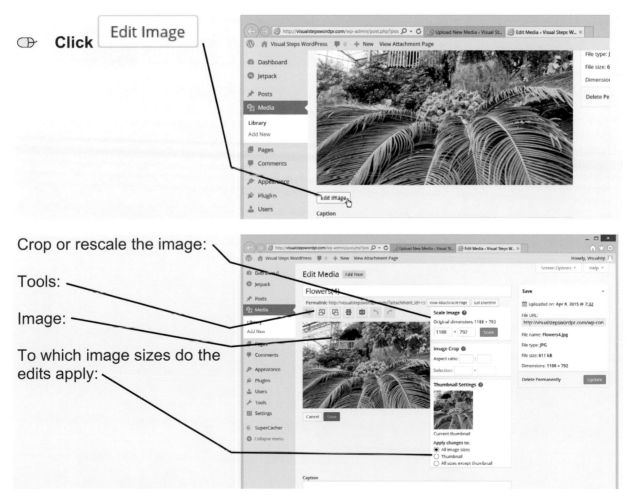

💡 Tip

Editing help
You can read more about the editing options, such as rescaling an image, by clicking ❓ by the edit label or icon.

For example, this is how you flip an image horizontally:

☞ **Click**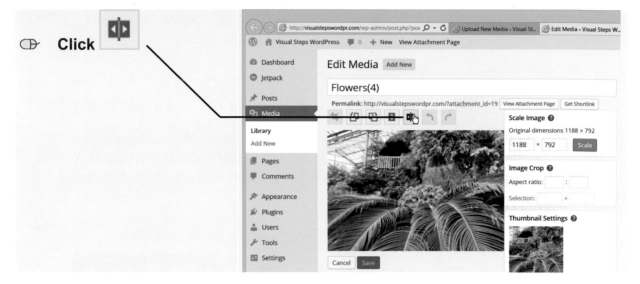

By clicking one of the icons shown in this list, the following edits can be applied:

🔄	Rotates to the left.
🔄	Rotates to the right.
🔁	Flip an image vertically.
◀▶	Flip an image horizontally.
↶	Undo an edit.
↷	Redo an edit.

In order to save the edited image in the media library:

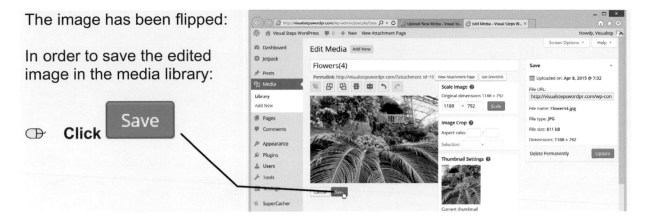

⊕ **Click** Save

At the bottom of the window there are other settings you can apply to the image:

Caption   A brief explanation that is displayed directly below the image. If this text is filled in, the **Alternative Text** will not be necessary.

Alternative Text   Text that is displayed if the image cannot be displayed in the Internet browser. Also used for accessibility.

Description   Text that describes the image, but is only displayed in the Dashboard.

It is often not necessary to fill in all this information. There are many websites where the photos do not have a caption. In this example, you can edit the title of the image, and add a caption:

⌨ **In the title box, type:**
Hidden tree house

⌨ **By Caption, type:**
Hidden tree house

⊕ **Click** Update

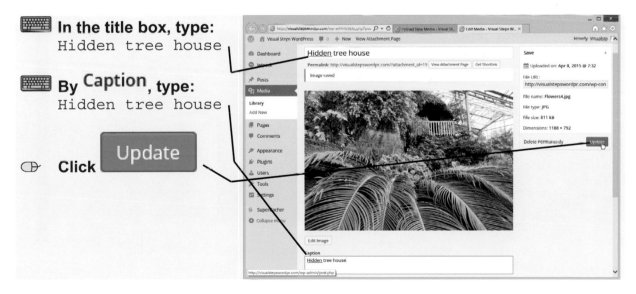

Now you can also edit the other image:

☞ **Click** **Library**

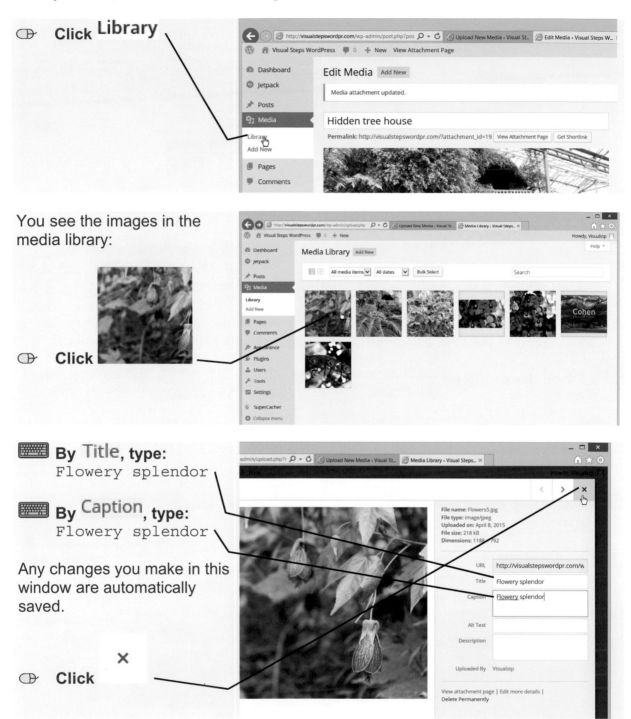

You see the images in the media library:

☞ **Click**

⌨ **By** **Title**, **type:**
Flowery splendor

⌨ **By** **Caption**, **type:**
Flowery splendor

Any changes you make in this window are automatically saved.

☞ **Click** **×**

You will see the media library:

☞ **Close the**

🔲 Upload New Media ‹ Visual S

tab 👣³

4.12 Adding an Image to a Web Page

Now you can add the images from the media library to a page on your website:

☞ **Place the pointer on**
  ⬜ **Pages**

☞ **Click** All Pages

☞ **Click** Home

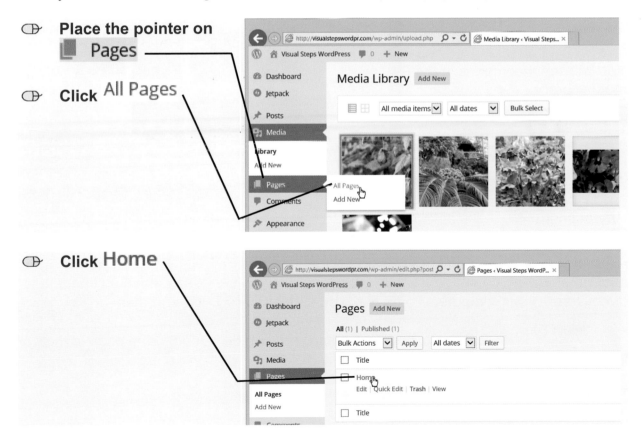

The *Edit Page* window is opened:

When an image is inserted in the text, the position of the cursor will be taken into account:

☞ **Set the cursor to the right of practice website.**

☞ **Click** 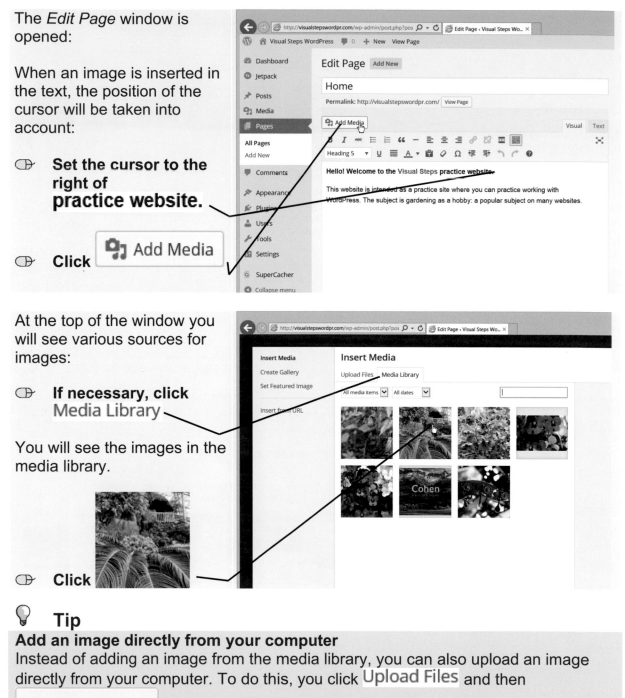 Add Media

At the top of the window you will see various sources for images:

☞ **If necessary, click** Media Library

You will see the images in the media library.

☞ **Click**

💡 Tip

Add an image directly from your computer
Instead of adding an image from the media library, you can also upload an image directly from your computer. To do this, you click Upload Files and then

Select Files . After uploading the image, it can be added to the page in the same way.

You can enter various settings for an image before adding it to your web page. For example, you can edit the description that was previously entered, set the alignment or set one or more of the other settings:

Details of the image:

The display settings can be found at the bottom:

Position of the image with regard to the text:

Link to the image, yes or no:

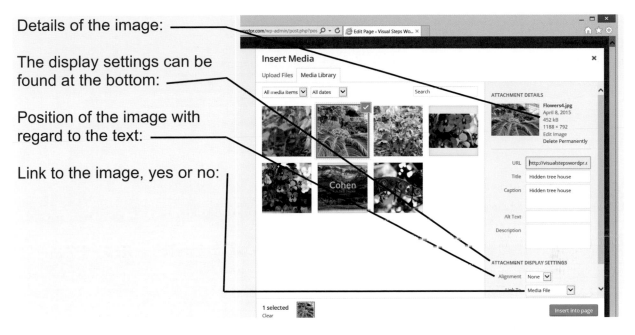

Each image receives its own web address in *WordPress*. You can add a hyperlink to the image if you want, by selecting Link To. This hyperlink will refer to the original, full-size version of the photo.

The Alignment setting lets you determine the position of the image with regard to the text: left, right or centered.

You can now enter the settings for the image. If the image does not seem to fit the web page with these settings, you can always adjust the settings later on.

☞ **By** Alignment**, click**

☞ **Click Left**

☞ **Click** Insert into page

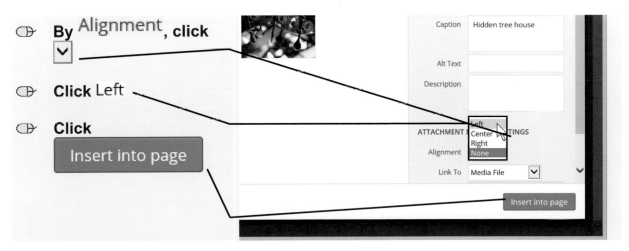

You will see the *Edit Page* window showing the position of the image with regard to the text:

Select the image:

☞   **Click the image**

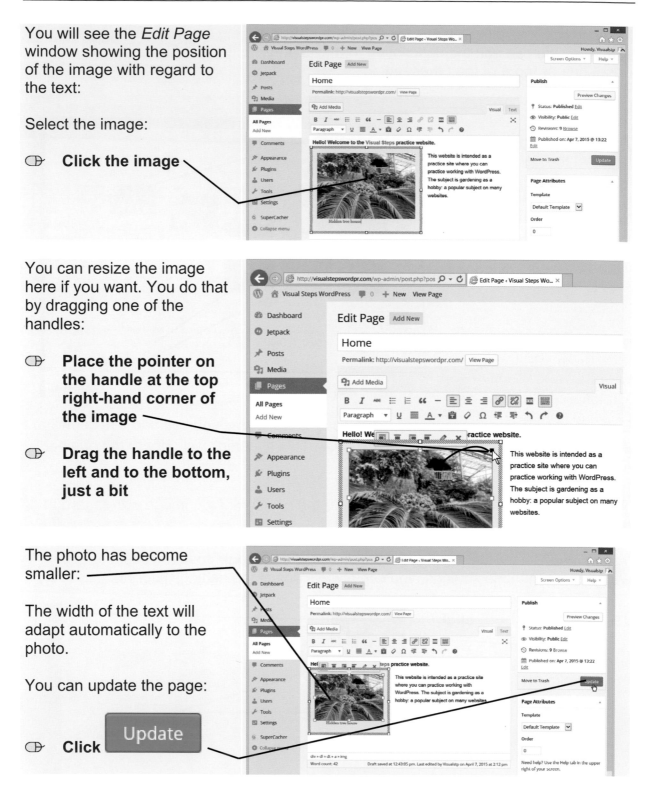

You can resize the image here if you want. You do that by dragging one of the handles:

☞   **Place the pointer on the handle at the top right-hand corner of the image**

☞   **Drag the handle to the left and to the bottom, just a bit**

The photo has become smaller:

The width of the text will adapt automatically to the photo.

You can update the page:

☞   **Click** Update

☞ **Click** View page

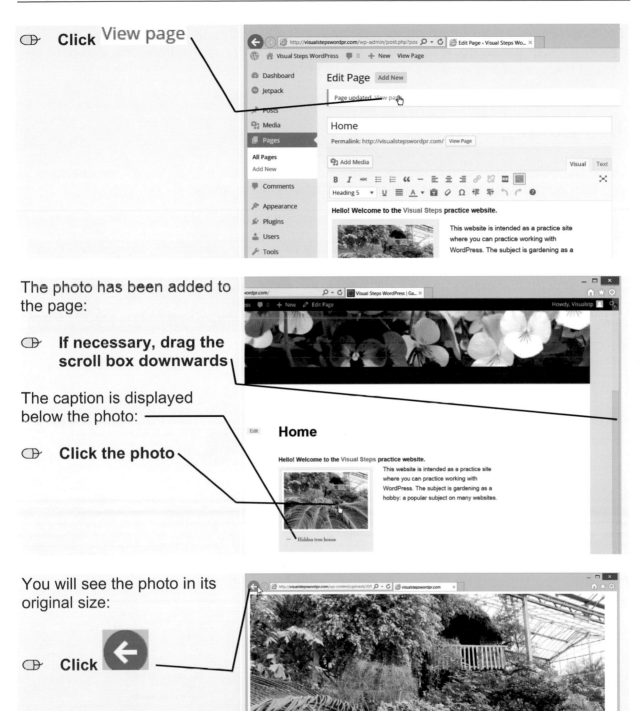

The photo has been added to the page:

☞ **If necessary, drag the scroll box downwards**

The caption is displayed below the photo:

☞ **Click the photo**

You will see the photo in its original size:

☞ **Click** ⬅

You can use this same method to add other images to the page. Or you can add other types of media such as a PDF file, a *PowerPoint* presentation, or a video. In the *Tips* at the end of this chapter you can read how to do this.

4.13 Editing an Image

Once an image has been added to a page, you can edit it some more. For example, you can adjust the alignment of the image, or add a hyperlink:

☞ **Click** *Edit Page*

On the *Edit Page* window:

☞ **Click the photo**

A toolbar appears, with icons for aligning, editing, and deleting the image:

Please note: with some images, the toolbar is not fully visible.

You can use the handles to resize the image, if you wish:

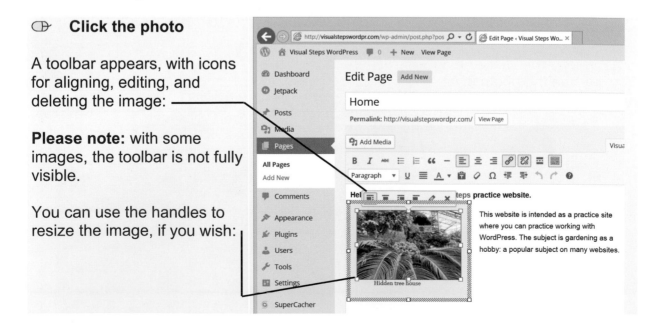

💡 Tip

Creating a hyperlink by an image

You can set a hyperlink by an image. By doing this, you can link the image to a larger version of the same image, or link the image to another web page:

On the *Edit Page* window:

👉 **Click the image**

👉 **Click** 🔗

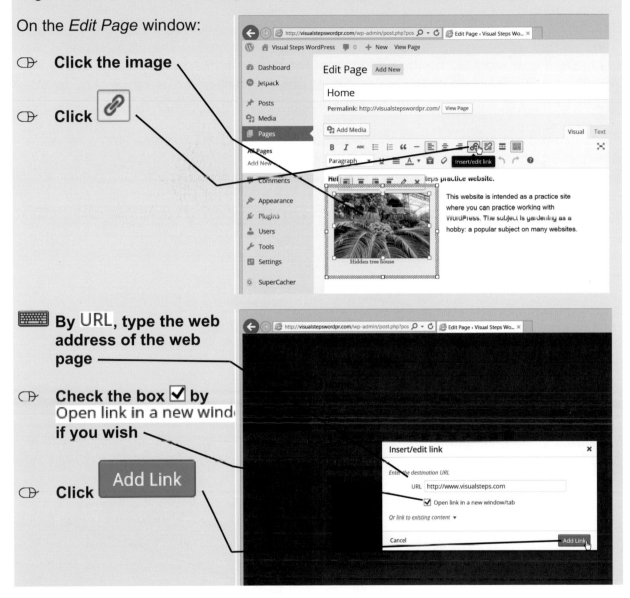

⌨ **By URL, type the web address of the web page**

👉 **Check the box ☑ by** Open link in a new windo if you wish

👉 **Click** Add Link

4.14 Working with Menus

Up till now, you have seen that the menu in *WordPress* is updated automatically and that it contains each page of the website. The location of the menu depends on the theme you use.

But you can also create one or more menus yourself, and add them to your website. You can use a new menu to replace the existing theme menu. This can be useful, for example, if you want to change the order of the pages in the menu. You can also create a new menu with handy hyperlinks to other websites, for instance. You can add this menu to your website in several places, such as in a sidebar.

First, you will learn how to replace the existing menu on your website with a menu where the pages are placed in a different order.
Before you do this, you will need to create another new page first:

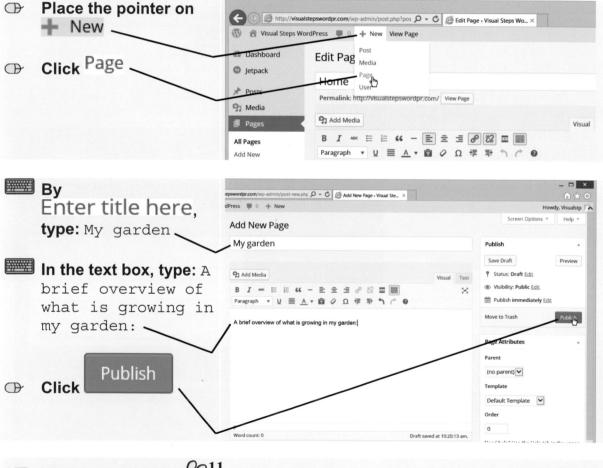

☞ **Place the pointer on**
  ➕ **New**

☞ **Click** Page

⌨ **By**
  Enter title here,
  type: My garden

⌨ **In the text box, type:** A
  brief overview of
  what is growing in
  my garden:

☞ **Click** Publish

☞ **View your website** 🐾 11

You will see that the website now consists of two pages:

Currently, the *Home* page is shown in the first position in the menu:

⊕ **Click** My garden

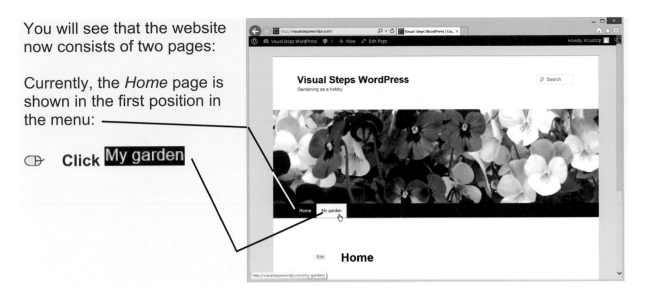

The page called *My garden* is opened. Now you can create a new menu, in which you change the order of the pages:

⊕ **Place the pointer on the name of your website**

⊕ **Click** Menus

You will see the *Edit Menus* page:

You need to enter a name for the new menu:

⌨ **By** *Menu Name*, **type:** Pages

⊕ **Click**

    Create Menu

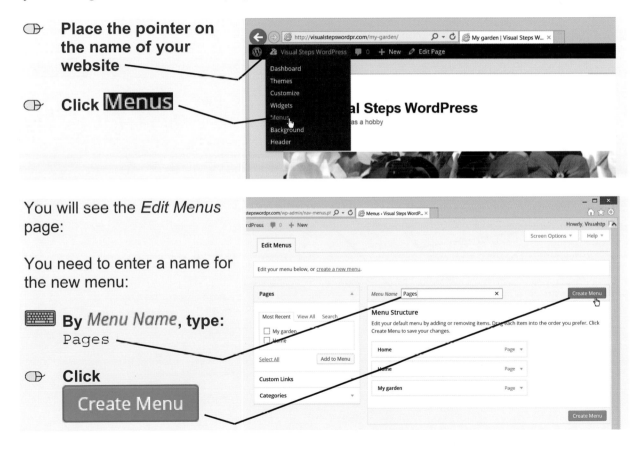

The second step is to fill the menu with menu options. These are the choices you have:

By **Pages** you can enter the pages of your website: ⎯⎯⎯

By **Custom Links** you can enter your own hyperlinks, for example, links to other useful websites: ⎯⎯⎯

By **Categories**, you can enter categories with links: ⎯⎯⎯

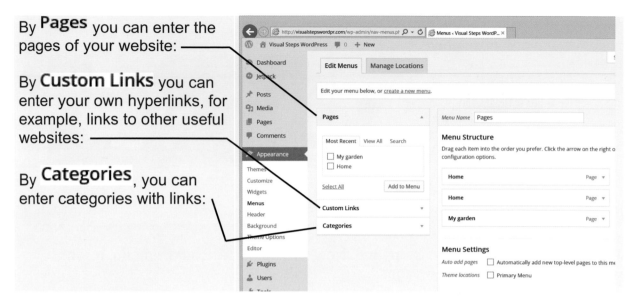

If you want to add the web pages to the menu:

By default, the pages of your site have already been added to the new menu: ⎯⎯⎯

If you want to add individual pages, you check the box ☑ by the pages. In order to add all the pages, you click **Select All**: ⎯⎯⎯

Afterwards, you click

Add to Menu:

In this example there are two *Home* pages in the menu. This is not how it should be. You can delete one of them:

☞ **By the first Home, click ▼**

☞ **Click Remove**

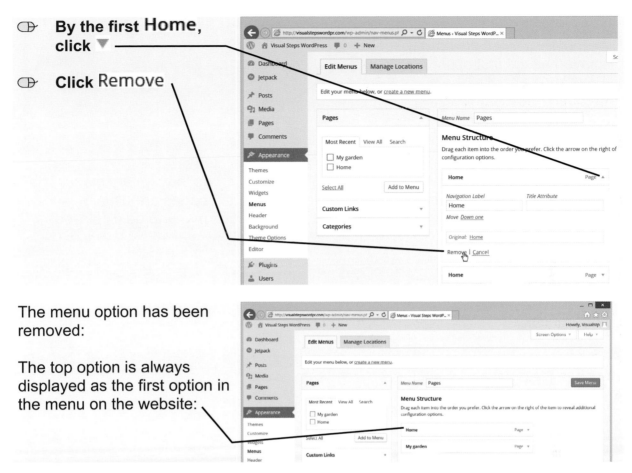

The menu option has been removed:

The top option is always displayed as the first option in the menu on the website:

You can set the order of the menu options yourself. You will usually start with *Home*, but in this example you can practice switching the options:

☞ **Drag the My garden option to the top position**

The option will be placed above the other option(s) in the menu: ——————

Now the *My garden* option is displayed as the first option in the menu.

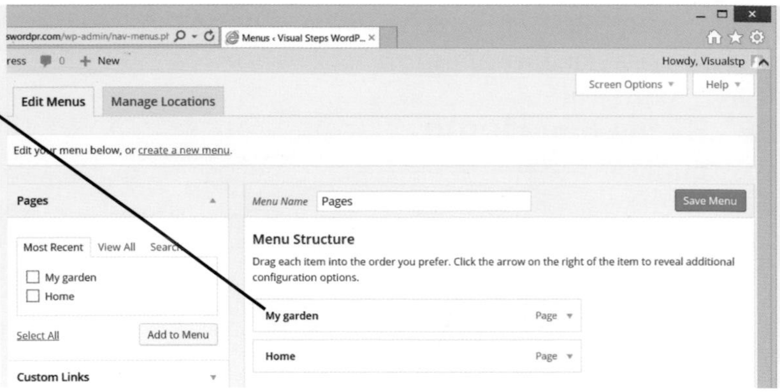

The last thing to do is to decide which menu is to be used as the *primary menu*. The primary menu is the main menu of the theme, in which the pages are usually displayed. In many themes, this menu is set as the default menu to be displayed.

☞ **Check the box ☑ by** Primary Menu ——————

☞ **Click** Save Menu

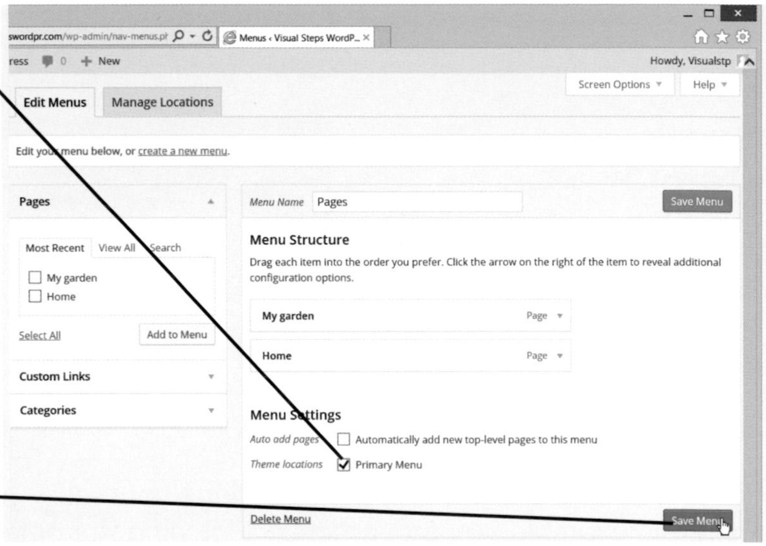

💡 **Tip**

Default menu as primary menu
If the settings for the Primary Menu have not been filled in, the default menu of the theme will be used as the main menu of the website.

You can take a look at the current menu:

☞ **View your website** 👣 11

You will see that the *Home* page is now the second option in the menu:

You can see that it is easy to change the order of the pages in your menu.

If you want to restore the old menu:

☞ **Place the pointer on the name of your website**

☞ **Click Menus**

☞ **Uncheck the box ☑ by** Primary Menu

☞ **Click Save Menu**

Now the default menu of *WordPress* is enabled again. The *Home* page is displayed as the first option in the menu again.

You can also create a menu consisting of hyperlinks, for example, a menu with links to other useful websites.

In order to create a new
menu:

⊕ **Click**
   create a new menu

⌨ **By** *Menu Name*, **type a**
   name, for example:
   Useful links

⊕ **Click**
   Create Menu

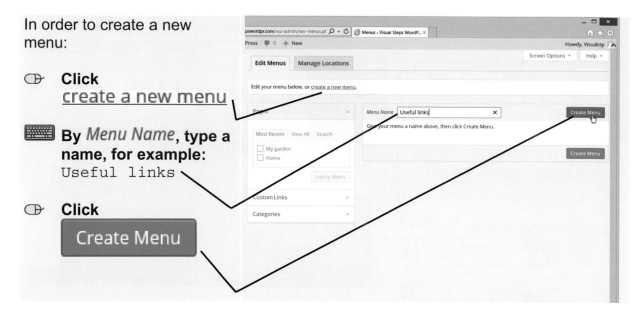

Next, you can add the hyperlinks to the new menu:

⊕ **Click Custom Links**

⌨ **By** *URL*, **type:**
   www.gardens.com

Make sure that http:// is typed
at the beginning of the link.

⌨ **By** *Link Text*, **type:**
   Website on gardens

This name will appear on the
website.

⊕ **Click** **Add to Menu**

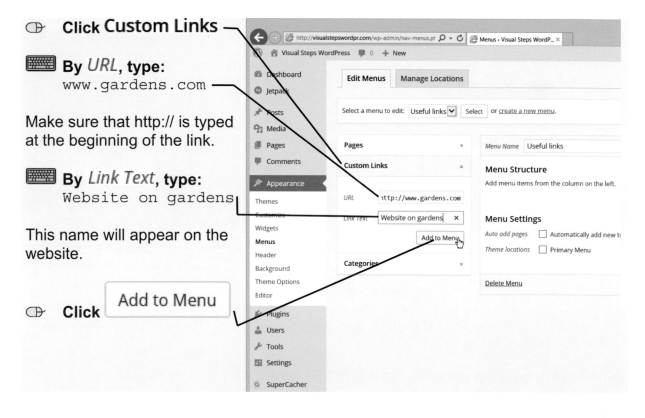

The menu option will be added to the menu. Now you can add a second link:

⌨ **By *URL*, type:**
www.finegardening.
com

Make sure that http:// is typed at the beginning of the link.

⌨ **By *Link Text*, type:**
Magazine on
gardens and
gardening

☞ **Click** Add to Menu

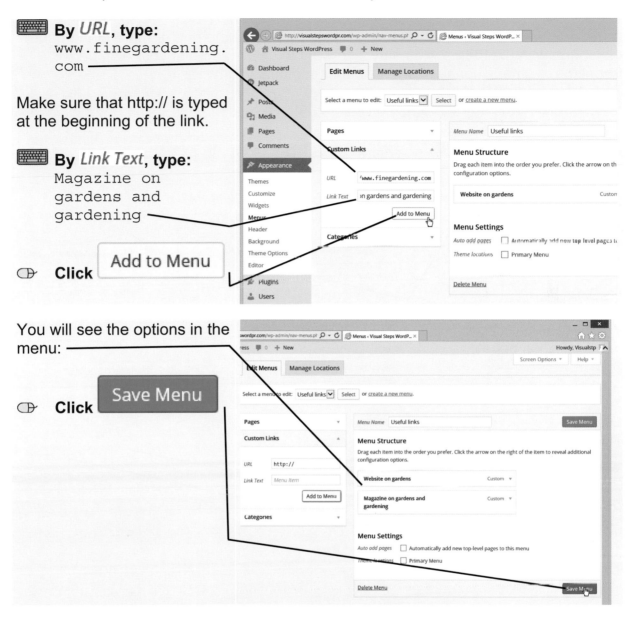

You will see the options in the menu:

☞ **Click** Save Menu

You will learn how to use the *Useful links* menu in the next chapter.

💡 **Tip**

Delete a menu
You can easily delete a menu by clicking Delete Menu in the menu frame.

4.15 Deleting a Page

If you are using a theme, you will most likely want to delete one or more of the pages that came with the theme. You may also want to delete some of your own pages, from time to time, when they are no longer useful to your website.

You can delete a page through the Dashboard:

☞ **Place the pointer on** Pages

☞ **Click** All Pages

You will see the pages administration page:

Actions for the selected pages:

Title of the page:

Author of the page:

Date of creation:

☞ **Place the pointer on** My garden

You will see a number of options:

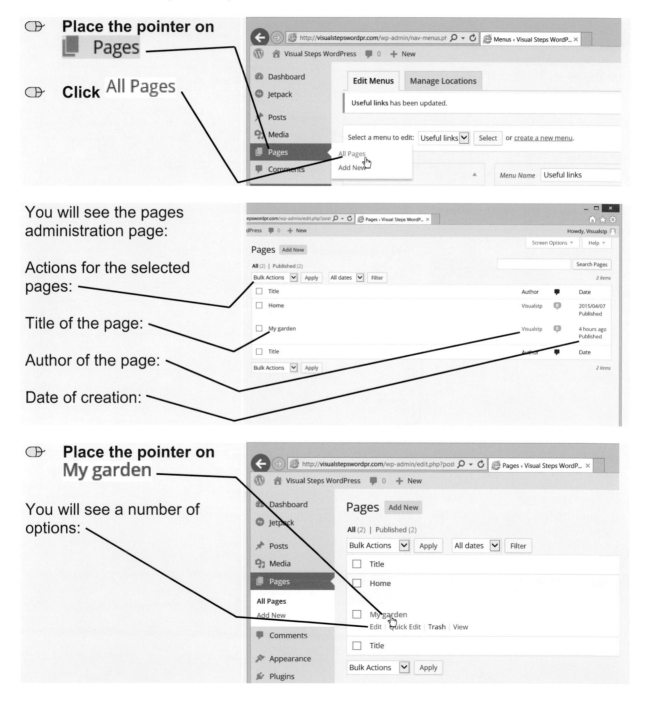

You can apply various actions to a page:

Edit	Edit the page and the text.
Quick Edit	Edit the page settings.
Trash	Move the page to the *Trash*.
View	View the page in the Internet browser.

To practice using one of these actions, you can place the *My garden* page in the *Trash*. It will not be permanently deleted.

☞ **If necessary, place the pointer on** My garden

☞ **Click** Trash

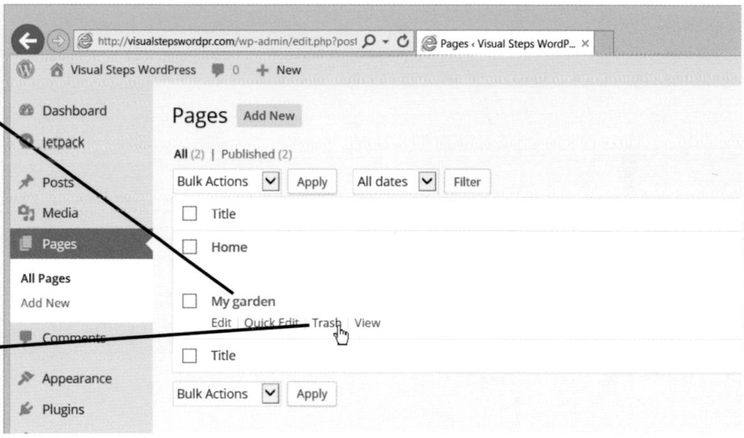

The page will be moved to the *Trash*:

☞ **Click** Trash

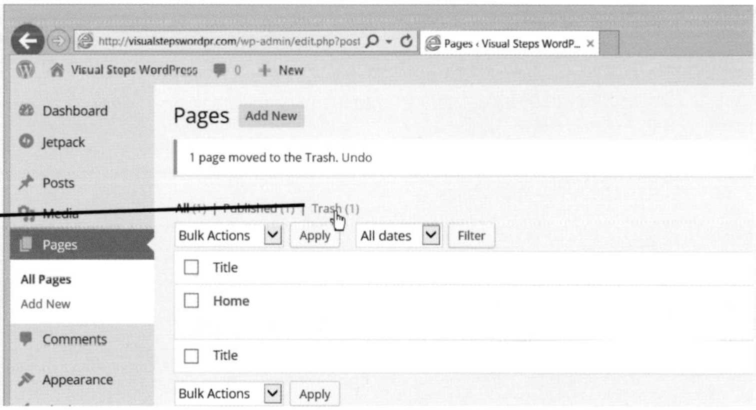

You will see the content of the *Trash*:

☞ **Place the pointer on My garden**

You can restore the page again by clicking Restore. Click Delete Permanently if you are sure you want to permanently delete the page:

☞ **Click** Restore

Now you can log out of *WordPress*:

☞ **Log out of *WordPress* ⬤⬤10**

In this chapter you have learned how to adapt a theme in order to build your own website. In the next chapter you will learn how to expand your website further, by adding new elements.

4.16 Background Information

Dictionary

Draft	A temporary version of a web page that is not quite finished or one that you want to save to be published at a later date.
Editor	The text editing component for *WordPress.* It allows you to add, edit and delete the text on a web page. Works much the same way as a regular text editor such as *Word*.
Home page	The first page that is seen by a visitor to your website. This is also the starting point for the rest of the website. Usually you will use the home page as a brief introduction to your website. You welcome your visitors and tell them more about your website. It is also called the start or default page.
Hyperlink	A clickable text or image that refers to other web pages.
Media library	A component in *WordPress* where you can save various types of media files, such as images and videos.
Metatags	Keywords that can help a website be found by search engines.
Page attributes	Properties of a web page.
Post page	A page where new messages are posted on a regular basis. Blogs consist mainly of this type of page.
Primary menu	The main menu of the theme that usually displays all the pages. This menu is often the default menu that is displayed by a particular theme.
Scale	To reduce or enlarge an image by maintaining the aspect ratio.
Static page	A page that is not updated with new posts on a regular basis. The text on this page usually remains unchanged for longer periods of time; that is why it is called static. Regular websites are usually made up of static pages.

- Continue on the next page -

Style	Default formatting of a text with a fixed font size. Used for headers, for example.
Subpage	A page referred to from a main page. You can use subpages to arrange your website in a more orderly manner.
Template	This determines the layout of a page within a theme.
Trash	A temporary depository for deleted web pages. You can permanently delete a web page from the *Trash*, if needed.

Source: WordPress Help

4.17 Tips

💡 Tip

Continue working on a draft

If you have saved a page as a draft, you can continue working on it later on. This is how you open a draft page:

☞ **Place the pointer on**
   Pages

☞ **Click** All Pages

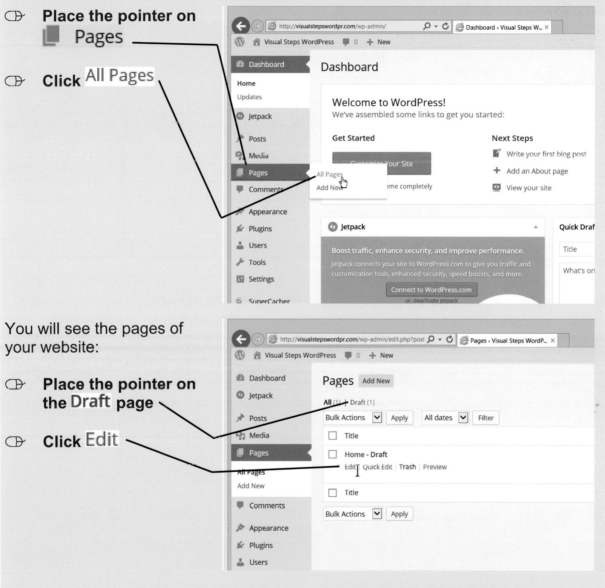

You will see the pages of your website:

☞ **Place the pointer on**
   the Draft **page**

☞ **Click** Edit

You will see the edit page window where you can further edit the draft page.

💡 **Tip**

Edit or delete multiple pages at once
You can edit or delete multiple pages at the same time in *WordPress*:

☞ **Check the box ☑ by the desired pages**

☞ **By Bulk Actions, click ☑**

☞ **Click the desired action**

☞ **Click Apply**

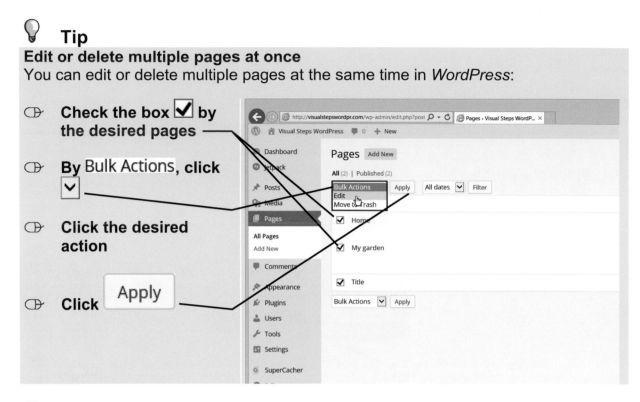

💡 **Tip**

Insert an image from the Internet
Besides inserting an image from your computer, or the media library, you can also insert an image from the Internet. For example, you can search for images with *Google*. Then you can use the address of the web page with the image in your own website. Just make sure you are not infringing on any image copyrights.

In the Dashboard:

☞ **Place the pointer on** 📄 Pages

☞ **Click** All Pages

☞ **Click the desired page**

- Continue on the next page -

You will see the *Edit Page* window:

⊕ **Click** 🖼 Add Media

⊕ **Click** Insert from URL

⌨ By Insert from URL, **type the web address of the image**

You can also copy and paste the web address.

☞ **Enter a different setting, if you wish**

⊕ **Click** Insert into page

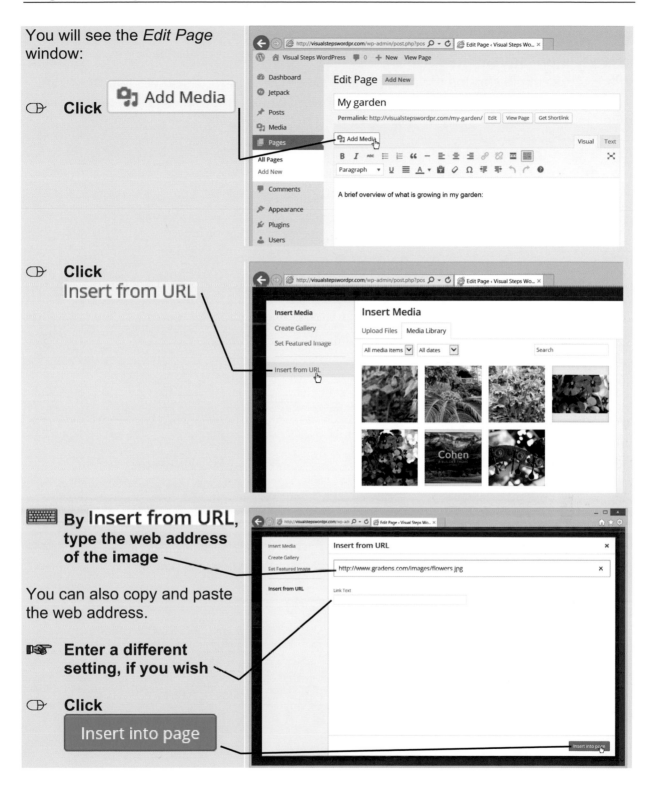

💡 Tip

Quickly edit a page
In the page administration window you can also edit a page. If you want to fully edit the page, you select Edit. But if you do not want to edit the text, you can select the quick edit option:

☞ **Place the pointer on the title of the page**

☞ **Click Quick Edit**

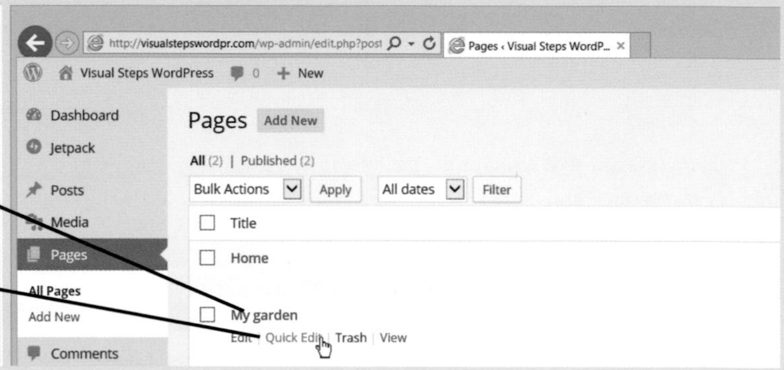

You can adjust several of the page settings here:

After you have finished:

☞ **Click Update**

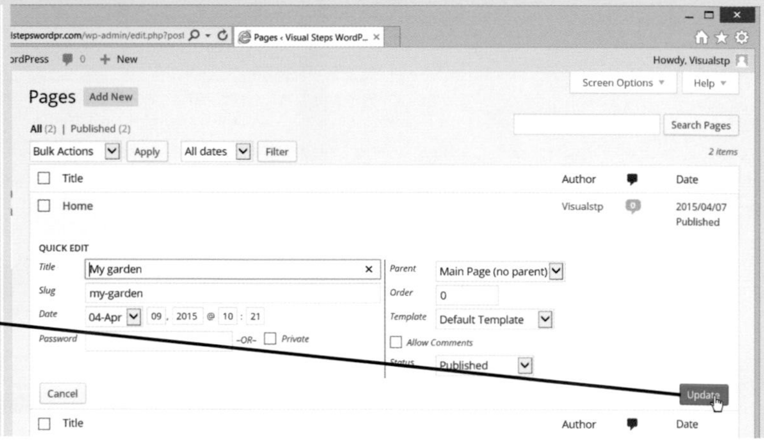

💡 Tip

Add a PDF file or PowerPoint presentation to a hyperlink

By clicking the 🗐 **Add Media** option you can place a PDF file or a *PowerPoint* presentation on your website. Here is how you do that:

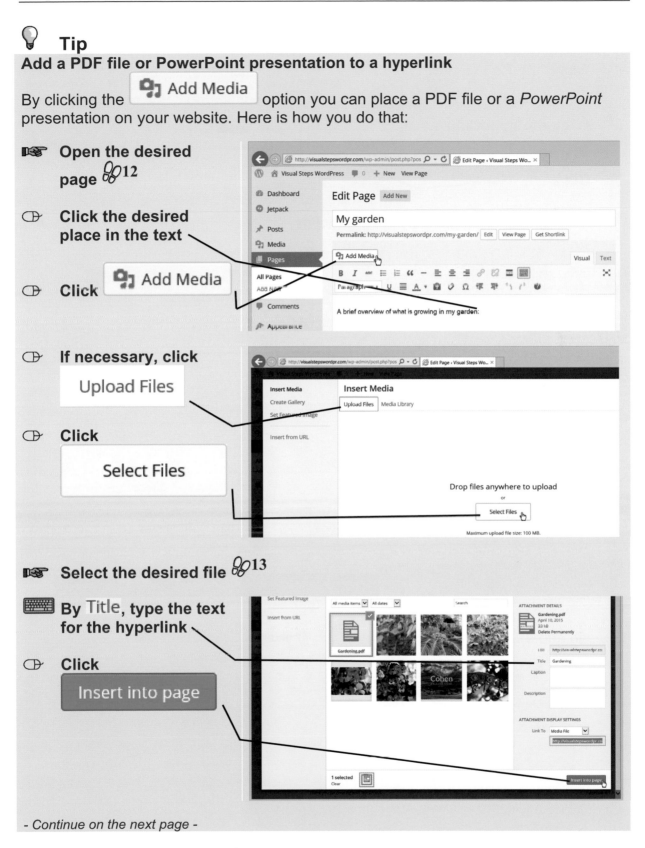

☞ **Open the desired page** 𝄞12

⌕ **Click the desired place in the text**

⌕ **Click** 🗐 **Add Media**

⌕ **If necessary, click** **Upload Files**

⌕ **Click** **Select Files**

☞ **Select the desired file** 𝄞13

⌨ **By** Title, **type the text for the hyperlink**

⌕ **Click** **Insert into page**

- Continue on the next page -

The PDF file will be opened in the same window. You can also display the file in a new window:

☞ **Click the hyperlink**

☞ **Click**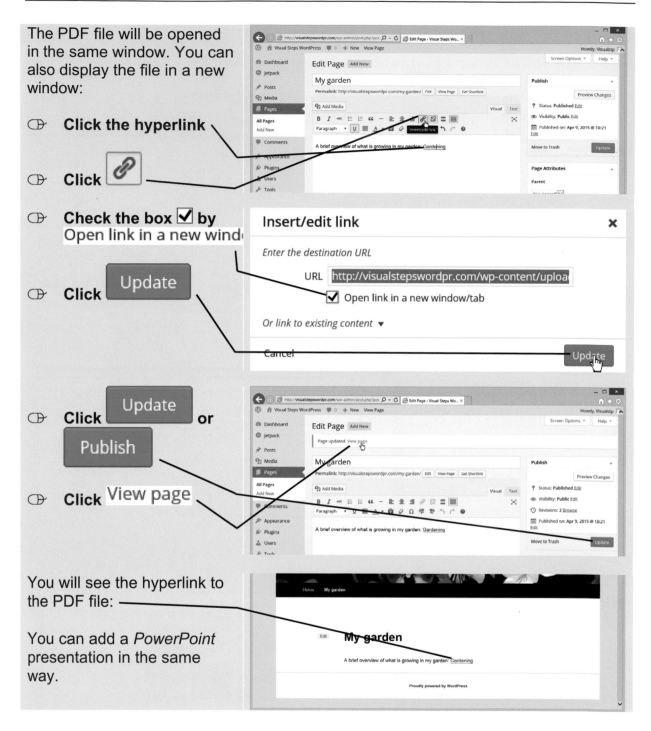

☞ **Check the box ☑ by**
Open link in a new wind

☞ **Click** Update

☞ **Click** Update **or** Publish

☞ **Click** View page

You will see the hyperlink to the PDF file:

You can add a *PowerPoint* presentation in the same way.

💡 Tip

Creating a subpage

By default, a web page is always a *main page*. But you can also link one page to another web page. Then the page will become a *subpage* or child page. This can be useful if the new page is one of multiple pages in a specific category.

For example: you are creating a website for a restaurant with multiple pages for the food menus. You have a separate page for dinner. You can make a new page for the desserts. Then you can indicate that this page is a subpage of the dinner page. You will see the result of this action in the page's web address. The web address of the dessert page as a main page would be www.myrestaurant.com/dessert. As a subpage, this would be www.myrestaurant.com/dinner/dessert. Subpages are also displayed in page menus as part of a main page. This means you can arrange your website in a better way by using subpages. You can only use subpages if there is already another main page.

In order to set a page as a subpage:

☞ **By Parent, click** ☑

☞ **Click the page that is to be the main page for this page**

💡 Tip

Hyperlink for email
You can also send an email from your website with a hyperlink. The email link will look like a regular hyperlink on your website. But by clicking it, the visitor's email program will be opened and they can then send you an email.

⌨ **Type an email address in the text box**

☞ **Select the email address**

☞ **Click** 🔗

The email address is already filled in by **URL**:

Always check to make sure that mailto: is written before the email address:

☞ **Click** Add Link

5. Adding Extra Components

You can create a good basic website with the themes you find in *WordPress*. But if you add some additional components, called *widgets* and *plugins*, you can extend the *WordPress* interface and your website to give them extra functionality.

A widget is a special component that can be added to the so-called *sidebar* of your website. The sidebar is a column that is displayed at the top, bottom, left or right of a web page. The exact placement of the sidebar depends on the theme you use. There are widgets available for all sorts of functions. For instance, there are widgets to display a calendar or an additional menu in the sidebar. A theme will often include a number of widgets that you can use right away. There are also some widgets provided by *WordPress* itself. You can search the *WordPress* website for other widgets.

Plugins also add extra functionality to your website and they are usually much more extensive than widgets. They can sometimes be used in other locations of your website, not just in the sidebar. There are special plugins than can secure your website and other plugins that let you add a complete webshop to your website. Some of the themes already contain plugins, and *WordPress* itself has some plugins too. You can search the large number of plugins on the *WordPress* website and find one or more that are suitable for your own website.

There are some plugins that will let you add a *photo gallery* to your website. A photo gallery can display multiple thumbnail images on a single page. If you click the thumbnail, you will see a larger version of the image.

In this chapter you will learn how to:

- install a widget;
- find a plugin;
- install a plugin;
- create a photo gallery.

➥ Please note:

In this chapter you can use the practice files that accompany this book. You can read how to copy the practice files to your computer in *Appendix B Downloading the Practice Files* at the end of this book.

5.1 Installing a Widget

In the previous chapter you learned how to create a menu with useful hyperlinks. Now you can add this menu as a widget to a sidebar on the *My garden* page:

☞ **Open the *WordPress* login window** 𝒫𝒫7

☞ **Log in to *WordPress*** 𝒫𝒫8

You will see the *WordPress* Dashboard. First, you will need to change one of the page attributes of the *My garden* page so that it will show a sidebar:

👆 **Click** ▯ **Pages**, All Pages

👆 **Click My garden**

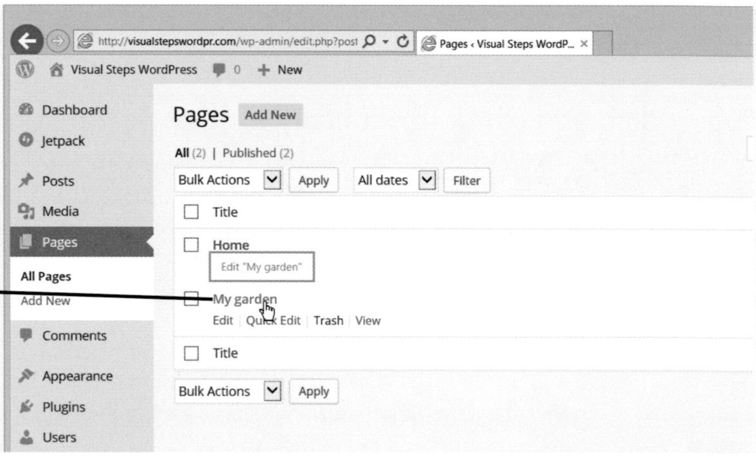

👆 **By Template, select the option Sidebar Template**

👆 **Click Update**

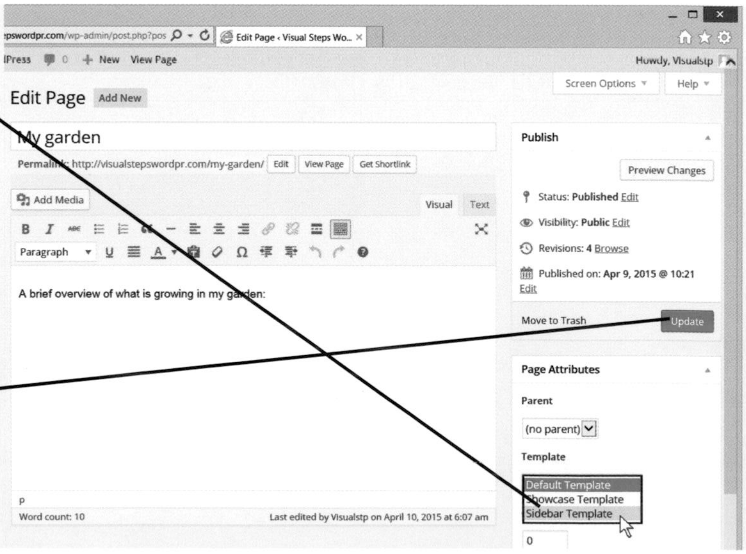

Take a look at the page:

☞ **View your website** ✂11

🖱 **Click** My garden

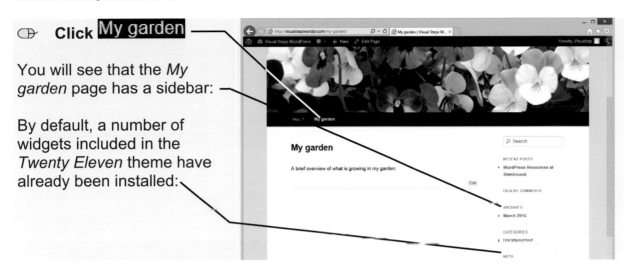

You will see that the *My garden* page has a sidebar:

By default, a number of widgets included in the *Twenty Eleven* theme have already been installed:

Now you can add a widget to the sidebar. Here is how you do that:

🖱 **Click the name of your website**

🖱 **Click** 📌 Appearance

🖱 **Click** Widgets

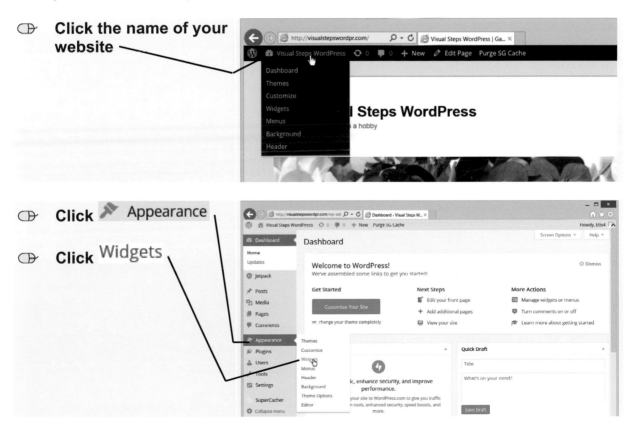

The *Widgets* window is opened:

Installed widgets:

Widgets that have been added to the website:

Available sidebars:

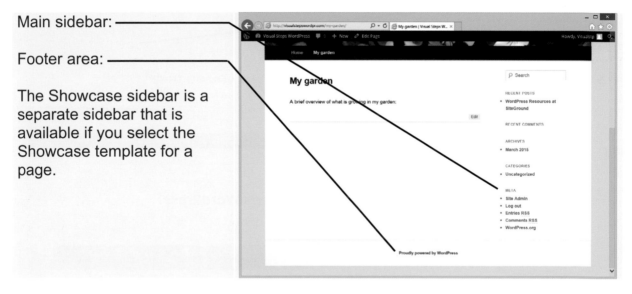

There are multiple sidebars available with the *Twenty Eleven* theme:

Main sidebar:

Footer area:

The Showcase sidebar is a separate sidebar that is available if you select the Showcase template for a page.

You can read what their function is by the installed widgets. You add a widget to the website by dragging it to the desired sidebar:

If the options by **Main Sidebar** are not visible:

☞ By **Main Sidebar**, **click** ▼

You can add the menu you created in the previous chapter as a widget:

In this example, a number of widgets have already been installed:

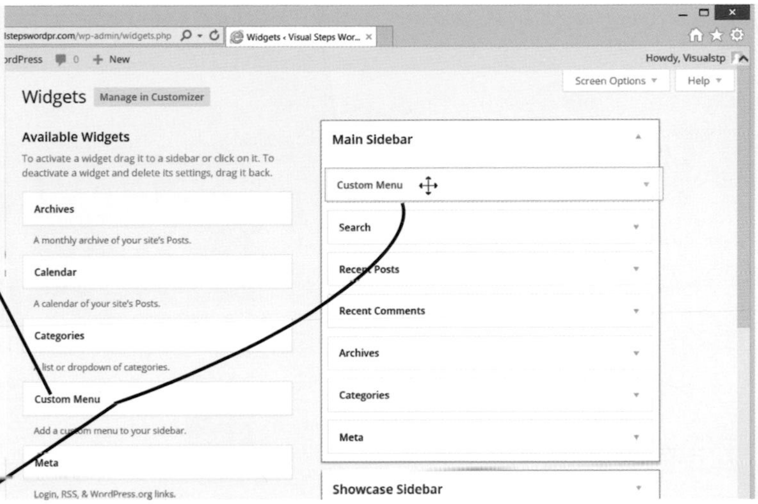

☞ **Place the pointer on the Custom Menu widget**

☞ **Drag the widget to an empty spot below Main Sidebar**

You see that the widget has been added:

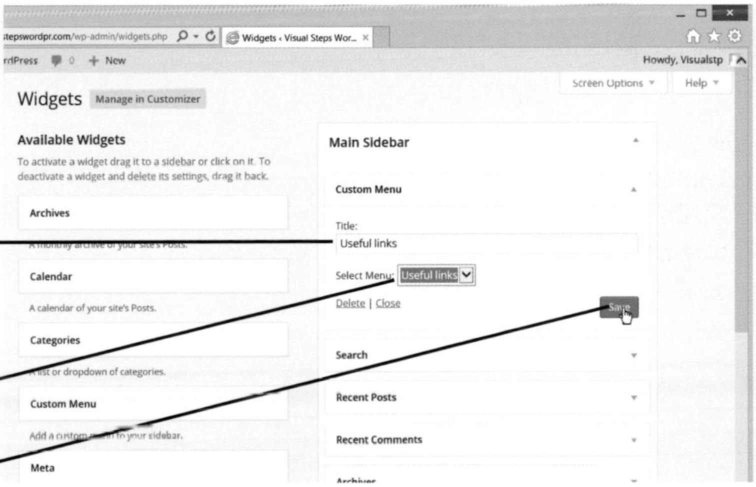

⌨ **By Title:, type:**
Useful links

☞ **By Select Menu:, select the Useful links menu**

☞ **Click** Save

☞ **View your website** 🦶11

☞ **Click My garden**

You will see that the *Useful links* menu has been added:

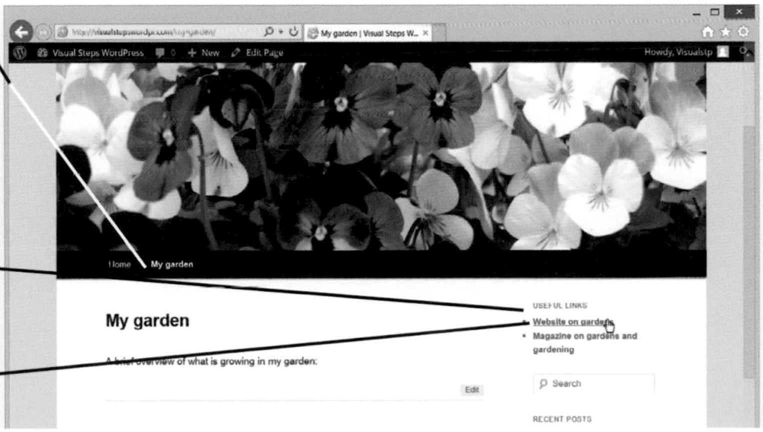

☞ **Click Website on gardens**

You will see the website to which the link in the menu refers:

☞ **Click**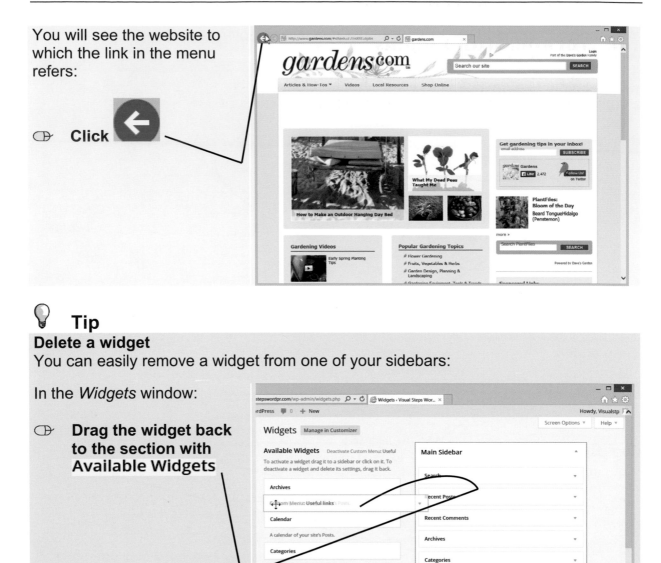

Tip

Delete a widget
You can easily remove a widget from one of your sidebars:

In the *Widgets* window:

☞ **Drag the widget back to the section with Available Widgets**

Tip

Download a widget
A widget is actually a very specific type of plugin. If you want to use other widgets, apart from the default widgets that come with your theme, you can download and install them in the same way as a plugin. See *section 5.3 Installing a plugin*.

5.2 Working with Plugins

There are many different plugins that can add extra functions to your website. Some of these plugins are already present in *WordPress* itself, and in certain themes.

This is how you view the plugins already installed in *WordPress*:

☞ **Click the name of your website**

☞ **Place the pointer on**
    Plugins

☞ **Click**
    Installed Plugins

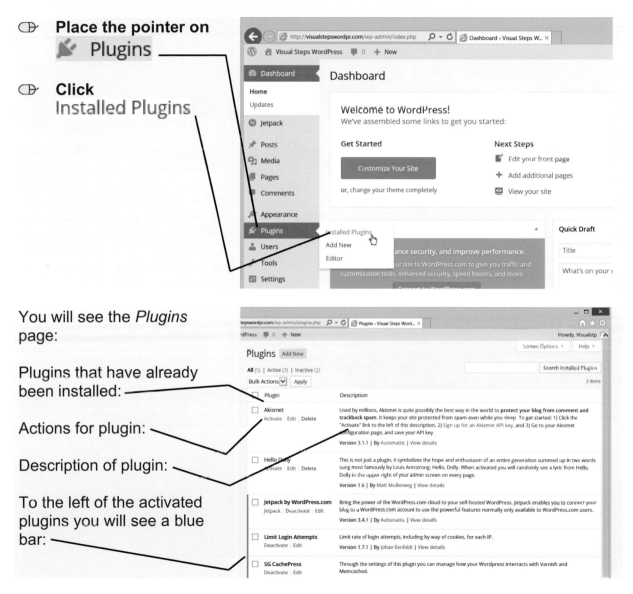

You will see the *Plugins* page:

Plugins that have already been installed:

Actions for plugin:

Description of plugin:

To the left of the activated plugins you will see a blue bar:

5.3 Installing a Plugin

It is easy to download and install a plugin from the *WordPress* website:

➥ Please note:

It is recommended that you only download plugins from the official *WordPress* websites, or from websites that *WordPress* acknowledges. Some of the websites that *WordPress* recommends which offer professional themes and plugins are fee-based and not free. If you download plugins from other websites, there is a chance that your computer will be infected with viruses or spyware.

☞ **By** **Plugins**, **click** **Add New**

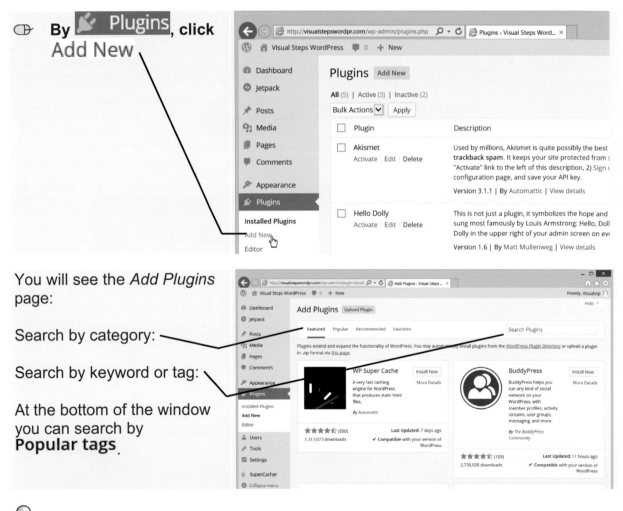

You will see the *Add Plugins* page:

Search by category:

Search by keyword or tag:

At the bottom of the window you can search by **Popular tags**.

💡 Tip
Finding widgets
On the *Add Plugins* page you can search for widgets by typing the keyword 'widget' in the search box Search Plugins, or by clicking widget by **Popular tags** at the bottom of the window.

You can practice a little by looking for a plugin that will allow you to display a photo gallery or photo album on your website.

In the Search Plugins **search box, type:**
gallery

Press Enter

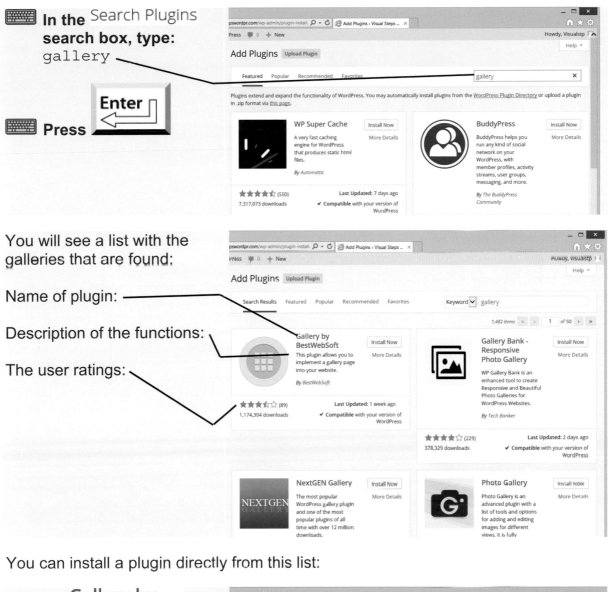

You will see a list with the galleries that are found:

Name of plugin:

Description of the functions:

The user ratings:

You can install a plugin directly from this list:

Gallery by **By** BestWebSoft,

click Install Now

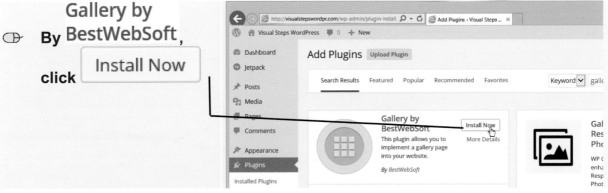

You may see this window:

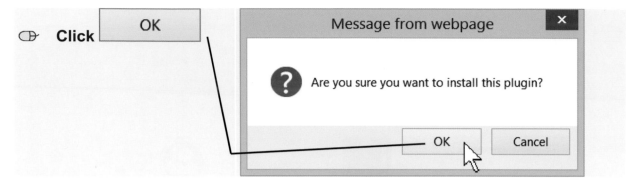

Now the plugin will be installed.

Once the installation is finished, you will see this window:

You still need to activate the plugin:

☞ **Click** Activate Plugin

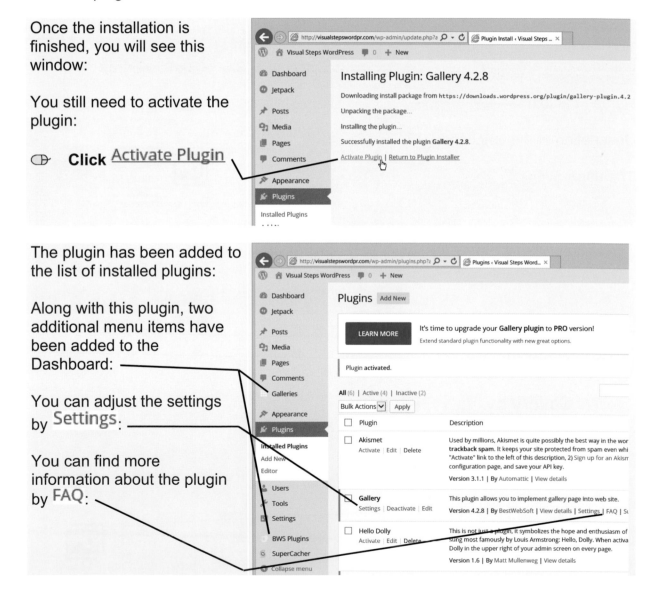

The plugin has been added to the list of installed plugins:

Along with this plugin, two additional menu items have been added to the Dashboard:

You can adjust the settings by Settings:

You can find more information about the plugin by FAQ:

You can create a photo gallery on a new page, but also on an existing page:

☞ **Click** 🖿 Pages, All Pages

☞ **Click** My garden

By activating the plugin, an extra gallery template has been added to the theme:

☞ **By** Template, **select the option** Gallery Template

☞ **Click** Update

Create a photo album:

☞ **Place the pointer on** ⊞ Galleries

☞ **Click** Add a Gallery

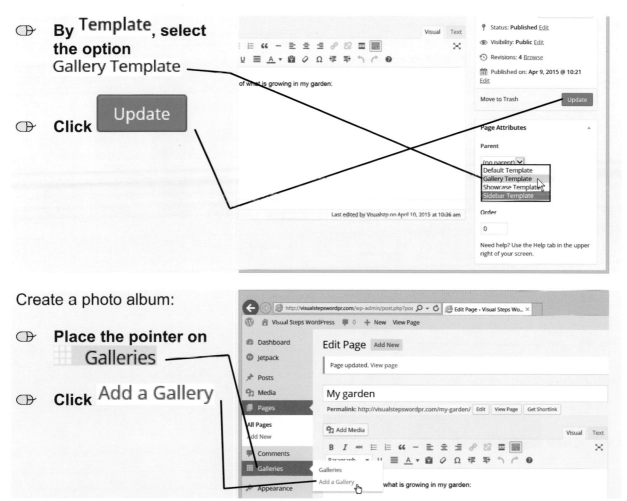

You will see the *Add New Gallery* window:

⌨ **In the title box, type:**
My photo album

Now you can upload photos to the album:

🖱 **If necessary, drag the scroll box downwards**

🖱 **Click** Upload a file

🖱 **Open the WordPress-Practice-Files folder** 🦶⁹

🖱 **Click** Flowers(9)

🖱 **Click** Open

The images will be added to the album:

You can upload more images:

🖱 **Click** Upload a file

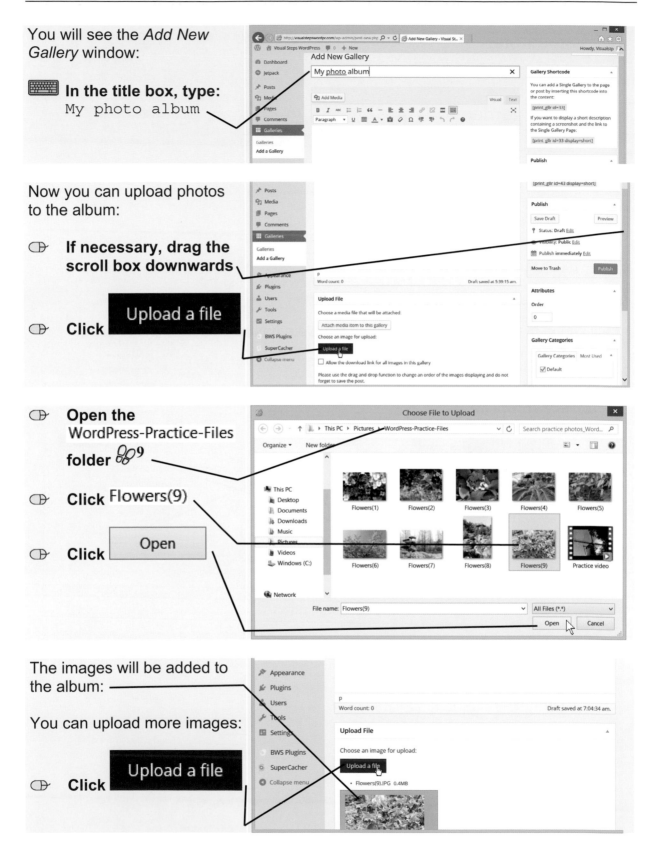

➡ **Please note:**

It is possible that the thumbnail image of the picture in this window is not displayed correctly. But when the page is published, this picture will be displayed in the right orientation.

☞ **Upload the images called** Flowers(3) **and** Flowers(6)

Now you can publish the photo album:

👆 **Click** Publish

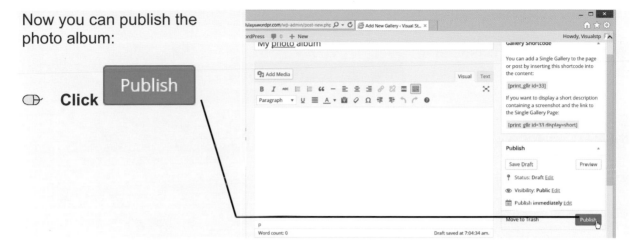

You can view the album:

☞ **View your website** 🦶¹¹

👆 **Click** My garden

A link to the photo gallery has been added to the *My garden* page:

👆 **Click** See images »

You will see the photo gallery on a separate page:

☞ **Click the photo with the little purple flowers**

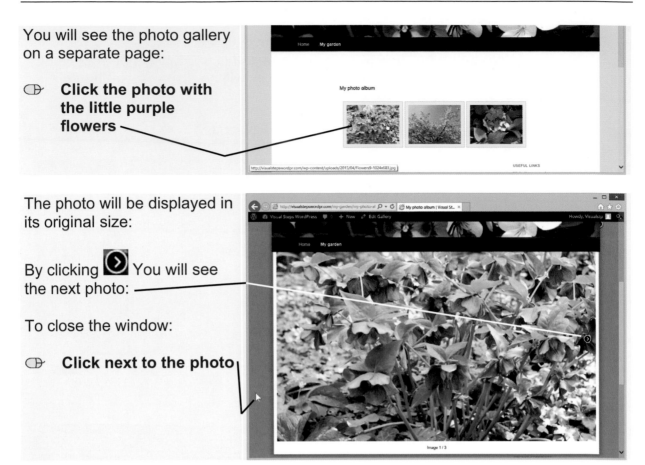

The photo will be displayed in its original size:

By clicking ⊙ You will see the next photo:

To close the window:

☞ **Click next to the photo**

HELP! The header appears on top of the photo.

It is possible that the header of your website appears on top of the photo, which means only half of the photo is visible. Here is how you solve this problem.

On the Dashboard:

☞ **Click** Appearance

☞ **Click** Editor

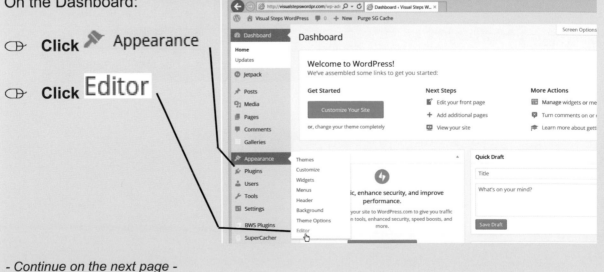

- Continue on the next page -

You will see the stylesheet of your website:

☞ **Drag the scroll box all the way downwards**

☞ **Click below the last character in the text box**

⌨ **Type:** #branding { z-index: 100 !important;}

☞ **Click** Update File

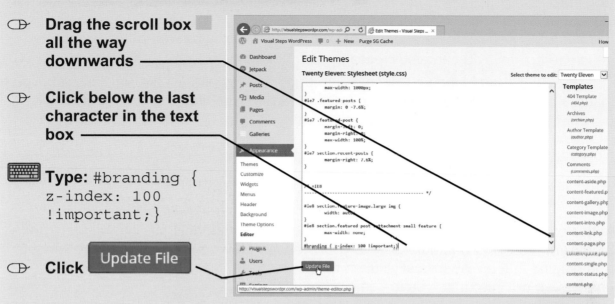

The stylesheet contains major codes regarding the look and feel of your website, and codes that make your website work in a proper way. It is recommended that you change the codes in the stylesheet as little as possible.

You will see the photo gallery again:

Photo galleries are assigned their own page.
You can use the web address to create a link to the photo gallery:

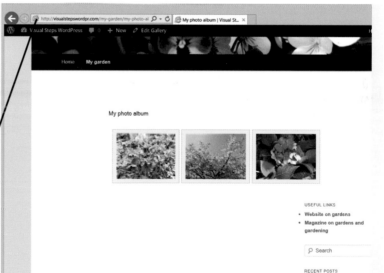

🔅 Tip

Do not use the photo gallery template
It is not really necessary to add a photo gallery to an existing web page through the gallery template. You can also create a new photo gallery with ▦ Galleries, Add a Gallery, and place a link on a web page to this gallery later on. You can even insert a link to the photo gallery on a totally different website. The web address of the photo gallery can be found by **Permalink:**.

Now you can log out of *WordPress*:

☞ **Log out of *WordPress*** 👣 **10**

In this chapter you have learned how to use extra components such as widgets and plugins that add extra functionality to your website. You can search for more widgets and plugins that are specifically suited to your website, if you wish. In the next chapter we will introduce you to some other useful plugins.

5.4 Background Information

Dictionary

FAQ   Frequently asked questions.

Footer area   The sidebar at the bottom of a web page.

Gallery   A plugin with which you can display images as thumbnails. By clicking the thumbnail, you will get to see the image in its original size.

Hyperlink   A clickable text or image that refers to other web pages.

Plugin   Plugins add extra functions to a website. They are more extensive than widgets. For example, there are special plugins that let you place a photo gallery on your website. Other plugins can add an entire webshop to your site. Other than widgets, plugins are usually not restricted to the sidebars.

Sidebar   A column at the top, bottom, left or right side of a web page. The sidebars that are available depend on the theme and the template you use.

Widget   An extra function that can be added to the sidebar of your website.

Source: WordPress Help

5.5 Tips

💡 **Tip**

Edit a photo gallery
This is how you edit a photo gallery:

☞   **Click** ⣿ **Galleries**

☞   **Click the photo gallery**

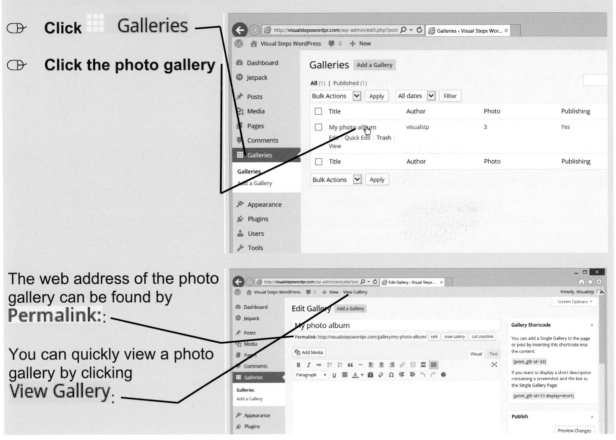

The web address of the photo gallery can be found by **Permalink:**:

You can quickly view a photo gallery by clicking **View Gallery**.

💡 **Tip**

Add social network buttons through a plugin
There are various plugins in *WordPress* with which you can add a link to your social network page, such as *Twitter* and *Facebook*, among others. For example, you can add an icon to your web page, which visitors can click to visit your social network page.
In order to find these types of plugins, you need to type the keyword 'social media' in the search box on the *Add Plugins* page. See also *section 5.3 Installing a Plugin*.

6. More Useful Plugins

In the previous chapter you were introduced to a couple of handy plugins that are available in *WordPress*. There are many more plugins that can be downloaded and used for various other functions. In this chapter you will get acquainted with some additional plugins that are very popular and frequently used by other websites.

You can add other types of media to your website such as video and audio files. You do this by adding a hyperlink to the web page or by using the so-called *embedded* function. Embedded means that the video is added directly to the page. It can then be played right from the same page. The user will not need to navigate to a page on another website (such as *YouTube*) by following a hyperlink. *WordPress* has a function with which you can embed videos.

Forms consist of boxes (called fields) that can be filled in, and other elements that will let a visitor send information to you. It may just be a name and address, but can also include more extensive information.

Many menus have options that can be viewed right away. But there are also menus where the options are hidden until a menu item is clicked. Then the menu expands and the options become visible. This type of menu is called a *dropdown menu*.

Metatags are keywords that are added to a web page to make it easier for search engines to find the web page. The metatags indicate what the subject of a website or a web page is. Some search engines use this information to determine whether the website is included in the search results.

A theme often uses a default font. By using a plugin you can use various other fonts for different elements on your web pages.

In this chapter you will learn how to:

- add a video;
- add a form;
- add a dropdown menu;
- add metatags;
- change fonts.

� Please note:

In this chapter you can use the practice files that accompany this book. You can read how to copy the practice files to your computer in *Appendix B Downloading the Practice Files* at the end of this book.

6.1 Adding a Video

Not just photos, but other types of media files can be added to your website, such as video and audio files. While images are displayed directly on a web page, *WordPress* adds video and audio files as a hyperlink, by default.

First, you open your web space:

☞ **Open your *WordPress* login window** ᏇᏇ7

☞ **Log in to *WordPress*** ᏇᏇ8

You will see the Dashboard. First, you need to add a new page to the practice website:

☞ **Place the pointer on**
   Pages

☞ **Click** Add New

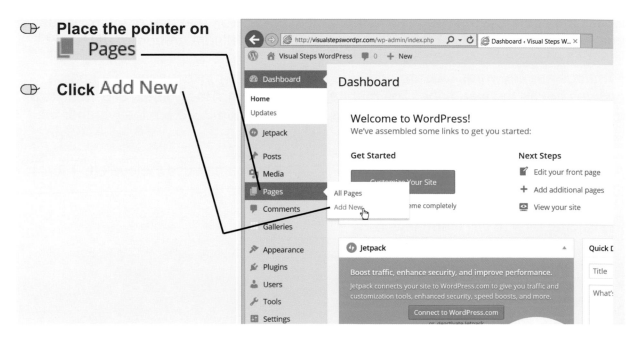

In the title box, type:
Media

In the text box, type:
Useful media
files:

Press Enter

Click Publish

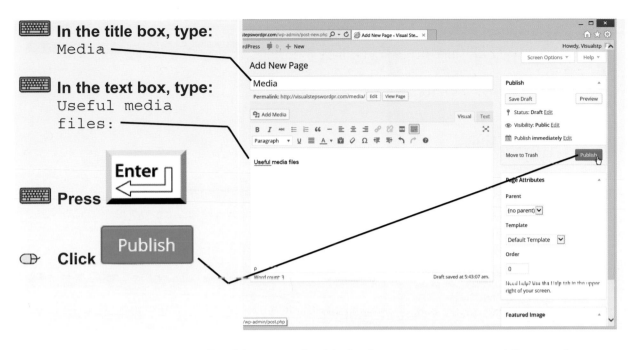

Now you can add a video file. You can do this in the same way as adding an image.

Please note:

Be sure to use the most current video file formats for your video files, such as AVI, MPG or WMV. Any video file that is added to a web page will be played with the video player installed on the visitor's computer. If you use an unknown type of video file, the visitor may not be able to play your video.

Click Add Media

☞ **If necessary, click**

Upload Files

☞ **Click**

Select Files

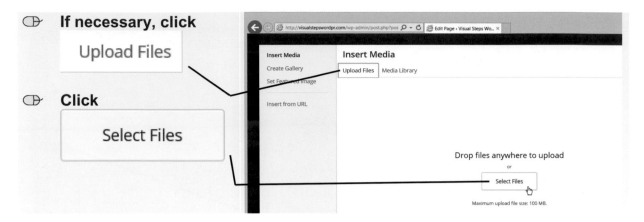

You will see the folders on your computer:

☞ **Open the**
WordPress-Practice-Files
folder ⚘⁹

☞ **Click Practice video**

☞ **Click** **Open**

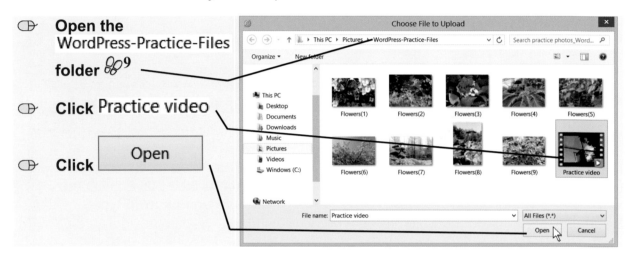

The file will be uploaded. After it has been uploaded, you can add a description and adjust other settings for the video:

Title of the video (this also
becomes the name of the
hyperlink on the page for this
video):

Caption by the video:

Text that is displayed by the
video in the Dashboard:

Create a link to the video:

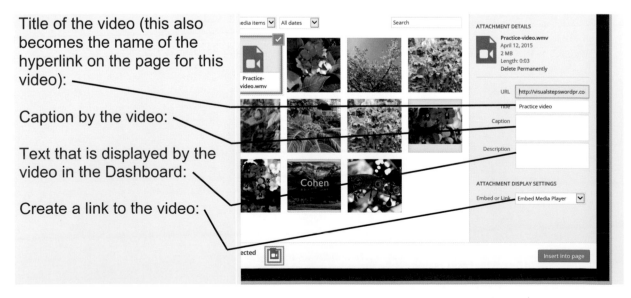

☞ **By** Embed or Link, **select the option** Link to Media File

⊕ **Click**
Insert into page

The hyperlink to the video has been inserted:

⊕ **Click** Update

The video link has been added:

⊕ **Click** View page

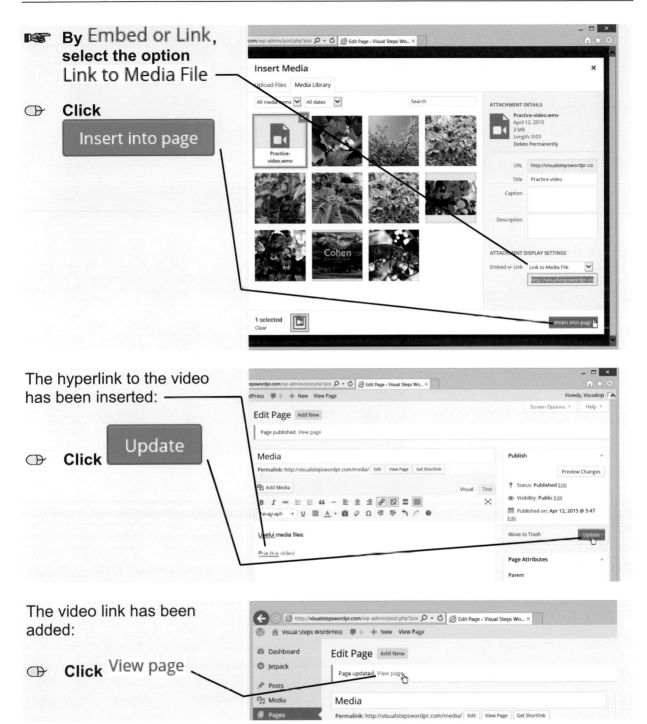

You will see the web page
with the hyperlink for the
video:

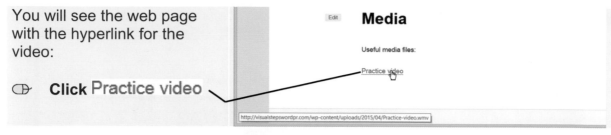

☞ **Click** Practice video

Now the video can be played
with a player installed on the
visitor's computer:

☞ **Click** ✕

💡 **Tip**

Add audio
Adding an audio file to a web page works the same way as adding a video file.

Although it is possible to play a video file via a hyperlink, it is even nicer if the video
file is embedded on the web page. Then the video can be played directly on the
same web page.

The best and easiest way of doing this, is to add the video from a video website, such
as *YouTube*. This way, you can make use of their safe embedding function.
If you want to embed your own video on the web page, you need to upload the video
to *YouTube*. You can also embed a *YouTube* video from somebody else on your web
page.

This is how you add a video to your web page, from *YouTube*:

⊕ **Click**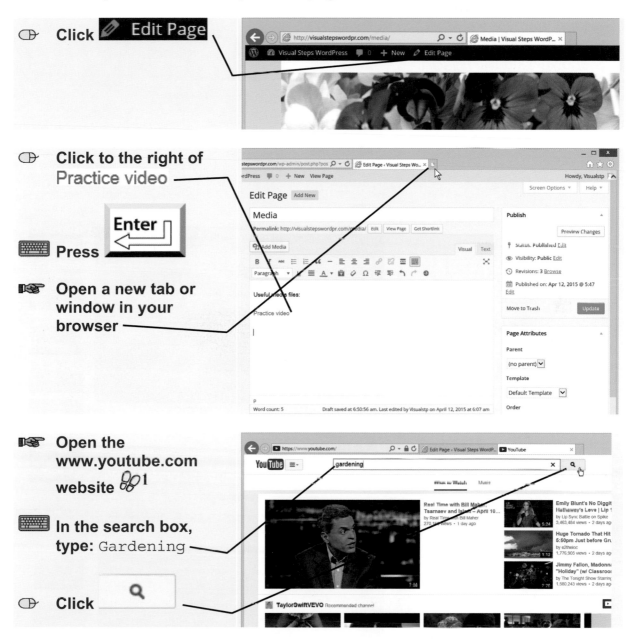

⊕ **Click to the right of**
Practice video

⌨ **Press** Enter

☞ **Open a new tab or window in your browser**

☞ **Open the www.youtube.com website** ℘1

⌨ **In the search box, type:** Gardening

⊕ **Click** 🔍

☞ **Click a video**

There will probably be a different list of videos shown in your own window. This will not affect the operations in this section.

The video is played:

☞ **By the video, click**
    ◄ Share

☞ **By the sharing options, click Embed**

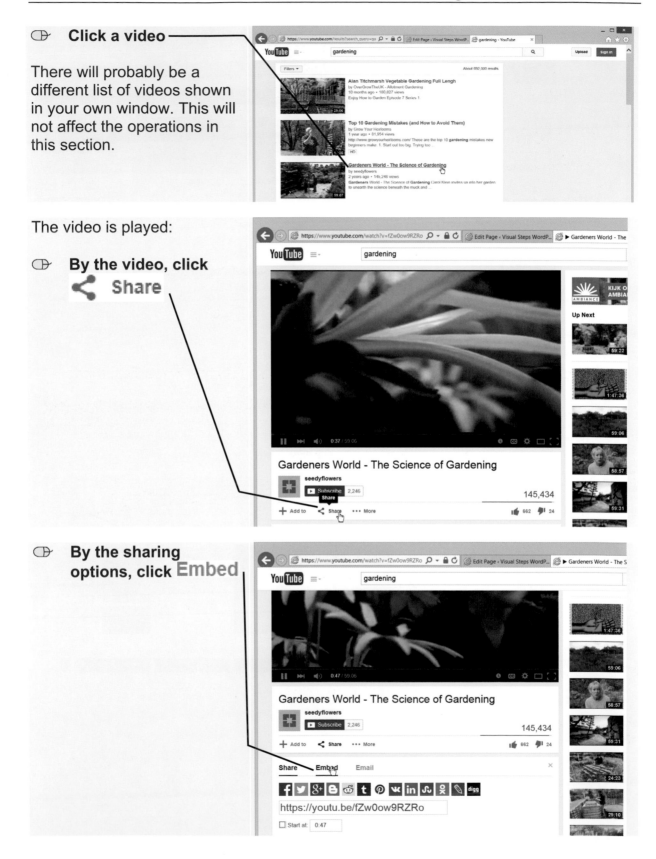

The code to embed the video is displayed: —

You can copy this code:

Press **Ctrl** + **C** simultaneously

☞ **Close the tab with the *YouTube* website** 👣³

Now you can add the video's URL to the web page. You do this in the Text mode:

⊕ **Click** **Text**

The HTML text appears: ⟶

⊕ **Click to the right of the last** ` `

Press **Ctrl** + **V** simultaneously

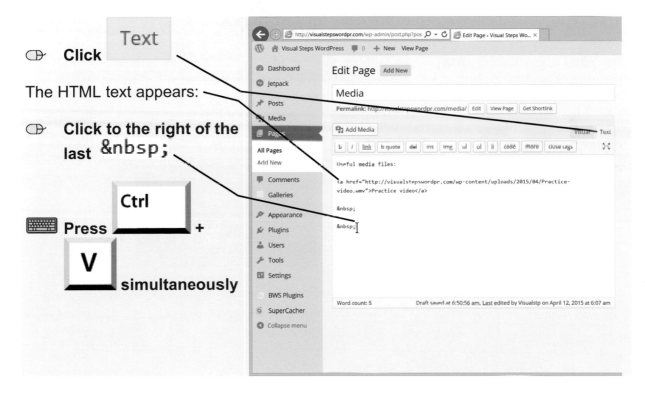

The URL of the video will be added:

Click Update

The video has been added:

Click View page

The *YouTube* video is now embedded on the web page:

Click ▶

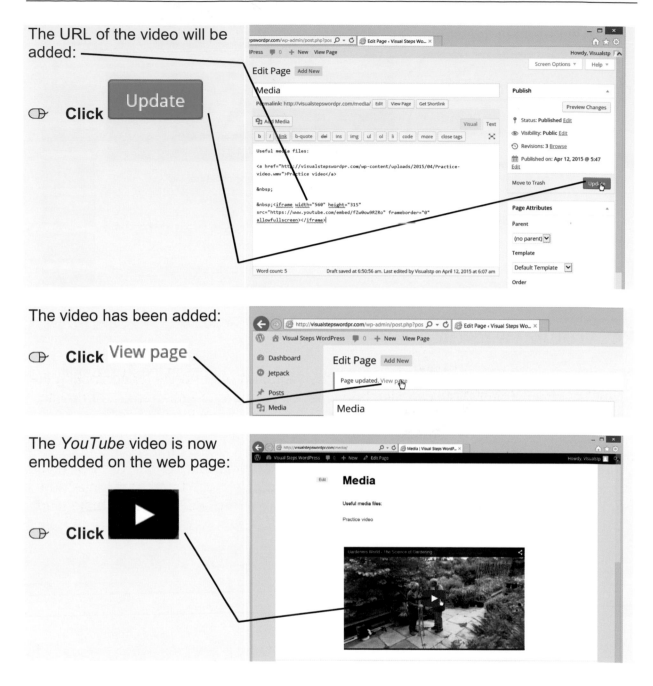

The video will be played right from the web page:

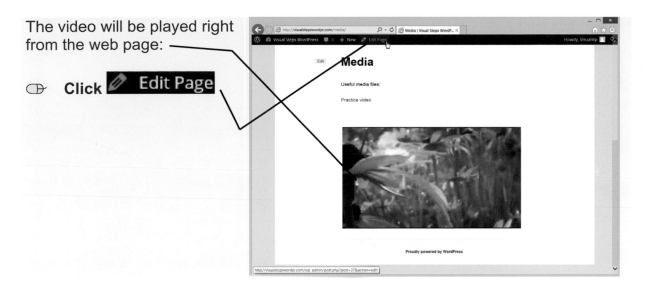

⊕ **Click** 🖉 Edit Page

6.2 Adding a Form

Forms are often used on websites to give the visitor an opportunity for contacting the website administrator. This can also be achieved through a regular email, of course, but the advantage of a form is that you can ask for more precise or specific information, such as the name and address of the visitor.

There are lots of different forms, and therefore lots of different plugins with which you can create a form in *WordPress*. For example, if you just want to present a standard form for entering address information and a comment, it is best to use a simple plugin for just this purpose.

You start by adding a new page to the website:

⊕ **Click** Visual

⊕ **Click** Add New

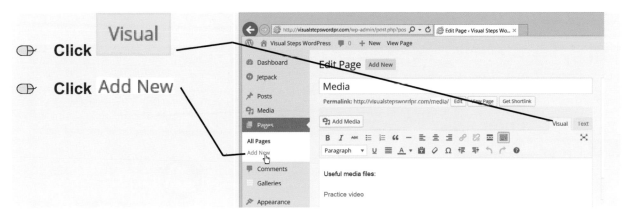

In the title box, type:
Contact

In the text box, type:
You can contact us
through this form:

Press Enter

Click Publish

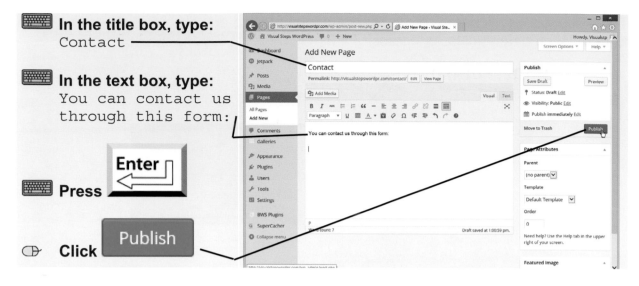

Now you can add a form:

Place the pointer on Plugins

Click Add New

By Search Plugins, **type:** contact form

Press Enter

You will see a list with the plugins that have been found and that will help you create a form. We will demonstrate the use of the plugin called *Contact Form*:

☞ **By** Contact Form by BestWebSoft **,**

click Install Now

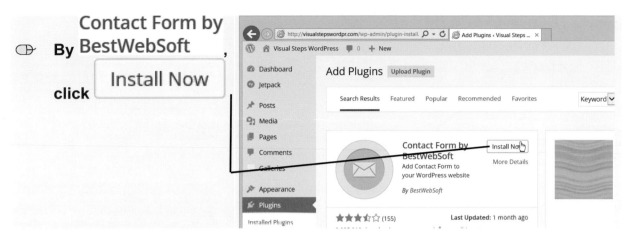

You may see this message.

☞ **If necessary, click** OK

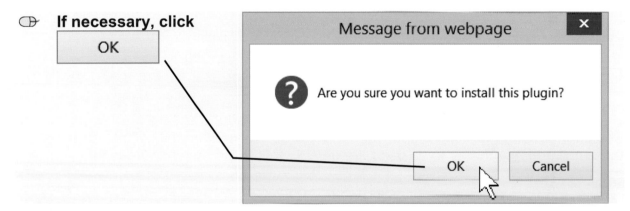

Now the plugin will be installed.

Once the plugin is installed, you will see this window:

You still need to activate the plugin:

☞ **Click** Activate Plugin

Before you add a form, you need to enter a few settings. These settings can be different for each plugin:

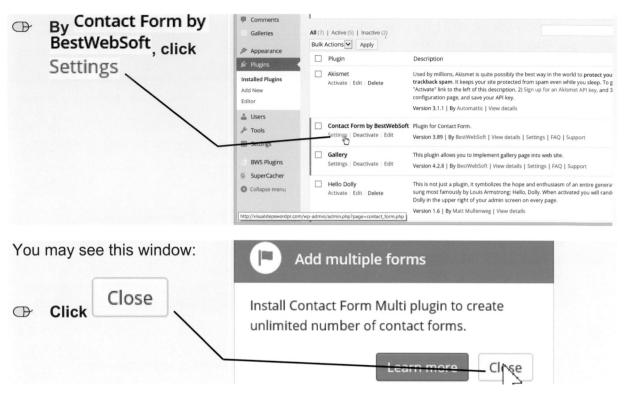

☞ By **Contact Form by BestWebSoft**, click **Settings**

You may see this window:

☞ **Click** Close

The information entered in a form will be forwarded to you by email. You can enter the email address that is to be used. By default, this is the email address that is also used by *WordPress*:

You will see the form settings:

By default, the user's email address is selected:

If you want to use another email address, you can enter this by **Use this email address::**

☞ **Click** **Additional settings**

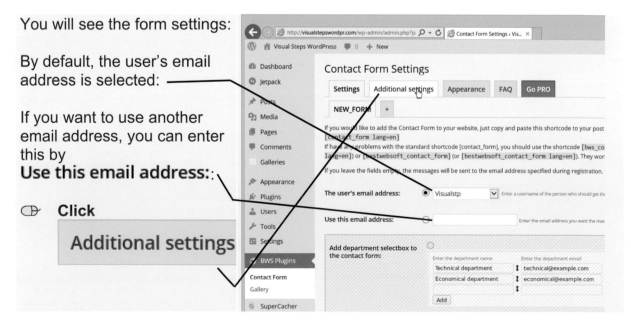

Here you see the extra settings for the form:

You can add extra fields to the form by checking the box ☑ by the field: ──────

If you want to see more information, hover the pointer over ❓ or click FAQ :

The default settings are often quite sufficient to start with.

At the bottom of the window:

☞ **Click**

Save Changes

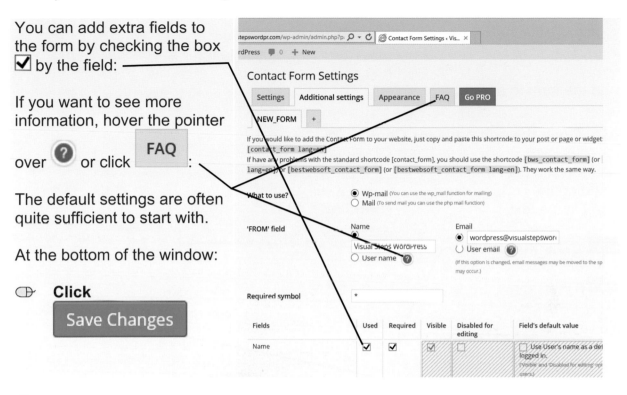

💡 **Tip**

Email address for messages sent to you by the form
If a visitor fills in the form on your website, you will receive the message in the Inbox of the email address that was entered by your user account. By **'FROM' field** you will see the name and email address that is used for the sender of this message.

By default, the email address by Email ends with the name of your website: ────

You can change this email address, if you wish. But if you do this, the email message may end up in the spam folder.

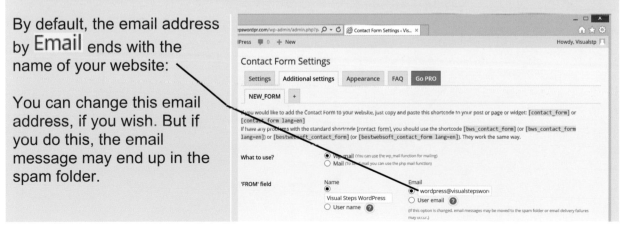

💡 Tip

Extended version of a plugin
Some plugins consist of a free version with limited options and a paid version with many extra options. The paid version may also be called the Pro version.

Add the form to a web page:

☞ **Open the edit page for *Contact* 👣12**

Add the contact form by inserting the code [contact_ form] in the text:

⌨ **Click the new line**

⌨ **Type:**
[contact form]

🖱 **Click** Update

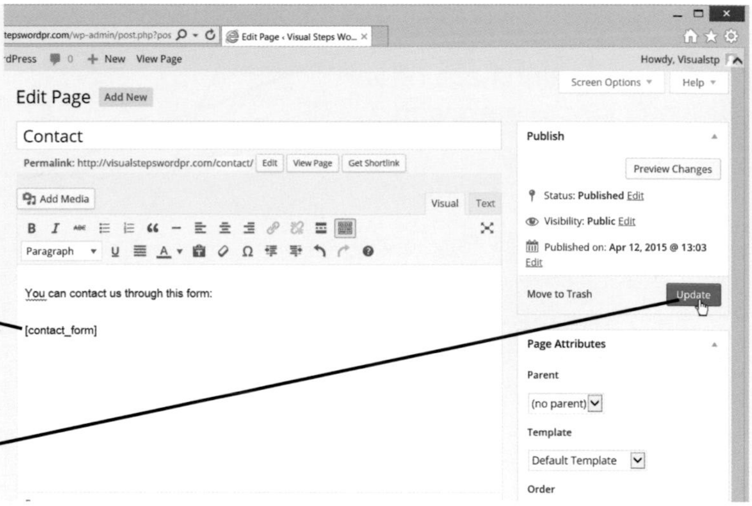

🐾 Please note:

The way in which you add a contact form can vary according to the form you use. You can find more information by clicking a link by the installed plugin, such as FAQ (Frequently Asked Questions), Support, or Website.

The form has been added:

🖱 **Click** View page

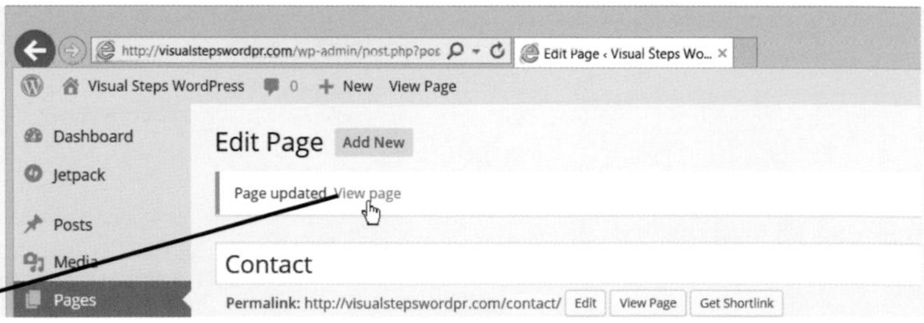

The form has been added to the web page:

You can enter the following data:

By Name: and Email Address:, type your own information

By Subject:, type: First message

By Message:, type: This is my first message using this form.

Click Submit

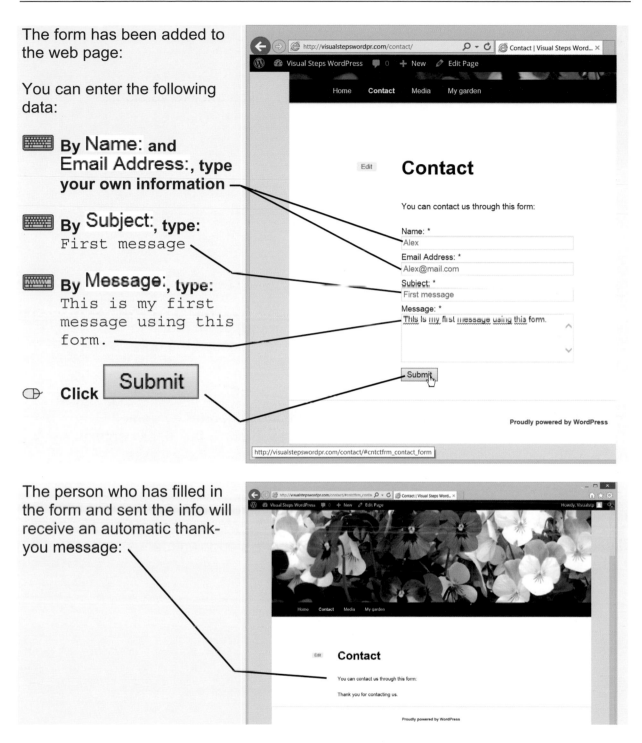

The person who has filled in the form and sent the info will receive an automatic thank-you message:

As the webmaster, you will automatically receive an email containing the information from the form:

You will receive this email at the email address you have entered by your user account.

⊞ E-mails	First message

First message
Visual Steps WordPress

Name	Alex
Email	Alex@mail.com
Subject	First message
Message	This is my first message using this form.
Site	http://visualstepswordpr.com

Date/Time:	April 12, 2015 1:53 pm
Sent from (referer):	http://visualstepswordpr.com/contact/
Using (user agent):	Mozilla/5.0 (Windows NT 6.3; WOW64; Trident/7.0; rv:11.0) like Gecko

6.3 Adding a Dropdown Menu

Although you can often include sufficient links to web pages and websites in a regular menu, it may sometimes be useful to add a dropdown menu to your website. This way you can add more options to your website, because the options in a dropdown menu remain hidden until somebody clicks them.

There are two options for a dropdown menu. The first option is to use a dropdown menu that is part of the installed theme: included in the header by default. The *Twenty Eleven* theme that has been used as an example in this book contains a menu with separate options to display the various pages of the website.
It is possible to change a theme with a regular menu into a theme with a dropdown menu. But you will need to edit all sorts of elements in the code for this theme. This is possible only if you have a more advanced knowledge of HTML and PHP.

If you want to use a different theme with one or more dropdown menus, you will need to select a theme that offers them:

☞ **Click** Edit Page

☞ **Place the pointer on** Appearance

☞ **Click** Themes

On the *Add Themes* page:

⊂⊃ **Click** **Add New**

You will see the search engine for the themes:

⌨ **In the search box, type:** dropdown

You will see the themes that include a dropdown menu:

If you want to install and activate a theme, then follow the instructions in *section 3.3 Installing a Theme* and *section 3.4 Changing a Theme*.

The second option is to add a dropdown menu by using a plugin. In this case you can add one or more dropdown menus to a sidebar as a widget:

⊂⊃ **Place the pointer on** **Plugins**

⊂⊃ **Click** Add New

⌨ **By** Search Plugins **, type:** dropdown menus

⌨ **Press** Enter

You will see a list with the search results for plugins with dropdown menus:

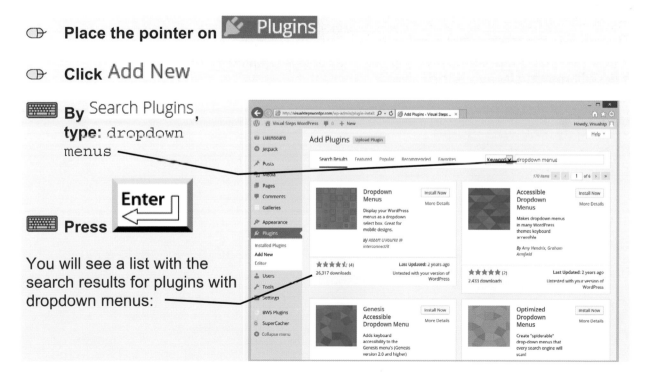

We will demonstrate the use of the plugin called *Dropdown Menus*:

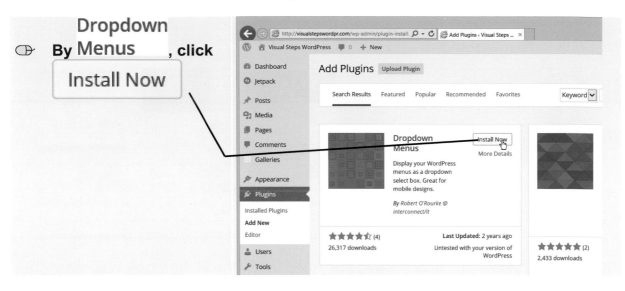

☞ By **Dropdown Menus**, click **Install Now**

You may see a message concerning the installation procedure:

☞ **If necessary, click** OK

Now the plugin will be installed.

You still need to activate the plugin:

☞ **Click** Activate Plugin

The dropdown menu is available as a widget. You can add this widget to a sidebar, and assign an existing menu to it.

💡 **Tip**

Create a new dropdown menu
You can also use a new menu for the dropdown menu. You will need to create this menu first; otherwise you cannot assign it to the dropdown menu. See also *section 4.14 Working with Menus*.

☞ **Place the pointer on** 🖌 Appearance

☞ **Click** Widgets

☞ **Place the pointer on the** Dropdown Menu **widget** ——

☞ **Drag the widget onto the empty area below** Main Sidebar

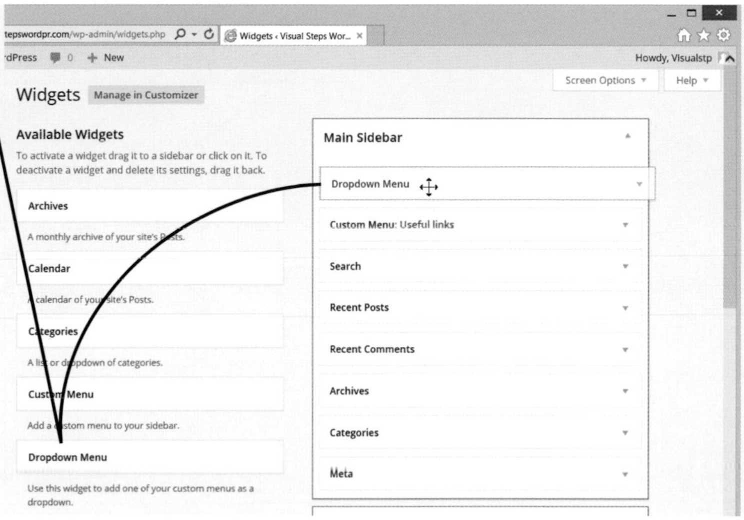

You will see that the widget has been added:

⌨ **By** Title:**, type:**
Useful links ——

☞ **By** Select Menu:**, select the** Useful links **menu** —

☞ **Click** Save

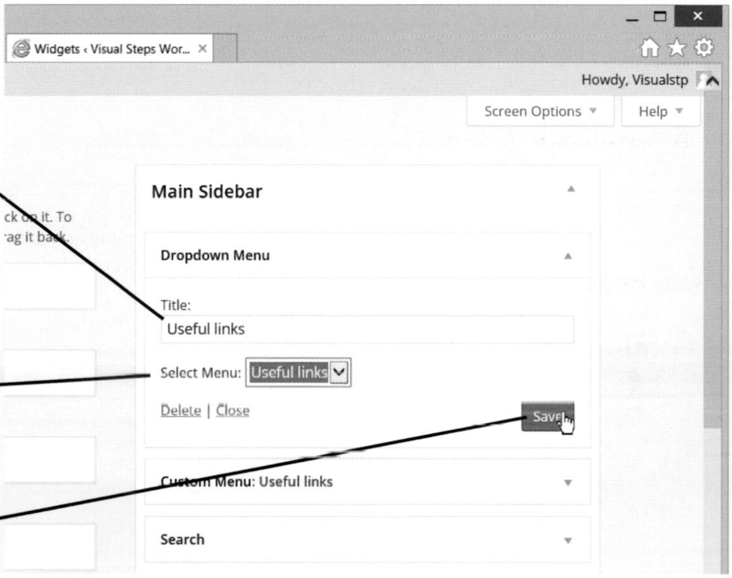

You can allow the sidebar to be displayed on the *Contact* page for example:

☞ **Open the edit page for** *Contact* ℅12

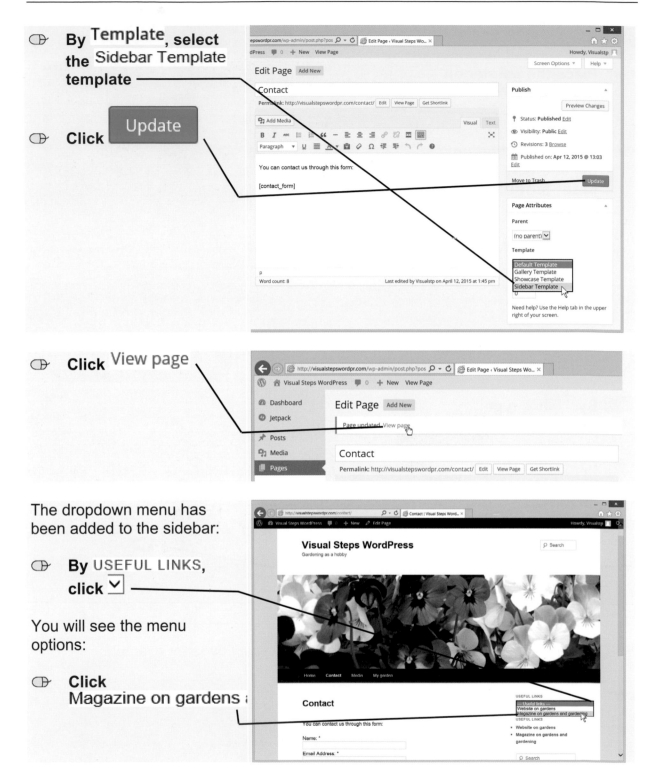

By **Template**, select the **Sidebar Template** template

Click **Update**

Click **View page**

The dropdown menu has been added to the sidebar:

By USEFUL LINKS, click ☑

You will see the menu options:

Click Magazine on gardens a

The website to which the link refers will be opened:

Click ⬅

💡 Tip

Add a dropdown menu to another page
You can add a dropdown for each individual page. The plugin offers you more choice and gives you the ability to add different dropdown menus to the various pages of your website.
This is how you add the dropdown menu:

👉 **Open the desired page** Ⱄ*12*

☞ **By** `Template`**, select the** `Sidebar Template` **template**

☞ **Click** `Update`

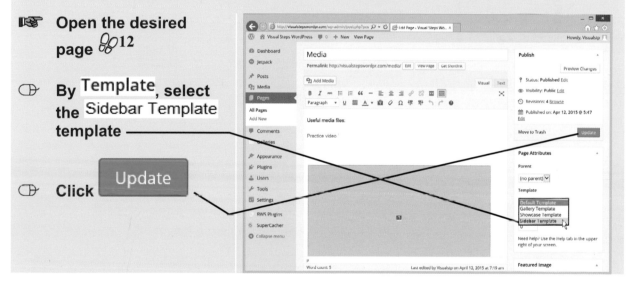

6.4 Adding Metatags

For a long period of time, metatags were added to web pages to help search engines find the web page, and to make sure that a website would reach a higher position in the search results. Metatags contain keywords that provide clues to the content of the web page or website. For example, frequently used metatags for a restaurant are: restaurant, dinner, lunch.

Currently, *Google*, the most frequently used search engine, no longer uses metatags, but scans the actual content of the page for keywords. The metatags however are still displayed in the *Google* search results.

Other search engines still use metatags in order to correctly include the website in their database. That is why it is still a good idea to add metatags to your web page. You can use a plugin for this:

☞ **Click** *Edit Page*

☞ **Place the pointer on** *Plugins*

☞ **Click** Add New

⌨ **By** Search Plugins, **type:** `meta tags`

⌨ **Press** Enter

You will see a list of search results for plugins that add metatags:

We will demonstrate the use of the plugin called *Add Meta Tags*:

☞ **By** Add Meta Tags, **click** Install Now

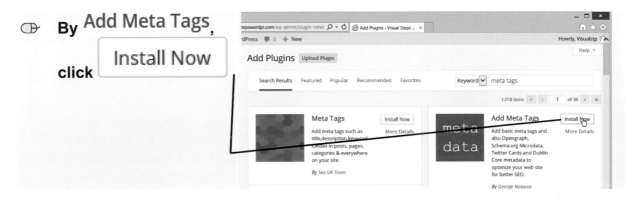

You may see a message concerning the installation procedure:

☞ **If necessary, click** [OK]

Now the plugin will be installed.

You still need to activate the plugin:

☞ **Click** Activate Plugin

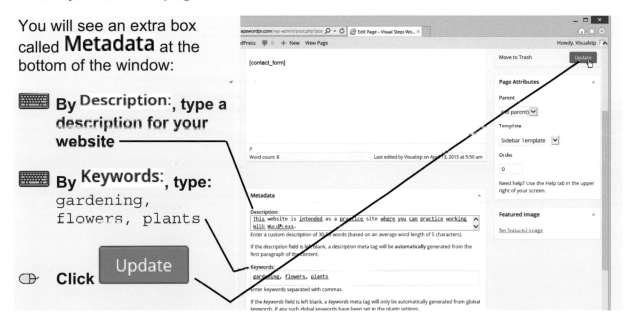

Now you can add metatags to your web pages. If you want to enter multiple tags, you need to separate them by a comma:

☞ **Open the edit page for** *Contact* 𝄞𝄞12

You will see an extra box called **Metadata** at the bottom of the window:

⌨ **By** Description:**, type a description for your website**

⌨ **By** Keywords:**, type:**
gardening, flowers, plants

☞ **Click** [Update]

Now the metatags have been added to the web page, and can be used by the search engines. In the same way you can add metatags to the other web pages.

Tip

Open the website to search engines
Do not forget to change the setting that enables search engines to find your website.

- Click ⊞ Settings, Reading
- Uncheck the box ☑ by Discourage search engines from indexing this site
- Click Save Changes

6.5 Changing Fonts

The text in a theme is often displayed with one or multiple default fonts. It may be useful or just fun, to use a different font sometimes. There are various plugins that will let you choose which font to use for each element on a page:

- Place the pointer on 🔌 Plugins
- Click Add New
- By Search Plugins, type: fonts
- Press Enter

You will see a list of search results with plugins that help you change fonts:

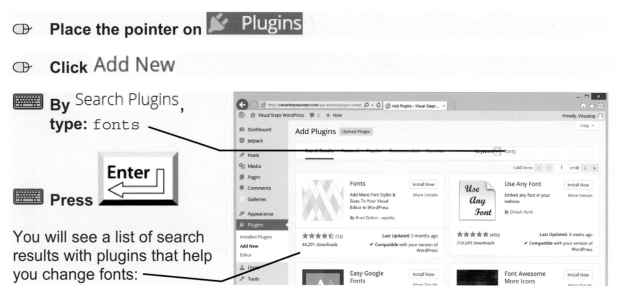

We will demonstrate the use of the plugin called *WP Google Fonts*:

- If necessary, drag the scroll box downwards
- By WP Google Fonts, click Install Now

You may see a message concerning the installation procedure:

⊕   **If necessary, click** | OK |

Now the plugin will be installed.

You still need to activate the plugin:

⊕   **Click** Activate Plugin

Now you can adjust the fonts for your web pages. You do this through the settings by the *WP Google Fonts* plugin:

⊕   **Drag the scroll box downwards**

⊕   **By WP Google Fonts, click Settings**

You can select a font by the settings for the various elements on the web page:

All	All text.
Headline	Header.
Blockquotes	Quotes.
Paragraphs	Paragraphs with regular text.
Lists	Lists.

☞ **By** Font 1**, select the** Almendra **font**

You will see additional settings:

☞ **Check the box** ☑ **by** Paragraphs

☞ **Click**

Save All Fonts

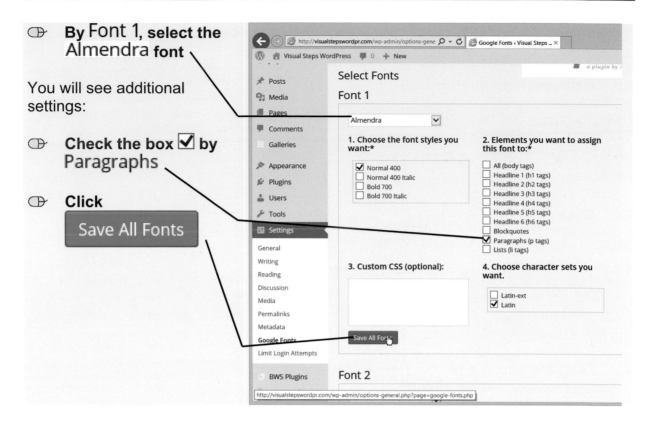

☞ **Open the edit page for** *Contact* 👣12

☞ **Click** View Page

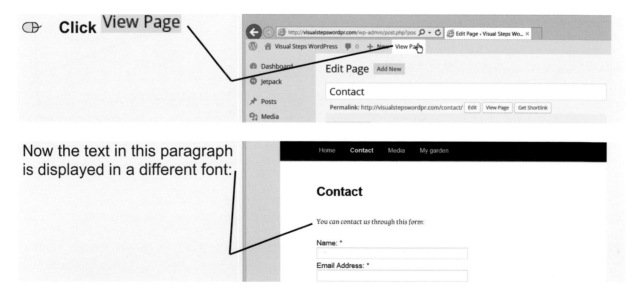

Now the text in this paragraph is displayed in a different font:

Tip

Restore the theme font
If you want to restore the original font for the text on the web pages, you can do that like this:

By the settings for the **WP Google Fonts** plugin:

☞ **By** Font 1, **select the option**
None (Turn off this font)

☞ **Click**

Save All Fonts

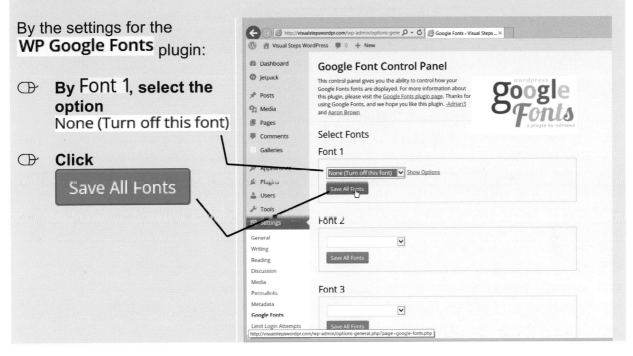

Now you can log out of *WordPress*:

☞ **Log out of *WordPress* ⌕⌕10**

In this chapter you have learned how to add additional functionality to your website by using various plugins. You now have acquired the basic skills to build your own website with *WordPress*.

You can edit and adjust the pages and elements you have created using *WordPress* and this book, and insert your own favorite theme, texts, images, and plugins. In this way, you can create a website just the way you want.

In this book you have learned basic skills for creating a website in *WordPress*. There is still more to discover on the *WordPress* website. You can find more information

Help ▾

about a specific component in *WordPress*, for example, by clicking the button in the top right corner of the window. You will also find more information and other resources by visiting the *WordPress* forum: http://wordpress.org/support

We wish you lots of luck in building your own website!

6.6 Visual Steps Website and Newsletter

By now we hope you have noticed that the Visual Steps method is an excellent method for quickly and efficiently learning more about computers, tablets, other devices and software applications. All books published by Visual Steps use this same method.

In various series, we have published a large number of books on a wide variety of topics including *Windows*, *Mac OS X*, the iPad, iPhone, Samsung Galaxy Tab, Kindle, photo editing and many other topics.

On the **www.visualsteps.com** website you will find a full product summary by clicking the blue *Catalog* button. For each book there is an extensive description, the full table of contents and a sample chapter (PDF file). In this way, you can quickly determine if a specific title will meet your expectations. You can order a book directly online from this website or other online book retailers. All titles are also available in bookstores in the USA, Canada, United Kingdom, Australia and New Zealand.

Furthermore, the website offers many extras, among other things:
- free computer guides and booklets (PDF files) covering all sorts of subjects;
- frequently asked questions and their answers;
- information on the free Computer Certificate that you can acquire at the certificate's website **www.ccforseniors.com**;
- a free email notification service: let's you know when a new book is published.

There is always more to learn. Visual Steps offers many other books on computer-related subjects. Each Visual Steps book has been written using the same step-by-step method with short, concise instructions and screenshots illustrating every step.

Would you like to be informed when a new Visual Steps title becomes available? Subscribe to the free Visual Steps newsletter (no strings attached) and you will receive this information in your inbox.

The Newsletter is sent approximately each month and includes information about
- the latest titles;
- supplemental information concerning titles previously released;
- new free computer booklets and guides;

When you subscribe to our Newsletter you will have direct access to the free booklets on the **www.visualsteps.com/info_downloads.php** web page.

6.7 Background Information

Dictionary

Dropdown menu	A menu where the options are hidden until the menu is clicked. Then the menu expands and the options become visible.
Embedded video	A video that is directly added to the page, and can be played from this same page afterwards.
Font	Another name for typeface.
Form	A collection of text boxes (also called fields) and other elements. A form gives you a way of collecting information from the visitors of your website. The information is sent to you by email.
Hyperlink	A clickable text or image that refers to other web pages.
Metatags	Keywords that are added to a web page, in order to make it easier for search engines to find the web page. The metatags give clues about the content of a website or web page. Some search engines use this information to determine whether the website is included in the search results.
Plugin	Plugins add extra functionality to a website. Plugins are much more extensive than widgets. For example, there are special plugins that will allow you to place a photo gallery on your website. With other plugins you can add an entire webshop to your website. Plugins can also be placed in other areas besides the sidebar.
Sidebar	A column at the top, bottom, left or right side of a web page. The sidebars that are available for your website depend on the theme and the template you have selected.
Widget	An extra function that can be added to the sidebar of your website.
YouTube	The largest and most popular online video website.

Source: WordPress Help

6.8 Tips

💡 Tip
Delete a plugin
If you no longer use a plugin, you can deactivate it, or even delete it. By deleting a plugin you can ensure that your *WordPress* installation remains uncluttered and well-ordered.
This is how to deactivate a plugin:

☞ **Click** **Plugins**

☞ **By the plugin, click** **Deactivate**

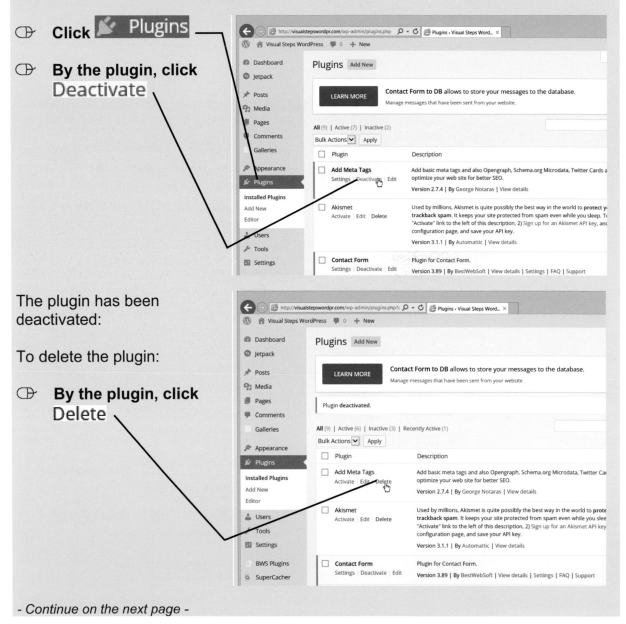

The plugin has been deactivated:

To delete the plugin:

☞ **By the plugin, click** **Delete**

- Continue on the next page -

You will see this window:

⊕ **Click**

  Yes, Delete these files an

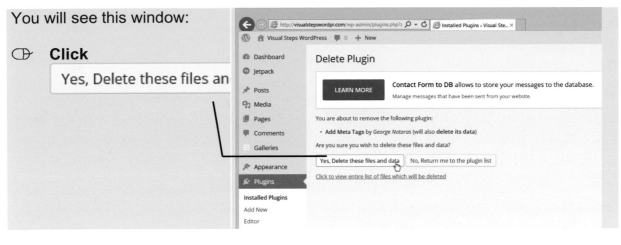

💡 **Tip**

Adapting your website for use on mobile devices
Nowadays mobile devices, such as smartphones and tablets, are often used for visiting websites, sometimes even more than computers. It is a good idea to take this into account when you are building your *WordPress* website: especially when you choose a theme.

The website will adapt automatically to the dimensions of a smartphone or a tablet with most themes. Although a website will be readable, some elements such as sidebars are not always displayed as you had designed them in the original website. For example, sidebars on the left and right are sometimes displayed at the bottom of the website. This could mean that a menu that has been included in the sidebar is displayed at the bottom of the screen.

If you prefer to build a website that is automatically adapted for use on mobile devices, it is a good idea to select a theme that is suitable for this:

☞ **Search for new themes with the keyword 'mobile'**

You will see themes that are suitable for use on mobile devices: —

Many paid themes, by the way, are already adapted for use on mobile devices.

💡 Tip

WordPress app

Although editing your *WordPress* website is easiest on your computer, you can also edit your site on a smartphone or tablet.

The first option for this is using an Internet browser on your mobile device. One of the biggest advantages of working with *WordPress* is that you can work with it while you are online. But the *WordPress* browser interface is primarily designed for use on a computer. It is more difficult to work on your website on a mobile device with a small screen and there are also other limitations.

There is a special app with which you can work with *WordPress*. You can download this app through the official app store of your smartphone or tablet. Use the keyword 'WordPress' to find this app.

The app is mainly directed at being able to quickly post and edit messages and comments on *WordPress* sites. It is not really intended for building and finishing an entire website. This is a thing that is best done on a computer.

You can take a look at the website:

View statistics:

Publish messages, reactions and pages:

Change settings:

Appendix A. How Do I Do That Again?

The actions and exercises in this book are marked with footsteps: 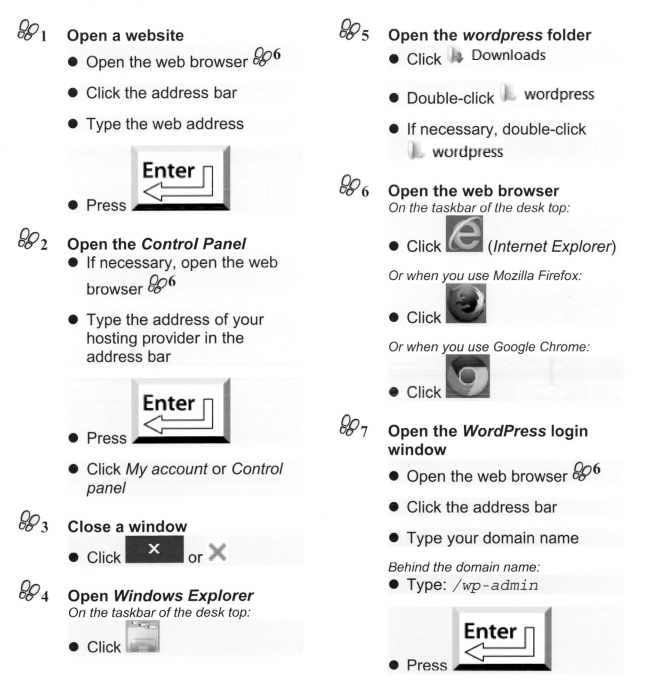**1**
If you have forgotten how to do something, you can read how to do it again by finding the corresponding number in the list below.

1 Open a website
- Open the web browser **6**
- Click the address bar
- Type the web address
- Press **Enter**

2 Open the *Control Panel*
- If necessary, open the web browser **6**
- Type the address of your hosting provider in the address bar
- Press **Enter**
- Click *My account* or *Control panel*

3 Close a window
- Click **X** or **X**

4 Open *Windows Explorer*
On the taskbar of the desk top:
- Click

5 Open the *wordpress* folder
- Click **Downloads**
- Double-click **wordpress**
- If necessary, double-click **wordpress**

6 Open the web browser
On the taskbar of the desk top:
- Click **e** (*Internet Explorer*)

Or when you use Mozilla Firefox:
- Click

Or when you use Google Chrome:
- Click

7 Open the *WordPress* login window
- Open the web browser **6**
- Click the address bar
- Type your domain name

Behind the domain name:
- Type: `/wp-admin`
- Press **Enter**

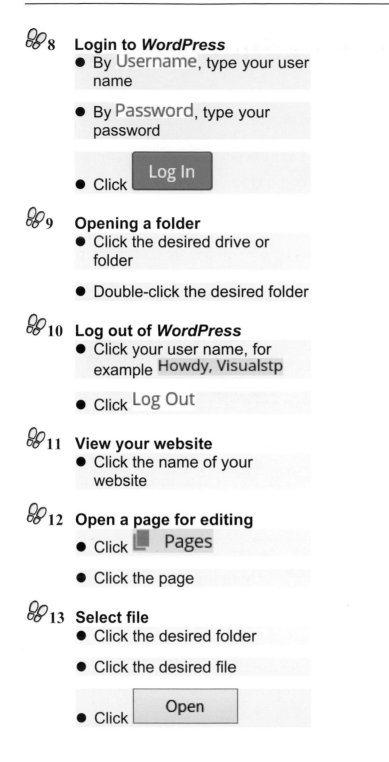

8   Login to *WordPress*

- By Username, type your user name

- By Password, type your password

- Click Log In

9   Opening a folder

- Click the desired drive or folder

- Double-click the desired folder

10   Log out of *WordPress*

- Click your user name, for example Howdy, Visualstp

- Click Log Out

11   View your website

- Click the name of your website

12   Open a page for editing

- Click Pages

- Click the page

13   Select file

- Click the desired folder

- Click the desired file

- Click Open

Appendix B. Downloading the Practice Files

In this appendix, we explain how to download and save the practice files from the website accompanying this book. Downloading means you are transferring files to your own computer.

☞ **Open the www.visualsteps.com/wordpress web page** 𝒪𝒪¹

Now you will see the website that goes with this book. You can download the practice files from the *Practice files* page:

👆 **Click** **Practice files**

👆 **Right-click**
[WordPress-Practice-Files.

You will see a menu:

👆 **Click** Save target as...

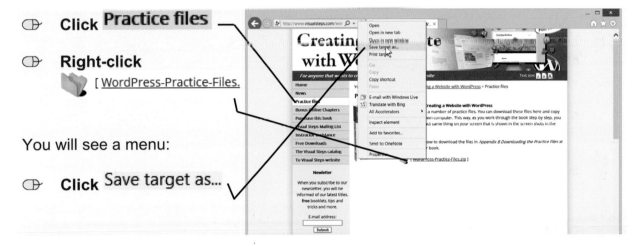

The *WordPress-Practice-Files.zip* folder is a compressed folder. You can save this folder in the (*My*) *Pictures* folder.

👆 **Click** Pictures

👆 **Click** Save

When the file has finished downloading:

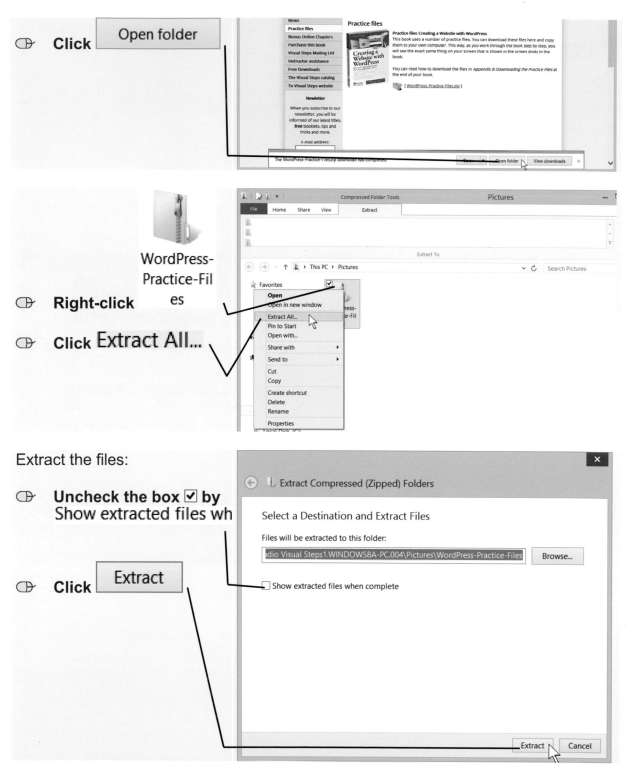

☞ **Click** Open folder

☞ **Right-click**

WordPress-
Practice-Fil
es

☞ **Click** Extract All...

Extract the files:

☞ **Uncheck the box** ☑ **by**
Show extracted files wh

☞ **Click** Extract

Now the *WordPress-Practice-Files* folder has been saved in the (*My*) *Pictures folder*:

You can delete the
compressed folder:

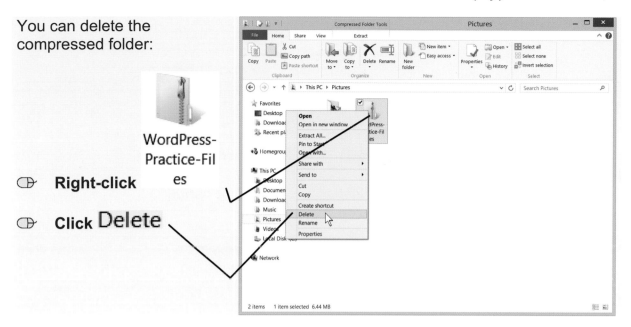

WordPress-
Practice-Fil
es

☞ **Right-click**

☞ **Click** Delete

In *Windows 8.1*, the folder will be deleted at once. In *Windows 7* and *Vista* you will see the *Delete Folder* window:

☞ **If necessary, click** [Yes]

The compressed folder has been deleted:

☞ **Close all windows** ⚫²

Appendix C. Index

Photo Editing on the iPad for SENIORS

There is so much you can do with an iPad. But one of the best applications is surely working with photos! There are many apps available that come with a variety of tools for enhancing your photos. You can spruce up the photos you took from a memorable event or vacation for example, and share them with others. And what about making a collage, slideshow or photo album?

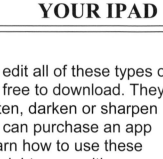

HAVE FUN AND BECOME A PHOTO EDITING EXPERT ON YOUR IPAD

This user-friendly book shows you in a jiffy how to create and edit all of these types of projects. A number of photo editing apps are easy to use and free to download. They offer lots of preset filters, plus useful tools to crop, repair, lighten, darken or sharpen your photos. And if you want additional editing capability, you can purchase an app for a small amount with even more great features. You will learn how to use these apps with clear step-by-step instructions. You can get started right away with exercise pictures that can be downloaded from our website.

With the knowledge and experience you gain, you will soon be able to edit your own photos and turn them into works of art. It will surprise you how much is possible with photos on the iPad!

Author: Studio Visual Steps
ISBN 978 90 5905 731 9
Book type: Paperback, full color
Nr of pages: 312 pages
Accompanying website:
www.visualsteps.com/photoipad

Full color!

Learn how to:
- Crop, rotate and straighten photos
- Adjust exposure and contrast
- Add effects, text and other objects
- Create a collage and slideshow
- Share your photos

Suitable for:
iPad 2, iPad 3rd generation, iPad 4th generation, iPad Air, iPad Air 2, iPad mini, iPad mini 2 and iPad mini 3. If you have a new type of iPad, you can also use this book.

Windows 10 for SENIORS

Windows 10 for SENIORS is the ideal book for seniors that have already worked with an earlier version of Windows and want to get up and going with Windows 10 on a desktop or laptop computer. All of the important basic functions are discussed, such as

GET STARTED WITH WINDOWS 10!

browsing the Web safely, sending and receiving email, and organizing files and folders. You will also get familiar with the apps for viewing photos and videos, and listening to music.

Learn step-by-step and in your own tempo how to work with the new programs and features in Windows 10. Learn about the applications that have been updated and how to use the new ones. You will also learn how to configure Windows 10 to make your computer more user-friendly. The book offers additional exercises to practice what you have learned and there are instructional videos available online on the book's support website that show you how to perform a variety of different tasks. With this book, you will quickly get accustomed to Windows 10 and become comfortable using it!

Author: Studio Visual Steps
ISBN 978 90 5905 451 6
Book type: Paperback, full color
Nr of pages: 320 pages
Accompanying website:
www.visualsteps.com/windows10

Topics covered include:
- Getting acquainted with Windows 10 step by step
- Managing files and folders
- Sending email and surfing the internet
- Working with photos, videos and music
- Useful configuration settings
- Computer safety

Suitable for:
Windows 10 on a desktop computer or laptop.

Mac OS X Yosemite for SENIORS

The Macintosh line of desktop computers and laptops from Apple has enjoyed enormous popularity in recent years amongst a steadily growing group of users. Have you recently found your way to Apple's user-friendly operating system but are still unsure how to perform basic tasks? This book will show you step by step how to work with Mac Yosemite.

LEARN STEP BY STEP HOW TO WORK WITH MAC OS X YOSEMITE

You will learn how to use basic features, such as accessing the Internet, using email and organizing files and folders in Finder. You will also get acquainted with some of the handy tools and apps included in Mac OS X Yosemite that makes it easy to work with photos, video and music. Finally, you will learn how to set preferences to make it even easier to work on your Mac and learn how to change the look and feel of the interface. This practical book, written using the well-known step-by-step method from Visual Steps, is all you need to feel comfortable with your Mac!

Author: Studio Visual Steps
ISBN 978 90 5905 360 1
Book type: Paperback, full color
Nr of pages: 312 pages
Accompanying website:
www.visualsteps.com/ macyosemite

Full color!

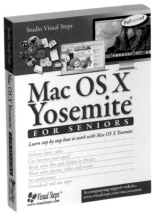

Learn how to:
- Perform basic tasks in Mac OS X Yosemite
- Use Internet and email
- Work with files and folders in Finder
- Work with photos, videos and music
- Set preferences
- Download and use apps

Suitable for:
Mac OS X Yosemite on an iMac or Macbook